ACTION RESEARCH IN STEM AND ENGLISH LANGUAGE LEARNING

Responding to the linguistic and cultural diversity of the U.S. K–12 student population and an increasing emphasis on STEM, this book offers a model for professional development that engages teachers in transformative action research projects and explicitly links literacy to mathematics and science curriculum through sociocultural principles. Providing detailed and meaningful demonstrations of participatory action research in the classroom, Razfar and Troiano present an effective, systemic approach that helps preserve teachers support students' funds of knowledge. By featuring teacher and researcher narratives, this book centers teacher expertise and offers a more holistic and humanistic understanding of authentic and empathetic teaching. Focusing on integrating instructional knowledge from ESL, bilingual, and STEM education, the range of cases and examples will allow readers to implement action research projects in their own classrooms. Chapters include discussion questions and additional resources for students, researchers, and educators.

Aria Razfar is Professor of Education & Linguistics at University of Illinois Chicago.

Beverly Troiano is Associate Professor of Education at Elmhurst University, Elmhurst, Illinois.

ACTION RESEARCH IN STEM AND ENGLISH LANGUAGE LEARNING

An Integrated Approach for Developing Teacher Researchers

Aria Razfar and Beverly Troiano

Routledge
Taylor & Francis Group

NEW YORK AND LONDON

Cover image: © Getty Images

First published 2022
by Routledge
605 Third Avenue, New York, NY 10158

and by Routledge
4 Park Square, Milton Park, Abingdon, Oxon, OX14 4RN

Routledge is an imprint of the Taylor & Francis Group, an informa business

© 2022 Taylor & Francis

Library of Congress Cataloging-in-Publication Data
A catalog record for this title has been requested

ISBN: 978-1-138-54924-1 (hbk)
ISBN: 978-1-138-54925-8 (pbk)
ISBN: 978-1-351-00116-8 (ebk)

DOI: 10.4324/9781351001168

Typeset in Bembo
by SPi Technologies India Pvt Ltd (Straive)

CONTENTS

ACKNOWLEDGMENTS

We would like to acknowledge all the teachers, school administrators, research assistants, faculty, students, families, and communities that made this book possible. We would like to express our deepest appreciation for all the reviewers of this manuscript. In particular, we would like to thank Professors Krisanna Machtmes and Judith Green for their valuable feedback and for writing the foreword.

These projects would not have been possible without the generous support from the U.S. Department of Education's Office of English Language Acquisition (OELA) National Professional Development (NPD) program. We would especially like to thank Samuel López, our NPD program manager, for his support.

While the contributions and names are too numerous to list, we would like to especially recognize and thank the LSciMAct (2007–2012) and ELMSA (2011–2017) research teams at the University of Illinois Chicago, whose spirit and dedication made this book possible.

The doctoral students whose dissertations were drawn from these projects: Dr. Eunah Yang (2012), Dr. Zayoni Torres (2015), Dr. Marcine Adams (2019), Dr. Adrian Allen (2019), and Dr. Joanna Maravilla (2020). A special thanks to Dr. Zayoni Torres, Dr. Marcine Adams, and Alex Carstensen for their roles in preparing the book.

The graduate and undergraduate research assistants: Jing Wang, Syeda Raza, Adriana Servin, Norma Noriega, and Diala David.

We would also like to especially acknowledge UIC colleagues whose support was critical during the early stages of the project(s): Dr. Flora Rodrigues-Brown, Dr. Karen Sakash, and Dr. Lena Licón Khisty. They left a powerful legacy for serving English learners, emergent bilinguals, their families, and communities. Dr. P. Zitlali Morales, whose presence at UIC since 2009 has helped sustain and build upon the rich legacy we inherited. We truly appreciate her vital role as mentor and dissertation committee member for the project teachers and doctoral students.

Finally, we would like to thank our family members, whose love and support made it all possible. I, Aria, would like to thank my wife, Hanieh, my daughter, Mariam, and my son, Ali, for their patience and encouragement throughout. I would also like to thank my uncle Mohandes Mehdi Behinfar, whose inquisitive and scientific spirit was present with us throughout this work. I, Beverly, would like to thank my husband, Chris, and daughter, Ines, for their support and love throughout the project.

AUTHORS

Aria Razfar is Professor of Education and Linguistics at the University of Illinois Chicago. He earned his PhD from the University of California, Los Angeles in 2003. He has authored theoretically driven empirical studies and conceptual pieces that draw on qualitative and quantitative methods, sociocultural theories of learning, and the application of language ideologies in urban schools. His publications have appeared in premiere academic journals such as *Anthropology of Education Quarterly, Human Development, Linguistics and Education, Mind, Culture, and Activity, Urban Education, TESOL Quarterly*, and a top-selling book titled *Applying Linguistics in the Classroom: A Sociocultural Perspective* (Routledge, 2013). The U.S. Department of Education and the National Science Foundation have provided major funding for his research on language learning, mathematics, and science education. In 2014, he was recognized for his scholarship by being named University of Illinois Chicago's Researcher of the Year for the Social Sciences. He currently serves as one of the editors for the *Journal of Literacy Research*.

Dr. Beverly Troiano is Associate Professor in the Department of Education at Elmhurst University. For 6 years, she served as the project coordinator and later as a postdoctoral fellow of Project LSciMAct at the University of Illinois Chicago, where she earned her PhD in Curriculum and Instruction. She developed and directs the undergraduate and graduate Teaching English Learners program, an ESL and bilingual endorsement program at Elmhurst University. She created the Elmhurst University Teacher Research Network with the goal to continue to support alumni as teacher researchers. For over 10 years she taught in P–12th-grade settings in Germany and Chicago. As a teacher and bilingual coordinator in Chicago Public Schools, she developed and coordinated a Newcomer Center for immigrants and refugees and directed ESL programs in community high schools throughout the city. Her research interests include teacher education and action research grounded in sociocultural theories of language and learning. She studies how in-service and preservice teachers use discourse analysis as an action research tool to reflect on their practice with English learners.

CONTRIBUTORS

Judith Green is a Distinguished Professor Emeritus in the Department of Education, University of California, Santa Barbara, where she worked from 1990–2016. Dr. Green has been teaching for more than five decades across levels of schooling (K–20). She received her MA in Educational Psychology from California State University, Northridge (1970), where she learned about child and language development. She received her PhD from the University of California, Berkeley, where she explored the relationships between teaching and learning, literacy and knowledge construction. Her recent research focuses on how classroom practices support access to students across academic disciplines in classrooms and in virtual communities. Her teaching and research focus on teaching–learning relationships, disciplinary knowledge as socially constructed, and ethnographic research and discourse studies of the patterns of everyday life in classrooms. As a founding member of the Santa Barbara Classroom Discourse Group, a collaborative community of teacher ethnographers, student ethnographers and university-based ethnographers, Dr. Green explores questions guided by theories on the social construction of knowledge.

Dr. Krisanna Machtmes holds a BS degree from University of Wyoming, an MS degree from Washington State University, and a PhD in Education from Purdue University. After completing her doctorate at Purdue University, Krisanna worked for 3 years as a program evaluator for the 4-H Youth Development Department at Purdue University. Krisanna's initial faculty position was at Louisiana State University in 2002. While at LSU, Dr. Machtmes earned promotion to Associate Professor with tenure. She joined Ohio University in the fall of 2013. Dr. Machtmes' research focuses on the methodology used to evaluate technology-based education programs. Current research examines the effects of immersive virtual learning on training adults. Responsibilities at Ohio University include teaching graduate courses in research methods and evaluation, including mixed methods. Dr. Machtmes has been active in myriad campus service and leadership committees at LSU, including the Honor Society of Phi Kappa Phi.

Dr. Ambareen Nasir is an accomplished researcher and senior educator leader in ESL and bilingual education with expertise in instruction, coaching, field supervision, policy advising, and program development and evaluation. She received her PhD in Curriculum and Instruction from the University of Illinois Chicago. She was a graduate research assistant for Project LSciMAct and later a postdoctoral fellow. Her dissertation work was based on the action research conducted at Genesis Elementary, which is the focus of Chapter 2. She has served large school districts, universities, and academic organizations for over 10 years. She has a record for high performance and results in the development, implementation, evaluation, and continuous improvement of challenging and inspiring curricula. Her passion and advocacy for educational equity, literacy, and promoting diversity is inspired by her strong commitment to the academic success of each student and supporting underserved diverse learner populations.

Dr. Joseph C. Rumenapp is a community-engaged scholar with more than 15 years of experience working in a variety of urban educational contexts. He received his PhD in Literacy, Language, and Culture from the University of Illinois Chicago. He was a graduate research assistant for Project LSciMAct and later a postdoctoral fellow with Project ELMSA. His dissertation work was based on the action research conducted at Warner Elementary highlighted in Chapter 5. He is currently an associate professor of literacy at St. John's University. Previously he served as an assistant professor of literacy research at Judson University. In addition to his teaching and scholarship, Joseph serves as an Emergency Medical Technician and is on the board of Project Education Plus, a community educational and athletic nonprofit organization in Chicago, Illinois.

FOREWORD

This book, written by Aria Razfar and Beverly Troiano, takes readers on a journey of understanding how teachers were introduced to and engaged in developing ways of building on and integrating Sociocultural Theory, Cultural Historical Activity Theory, Discourse Analysis, and Funds of Knowledge, as well as Third Space theories, to guide their participatory action research projects. Through this process, as the chapters will demonstrate, readers are introduced to, and can explore, how Razfar and colleagues (university researchers, teachers-as-learners in his action research program, and others) have created a theoretically grounded approach to undertaking and learning from *participatory action research* as they sought to transform traditional curriculum in their classes. Additionally, readers will gain insights into how a common framework guiding the focus of the work of both the teachers and the university researchers/instructors led to the transformation and development of ways of engaging the participating teachers' culturally, linguistically, socially, and academically diverse students.

Readers will also gain understandings of the growing relationships among teachers, students, and university-based researchers at the center of this approach to participatory action research. By engaging in the chapters that make transparent the relationship approach that Razfar and colleagues constructed to integrate theory-process relationships, and by exploring the teachers' local and situated processes, readers will have opportunities to take deep dives into decisions and actions that the teacher and university faculty faced and responded to in order to address the needs of the teachers' linguistically, culturally, socially, and academically diverse students. Thus, readers have a unique opportunity to learn from the cases ways of integrating instructional knowledge from the fields of bilingual and English as a Second Language, mathematics, and science education and ways of designing STEM-oriented curriculum for and with students.

What is unique about the journey that this book will take readers on is that the chapters provide a series of metanarratives, which make transparent how the university researchers and teachers engaged in participatory action research processes to develop professionally together in ways that supported learning of diverse learners in STEM-oriented classes. In this way, readers will be able to explore processes that teachers in different sites developed to engage their diverse learners in actively constructing with the teacher the opportunities for learning guided by the sociocultural theories introduced to them by the university-based program. Thus, this book provides readers with deep and grounded opportunities to engage with the program at multiple levels and from the perspective of different community members.

Another unique dimension of this book is that readers will be introduced to different teachers' action research processes that supported transformational educational opportunities with and for students that empowered students in learning previously unknown ways of knowing, being, and doing academic work. Additionally, across the chapters, readers will have opportunities to trace developing relationships within the participatory action research community that supported teachers in taking leadership in transforming the curriculum and instructional processes from predefined ones of the traditional curriculum to ones that engage students and teachers as active designers of and for their own learning. Readers will also gain insights into how Aria Razfar and his team supported five teachers in a cohort approach in the year-long action research process, in which the teachers were guided as they developed action research processes that formed a basis for communicating to students, administrators, and community members what students were learning and how these learnings met the district's standards.

The five case studies presented in this book demonstrate how each group of learners (teachers, university researchers, and students) took up new roles and developed new knowledge as they became participating action researchers. Additionally, through these case studies, readers will gain deep insights into how the teachers and students addressed often-unanticipated challenges in their journeys into this new learning venture. Through these case studies, readers will have a unique opportunity to explore how the teachers engaged in orienting their students to ways of engaging, thinking, interpreting, and evaluating the curriculum activities they were constructing with the university program's guidance. In these cases, therefore, readers will have the opportunity to explore how linguistically, culturally, socially, and academically diverse students and their teachers were encouraged to use their own knowledge and background to design and engage in STEM curriculum processes.

Through these case studies, readers will be able to trace how teachers, with the support of the participatory actions research model developed by Aria Razfar and his team led to reflexive processes that were iterative, recursive, and abductive in nature. Readers will also gain access to a series of theoretical and conceptually guided materials (templates) that were developed with and for teachers to guide them in taking a reflexive approach to teaching as well as curriculum development as they engaged students over time (1 year) in new curriculum processes. This volume, therefore, allows readers, whether teachers or university program developers, to gain understandings of how to develop participatory action research processes to support diverse learners in STEM-oriented classes.

Additionally, throughout the book, readers are offered opportunities to explore the kinds of questions that were asked by the teachers, and what ways the teachers in this program identified problems or defined areas of exploration. Readers will also learn about the different kinds of data that the teachers collected as well as how they collected each record for later analyses and how often such records were collected and analyzed across the school year. Furthermore, readers will be able to trace how the findings in each context were used and how they were applied in designing and engaging with students as well as others (administrators, university researchers, community members). Finally, readers will gain a deep understanding of how the reported findings, or rather outcomes of the actions within a particular site, were reported and what the teachers viewed as relevant to participants.

Across the chapters, therefore, readers will gain deep insights into how the teachers engaged English learners as well as speakers of other nondominant linguistic varieties such as African American Language (AAL) in this program of participatory learning. Readers will also be able to explore how activities were mediated by explicit and implicit *rules* for cultural practices in particular school settings. Thus, through these telling case studies, readers will be able to trace how learning processes were supported by the program designers as teachers developed a community of inquiry that focused on problem-solving strategies, peer assistance and sharing, public presentations, and rights and responsibilities at both the collective level of the university-based program and the local and situated level of the classroom community. In this way, readers will gain understandings of the importance of the *division of effort* critical to supporting teachers and students in becoming facilitators of learning. Finally, readers will come to understand how and why a longitudinal process is at the center of this dialogic community and how the different participants each learned from and contributed to the collective's as well as individual's processes of thinking, acting, and creating meanings to transform traditional views of teaching, teachers, and learning processes.

Krisanna Machtmes
Ohio University

Judith Green
University of California, Santa Barbara

1

INTEGRATING LANGUAGE LEARNING AND STEM THROUGH ACTION RESEARCH

We begin with final testimonial accounts of the teachers we worked with to reimagine and redesign STEM education that was linguistically and culturally sustaining, adaptive to restrictive mandates, and pedagogically transformative:

> We found that teacher collaboration strengthens our abilities as educators. While we initially found ourselves struggling to connect students' playground funds to the FOSS [mandated] curriculum, Ms. Abby's science expertise, Ms. Karen's knowledge of standards and curriculum planning, and Ms. Lorena's prominence in the community and Spanish language expertise helped us design transformative science curriculum through linguistic and science funds.
>
> Karen, First-Grade Teacher, Genesis Elementary **[Chapter 2]**

> I'm more confident in this way of teaching because it's better for my students. This year I feel like especially with all the changes in middle school [science curriculum] that I am doing what is best for my students and I have proof that inclusion is the best for my students and I think a lot of stuff that we did last year has empowered me to say I am doing what is best for my students. I don't care what your book says I am doing what is best for them.
>
> Dana, Fifth-Grade Special Education **[Chapter 3]**

DOI: 10.4324/9781351001168-1

Despite the fact that I valued other cultures and languages and had traveled and lived extensively overseas, I did not know how to value students' home language in my classroom. When I first began encouraging them to use Spanish in the classroom, they were pleasantly surprised. By the end of the year, many comfortably wrote and spoke in Spanish.

Susan, Seventh- and Eighth-Grade Language Arts Teacher **[Chapter 4]**

Language development is so important for English learners … that's what this action research project pointed out to me. Also, that science is there for them to develop their language and vocabulary.

Allison, Eighth-Grade Science Teacher **[Chapter 5]**

I came to change during the action research project, realizing how important it was to allow students to use their native language to clarify or communicate with classmates. During the beginning of the year, this change began, but ultimately once the project began. I would consistently use Spanish when I could to clarify and to encourage the EL students to speak. I also tried to encourage my African-American students to use African American Vernacular English.

Cara, Second-Grade Teacher **[Chapter 6]**

Introduction

Teachers enter the classroom every day to make an impact on their students' learning and increasingly more, looking for valuable resources to help engage and enhance their students' learning outcome(s). In particular, it is becoming more common for teachers to implement an alternative approach to their teaching practice and in turn seeking to do away with teaching paradigms that minimize teacher expertise and their central role in curriculum design. With an increase in students' lack of interest in the fields of science and mathematics, teachers are looking for more opportunities to implement purposeful and meaningful curriculum that help to create the most gains in the subject areas as well as center their pedagogical and content knowledge (Green, 1983; Kelly & Green, 2019; Shulman, 1986; Silberman, 1973).

Responsiveness to community needs and community engagement have become more prominent metrics in the evaluation of higher-education institutions (Driscoll, 2008). In 2005, after a thorough self-examination, the Carnegie Foundation for the Advancement of Teaching created the Community Engagement Classification as a way to address concerns about the lack of community engagement and insensitivity to the evolution of higher education (Campus Compact, 2016; Driscoll, 2008). This elective classification has given visibility and recognition for co-curricular growth, collaboration, and partnerships; increased student involvement in the community, and leveraged faculty expertise for cutting-edge initiatives that benefit the communities in which universities are located (e.g., Trent, 2020). Over the last 15 years, the Carnegie Foundation's community engagement classification has altered how we view the purpose of higher education (Driscoll, 2014). It has brought promise and prestige to community engagement, and now there are 361 universities with this classification (Vann & Firth, n.d.).

With the increase of diversity among students in urban contexts, for more than a decade, projects *Learning Science through Math and Action Research* (LSciMAct, 2007–2012)[1] and *English Learning through Mathematics, Science, and Action Research* (ELMSA, 2012–2017),[2] sponsored by the U.S Department of Education, Office of English Language Acquisition, set out to facilitate resources to educators wanting to make an impact in the classroom for their English learners (ELs). In addition, these projects answer a broader national call to integrate literacy and STEM education (National Research Council, 2014).

Over 100 teachers across 26 schools have participated in these action research projects designed to provide long-term professional development for K–8 teachers working with ELs in predominantly low-income areas (Razfar, 2007, 2011). Between 2009 and 2020, eight dissertations and more than 100 master's theses based on these action research projects were written (Razfar & Li, 2017; Razfar & Li, 2014). In contrast to off-the-shelf, cookie-cutter curriculum, our aim was to empower teachers to become researchers and designers of authentic curricular activities that fostered learning for all participants: teachers, students, and university-based researchers. Our goal was to cultivate a systematic approach, which implements curricular activities based on students' funds of knowledge and national mathematics, science, and literacy standards. This model for professional development focuses on integrating instructional knowledge from the fields of bilingual and English as a Second Language (ESL) education, mathematics education, and science education, with teachers doing action research and developing collegial communities. Our professional development program sought to engage teachers in a transformative action research model that explicitly linked literacy, mathematics, and science through sociocultural principles of teaching and learning.

Furthermore, these cases have broader applicability and implications beyond the schools and communities in which they were situated. They are part of a teacher professional development movement that goes beyond methods fetish (Bartolomé, 1994; Wells, 2000). Our professional development sought to go beyond simply "PD" by actively co-creating processes that lead to continuous opportunities for teachers and university researchers to develop professionally together (Green, Camilli, & Elmore, 2012). This book is the product of continuous dialogues over the last 15 years with teachers and teacher educators. It is a metanarrative of cultural practices, identity shifts, and processes that aim to fundamentally humanize K–12 education. By *humanizing*, we mean centering teacher expertise, student learning, and community epistemologies (Bartolomé, 1994). More specifically, the challenge is to provide a well-suited curriculum for English learner (EL) students. The preparation of teachers for linguistically and culturally diverse populations has been the subject of a growing body of research and discussion over the last six decades (Brisk, 2008; Cochran-Smith, Fieman-Nemser, McIntyre, & Demers, 2008, Green, 1983; Gupta, 2020; Silberman, 1973). As the increase in diversity becomes apparent in our classrooms across the country, the need for alternative approaches to teaching are of great need. For decades, teacher educators have been calling for an educational approach that is less focused on information transfer and more centered on relational cultural practices and humanizing values (Blume, 1971; Freire, 1993).

Humanizing teacher education and professional development is an intentional and strategic move away from deficit views of teachers and K–12 education. One way this is accomplished is when university-based researchers are embedded in authentic, empathetic, and committed partnerships with schools and communities (Andrews, Brown, Castillo, Jackson, & Vellanki, 2019; Mirra, 2018). We demonstrate throughout how participatory action research humanizes research and university-based researchers in contexts that are often dehumanizing (Irizarry & Brown, 2013). It emphasizes the unique role of university-based research partners to create opportunities for learning, growth, and development in spaces that have been historically constrained at best and dehumanizing at worst (Paris & Winn, 2013). University research partners and teacher education programs provide a critical space to unlearn many of the biases, stereotypes, and assumptions that inhibit a humanizing learning experience for teachers and students (Carter-Andrews & Castillo, 2016).

Action Research

What does a purposeful and meaningful curriculum consist of, and furthermore how is one created? We started our action research journey with several definitions spanning several decades of action research in education. From Lewin (1946) to Freire (1993), we considered a broad range of action research paradigms that have informed and inspired teacher professional development across the globe (Adelman, 1993). Action research

> seeks to bring together action and reflection, theory and practice in participation with others, in the pursuit of practical solutions to issues of pressing concern to people and more generally the flourishing of individual persons and their communities … a primary purpose of action research is to produce knowledge that is useful to people in the everyday conduct of their lives.
>
> (Reason & Bradbury, 2001, pp. 1–2)

Mills describes action research as (2003), "Action research is any systematic inquiry conducted by teachers to gather information about the ways that their particular school operates, how they teach, and how well their students learn." (2003, p. 4). Action research is fundamentally an orientation to make global change at a micro level by centering student knowledge and teacher agency (Mills, 2018). Teachers need to initiate and direct their own action research project with the end goal of improving their practice, and practitioners who engage in action research find it to be an empowering experience (Sagor, 2000). Action research is a broader movement to counteract the deprofessionalization of K–12 educators and prescriptive approaches to learning (Sagor, 2009):

> To counteract prescriptive approaches and realize the dream of universal student success requires restructuring the work and expectations of teacher performance so that they are in line with a professional model rather than a blue-collar model. The ethic of professionalism requires the professional educator to continuously ask, "How can my work be modified to produce better results?"
>
> (p. 10)

Embracing youth voice and Participatory Action Research (PAR) have been shown to have a positive impact on youth development and relationships with adults (Cater, Machtmes, & Fox, 2013; Serido, Borden, & Perkins, 2011).

More recently, Youth Participatory Action Research (YPAR) has focused on how students, especially those coming from nondominant communities, challenge dominant ideologies, narratives, and epistemologies. YPAR has an explicit focus on a pedagogy of transformational resistance to oppression (Morrell, 2006). Its roots are grounded in Brazilian educator and activist Paolo Freire's critique of banking and autocratic models of education that stymie student creativity, agency, and autonomy (1970). Thus, participatory action research has an explicit objective of liberation through building counter hegemonic consciousness and curricular activities. In recent years, YPAR has been specifically adopted in STEM and English learner education (Suárez, 2020). Morales-Doyle (2017) shows how high school youth take up advanced chemistry to significantly impact issues of social, racial, and environmental justice in their communities. In this book, all the cases to some degree demonstrate how sociocultural theory and YPAR can lead to changes in teachers, students, and the nondominant communities they serve.

Conceptual Readings and Design Tools: Sociocultural Theories and Third Space

Becoming teacher researchers means regular engagement with conceptual, theoretical, and empirical readings. Overall, sociocultural perspectives of language, learning, and human development informed our approach to action research. More specifically, four conceptual frameworks guided our conversations about design and implementation: (1) Sociocultural Theory (SCT); (2) Cultural Historical Activity Theory (CHAT); (3) Discourse Analysis; and (4) Funds of Knowledge (FoK). Readings about SCT led to the Social Organization of Learning Protocol (Appendix C). Readings about CHAT led to the activity triangle template serving as a curriculum design tool (Appendix A). Readings about discourse analysis led to the transcription conventions (Appendix F) and coding sheets (Appendix E). Readings about FoK led to the Funds of Knowledge inventory table (Appendix B). In addition, *third space* theory helped us develop more expansive and productive ways of understanding different types of tensions as they related to discourse analysis, learning, and development. While there was no specific third space tool like the ones mentioned earlier, teachers used the coding sheet to mark instances of tension and identify episodes where participants leveraged those tensions to mediate hybrid learning through third spaces. Given the complexity of this concept, robust third space episodes didn't generally emerge until later in the action research cycle, sometimes in unit 2 (e.g., Cara's Chapter 6) but mostly in unit 3.

Using elements of action research in these classrooms opened new doors for students to find purpose and meaning in science and mathematics in their everyday lives outside classroom walls and into the community. This led to projects such as building a safe playground from scratch, designing solar energy panels, using video games to develop authentic engineering design, engaging in real forensics experiments, and transformative urban community gardening.

The teachers had opportunities to create a curriculum that is more cohesive with their students' identities outside the classroom. Through their shift in practice, teachers became more willing to be inclusive of students' home language, cultural beliefs, or what we considered students' Funds of Knowledge (FoK). FoK frames the notion of curriculum and instruction, which "facilitates teachers' recognition and use of family and community resources for pedagogical purposes" (Rios-Aguilar, Kiyama, Gravitt, & Moll, 2011, p. 164). Teachers draw on this community and household knowledge to develop activities that are linguistically and culturally relevant (Lee & Smagorinsky, 2000). By linking school curriculum to students' lives, teachers are able to challenge deficit models of low-income students and their families in order to leverage STEM learning (Civil, 2016). Furthermore, teachers are challenged to begin with what is important to the students and take the role of a facilitator where students are the experts.

This openness to students as the experts stems from a discussion of cultural historical activity theory (CHAT) and sociocultural theory (SCT) and teachers taking a more sociocultural perspective (Razfar, Khisty, & Chval, 2011). Our project adopted a sociocultural approach to doing action research where sociocultural tools of language and learning were used to empower teachers to become teacher researchers and curriculum designers (Razfar, 2011). Current conceptualizations rely heavily on the work of Vygotsky. SCT argues that human mental functioning is fundamentally a mediated process that is organized by cultural artifacts, activities, and concepts (Ratner, 2002). Rogoff and Chavajay (1995) emphasized that "the intellectual development of children is inherently involved with participation in societal activities" (p. 871). Teachers are exposed to this theory and framework through articles and different tools to analyze the classroom data, including cultural-historical activity theory (CHAT) framework to learning and development (Engeström, 1999; Wertsch, 1998).

The historical foundation of discourse analysis in teacher development is rooted in sociological, psychological, linguistic, and anthropological perspectives for understanding student teacher verbal communication and its impact on learning of socially, culturally, and linguistically and academically diverse learners (Cazden, John, & Hymes, 1972). Discourse analysis as a conceptual and methodological framework also emphasized forms of speech that usually escape traditional forms of assessment (e.g., nonverbal communication, bilingualism, nondominant registers, mathematics and scientific registers). For the purpose of our action research projects, we drew on definitions of discourse and discourse analysis that emphasized micro and macro dimensions of communication (Brown, 2006; Gee, 2014; Hicks, 1995; Moschkovich, 2007). Gee's distinction of discourse (lowercase *d*) and Discourse (capital *D*) was particularly useful for introducing micro and macro dimensions of discourse analysis (Gee, 2014). More important, all these readings emphasize language use as indicative of a community. Communities span disciplines (e.g., mathematics and science) and classrooms (Brown, 2006; Moschkovich, 2007). In classrooms, one way teachers can assess student learning and growth is through discourse analysis (Rex & Schiller, 2009).

Third space learning theory is a valuable perspective for analyzing social interactions where participants have unequal power (Soja, 1989). Third spaces are the in-between, or hybrid, spaces, where the dominant first space and the nondominant second space intersect to generate a new third space. As a concept, in-betweeness has been used in various forms across the arts and sciences. In education, it has become popular with sociocultural and constructivist perspectives of learning because of its focus on empowering student learning and promoting egalitarian discourse structures (Gutiérrez, Rymes, & Larson, 1995). In typical classroom interactions, teacher-centered discourse positions students in asymmetric power relations that often erases their nonschool linguistic, cultural, and epistemological expertise. Teachers often initiate and determine content, process, and assessment of classroom activities. Teachers occupy the official or first space of the classroom. All talk and actions are legitimated through the teacher. The second space constitutes what students are thinking, doing, and saying without the teacher's recognition. The interactions are generally implicitly and/or explicitly hierarchical, where teachers are positioned as experts and students are perpetual novices. The third space is an in-between space where teachers and students can challenge existing structures and imagine novel possibilities.

The third space is a metaphor that provides an alternative framework for organizing learning in ways that centers student and community discourses.

In terms of action research, third space theory helps make this asymmetry visible to teachers. Third space theory helps teachers analyze the tensions, contestations, and conflicts that inevitably arise when learning is purposely organized to embrace differences. It is one of the more challenging concepts to apply because fostering third spaces means going beyond comfortable and predictable discourse practices. It fundamentally challenges the familiar teacher initiated, student response, and teacher evaluates (IRE) script found in traditional classroom interactions. It encourages more dialogic, expansive, and authentic learning by centering student and community-based epistemologies, discourses, and activities (Baquedano-López, Solis, & Kattan, 2005; Christoph & Nystrand, 2001; Gutiérrez, Baquedano-López, Alvarez, & Chiu, 1999).

Each of the cases presented in this book highlight some degree of cognitive, curricular design, content, and administrative-related tensions that teachers coded while analyzing the videos of their activity units. In general, when teachers coded such instances, it led to conversations about possible ways of mediating third space learning. Third space episodes were one of the more complex ideas to implement and observe. At Genesis (Chapter 2), there was significant tension with the administration around the alternative playground curriculum the teachers designed with their students. Similarly, at Jarman (Chapter 3), the teachers experienced tension between the mandated curriculum and their action research project. Thus, in both Genesis and Jarman, the teachers focused more on tensions and thirds spaces at the administrative and policy level. At Adams (Chapters 4 and 6) and Warner (Chapter 5), teachers were given more autonomy and hence were able to focus on tensions and third spaces in their classrooms.

Context: Our Teachers, Schools, and Communities

Our action research project over the years has provided a framework for apprenticing teachers as ethnographers and teacher researchers in high-poverty schools serving English learners. We applied sociocultural and ethnographic principles of learning and development to collaboratively design and implement curricular activities based on students' funds of knowledge and aligned with national mathematics, science, and literacy standards. Strong university–school partnerships play a key role in fostering such educational possibilities in these high-poverty and immigrant communities. Over the span of 10 years, we partnered with more than 100 teachers across 26 schools in a large, urban midwestern city. In this book, we focus on cases from four of the communities that we worked with during the first 5 years. We selected these cases based on the breadth and depth of research we have done. Furthermore, we have had the opportunity to better observe and document the longitudinal outcomes of these collaborations. These cases have been the subject of a wide array of publications and presentations, including doctoral dissertations, national and international academic conferences, peer-reviewed research articles, and handbook chapters. We provide a

TABLE 1.1 Teacher and School EL Demographics

Teacher	School	Grade	Years of Teaching	Language Fluency	% of ELs School
Karen	Genesis	1st	5	English	35%
Lola	Jarman	5th	7	Spanish/English	49%
Dana	Jarman	5th	3	English	49%
Susan	Adams	7th/8th	11	English	24.2%
Allison	Warner	6th	26	English	26%
Cara	Adams	2nd	2	Serbian/English	24.2%

brief overview of the context of each of the selected teachers, their schools, and communities: Genesis Elementary, Jarman Elementary, Adams Elementary, and Warner Elementary (Table 1.1).

Genesis Elementary

At the time of the study, Genesis Elementary was an underachieving school that was placed on academic probation with 35% of the school population identifying as English learners. Genesis consists of over 875 students with racial demographics of 95% Latinx, 3% African American/Black, and 2% classified as "Other" with 98% of students qualifying for free or reduced lunch.

Jarman Elementary

Jarman Elementary School is located in a large urban city in a historically immigrant neighborhood with an enrollment of 328. Of the student population, 94% are classified as low income. The population of the school is 92% Latinx, 6% African American/Black, and 2% Multiracial/Ethnic. Of these students, 49% are considered Limited English Proficient and are eligible for the school's transitional bilingual programs. The majority of the students at the school have Spanish as their first language, and 98% of students receive free and reduced school lunch. Most of the students at Jarman live in the neighborhood surrounding the school and walk to school.

Adams Elementary School

Adams Elementary is a small urban, public K–8 community elementary school with 269 students. Adams Elementary School is a community school with a math and science magnet program. Adams saw a substantial increase in reading and math ISAT scores with a ranked schoolwide reading proficiency of 70% and a ranked schoolwide math proficiency of 82%. The neighborhood has changed during the time of the study due to gentrification. Consequently, enrollment has decreased significantly. Latinx make up 82.5% of the enrollment, 24.2% of the student population identified as English learners, and 95.9% identified as low income (School Report Card).

Warner Elementary

Warner included 704 students, 93% of whom were Asian (most of whom were from families who had immigrated from Cantonese and Taishan regions of China), 6% African-American/Black, and 1% from other racial groups. Twenty-six percent of the students were identified as bilingual or requiring bilingual services, and 95% had free or reduced lunch.

Aligning Standards with Sociocultural Learning Activities

Throughout the cases presented in this book, each teacher was compelled to design a curriculum that was in alignment with state standards related to language arts and STEM education. Each school varied in terms of how scripted and dogmatic they were in relation to "sticking to the standards." For example, the Genesis teachers wrote about having to be "sneaky teachers" in order to design curriculum that was culturally relevant and grounded in "community science funds." At the beginning of the action research project, Karen and Abby lamented that there was absolutely "no space" provided by the school's administration for doing anything outside the mandated curriculum. In fact, it was one of the few times the project director (Aria Razfar) had to have face-to-face meetings with the principal in order to explain how our professional development and community-centered activities were *not* going to undermine the mandated curriculum or negatively impact standardized test scores.

On the other end of the spectrum, the administration at Adams was enthusiastic and welcoming of our culturally sustaining approach to STEM curriculum design and activities. In fact, the teachers at Adams were so implicitly trusted for their professional knowledge and expertise that they were one of the only schools where the principal did not mandate scripted lesson plans. Not surprisingly to us, they were designated as one of the "high-performing schools" with some of the highest standardized test scores in the city. The teachers at Adams already had a support system that aligned with the goals of our embedded action research program. Teachers systematically collaborated across disciplinary lines and were encouraged to integrate the curricular activities with students' linguistic, cultural, and STEM funds of knowledge.

In between Genesis and Adams was Jarman Elementary School, where fidelity to the mandated curriculum was expected. However, the administration provided some space for "extension units," where teachers could design more student-centered activities. Still, the curricular constraints were palpable in that these extension units had to be conducted during the time designated for social studies, and *not* language arts or STEM education. The rationale for this was that language arts and mathematics were two of the high-stakes assessment areas and shouldn't be fiddled with.

Warner Elementary School had an administration that was well intentioned and viewed our action research program as a valuable opportunity to foster a collaborative culture. The assistant principal initially enrolled in the program and matriculated into the introduction to action research course. Despite the good intentions and active involvement of the principals, we learned that because of Warner principals' involvement, many of the teachers at Warner resented the "mandated" professional development activities. Teacher autonomy and leadership became somewhat compromised. In fact, the leading teacher from Warner, Allison, highlighted in Chapter 5, was considered an exceptional, experienced, award-winning teacher who was singled out as "one of the best teachers in the state." She was well-positioned within the school as a coach for novice teachers, active in partnerships with the local Ivy League–level university, and known for her expertise in STEM content. Allison enjoyed a level of autonomy rarely seen for teachers in a large urban district. Despite all the accolades and status, Allison never realized how teacher-centered her classroom discourse pattern was. More important, she became a model of change through action research.

For each of these chapters, we address how teachers aligned their community-based curriculum with mathematics, science, language arts, and learning standards. We adapted the standards in order to show how teachers can create robust learning activities within a range of mandated curricular spaces. The overall objectives of the book are stated here.

Objectives

Upon completion of this book, educators at all levels will be able to:

1. Advance inquiry of teacher autonomy and student agency (teacher researchers);
2. Socially organize learning and development from a cultural historical framework;
3. Reimagine mathematics and science as discourses rather than isolated disciplines;
4. Build culturally sustaining curriculum;
5. Integrate fiction and nonfiction children and adolescent literature into STEM learning;
6. Develop a foundation for integrating language learning and STEM content;
7. Codesign an action plan to transform mathematics and science pedagogy for polylingual, multilingual, and English learners;
8. Advance multiple language use in the classroom and beyond;
9. Link mathematics, science, and language within the larger community; and
10. Move from teacher-centered to community-centered discourse practices.

These objectives were accomplished through various tools such as the cultural historical activity triangle.

Cultural Historical Activity Theory (CHAT) Triangle

Teachers begin by reading more about Sociocultural Theory and Cultural Historical Activity Theory (CHAT) to create an activity triangle (Engeström, 1999). The activity triangle template helps teachers conceptualize and design a systematic curricular process over a period of time, both synchronically and diachronically. Furthermore, it is critical for teachers to develop deeper understandings of sociocultural concepts of learning as best practice and not just as a "fad" (Wells, 2000, p. 51). Sociocultural concepts of learning are observable in three ways. First, they are observed through how the classroom is physically arranged for group work (space). Second, how is instructional conversation conducted through group work (classroom discourse)? Third, how are student responses, conversations, and funds of knowledge elicited (discourse analysis and funds of knowledge) (Gee, 2014; Rex & Schiller, 2009)?

The triangle outlines the activity design, the fundamental question that guides the learning process:

- the *object*, or immediate learning goal of the activity,
- the *mediational tools* (both material and ideational artifacts) that facilitate movement towards the learning goal,
- the *subjects* or immediate classroom participants,
- the *community* or distal participants,
- the *rules* that establish parameters for participation within the activity system, and
- the *division of effort*, which establishes roles and responsibilities for each learner.

Through this conceptual approach, the teacher supports students toward accomplishing the learning goals and finally *outcomes*, which are longitudinal effects suggesting a deeper shift in learner identity and consciousness. Outcomes help teachers think about practices and skills that transfer beyond the immediate learning goals or object of the activity (see Appendix A for a blank template).

Figure 1.1 illustrates how we conceptualized the entire professional development program as a cultural historical activity system. The system was guided by a central problem to integrate literacy, science, and mathematics curricular goals through participatory action research. The *object* was to move teachers from implementing scripted, mandated, "cookie-cutter" lessons toward teacher researchers who were agents of change, responsive to their students' communities, and curriculum designers. We accomplished this through *mediating artifacts* that leveraged egalitarian discourse structures, a situated view of language and learning, theoretical readings (e.g., CHAT, FoK, Third Space), and tools that

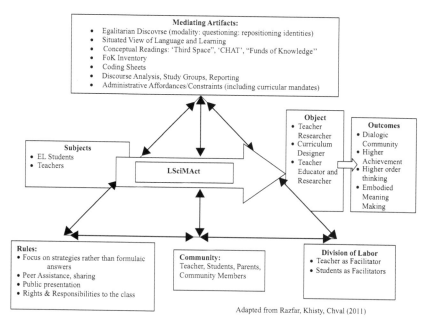

FIGURE 1.1 Activity Triangle for Action Research Program

would help them navigate curriculum design (e.g., FoK inventory table, discourse coding sheets, discourse analysis transcription conventions, study groups, and administrative affordances and constraints).

The primary *subjects* were English learners and teachers as well as speakers of other nondominant linguistic varieties such as African American Language. Activities were mediated by explicit and implicit *rules* for cultural practices such as focusing on problem-solving strategies, peer assistance and sharing, public presentations, and rights and responsibilities to the classroom community. The *community* consisted of teachers, parents, students, and community members with expertise that could be leveraged toward the activities' learning goal(s). The *division of effort* was designed to encourage teachers and students to be facilitators of learning. Finally, more longitudinal *outcomes* consisted of creating a dialogic community, higher-order or abstract thinking, and embodied meaning-making.

Language Learning through Science, Mathematics, and Action Research

This chapter seeks to provide a foundation to the organization of the book and the frameworks utilized. Each chapter offers case studies of practitioners that are reflective of the process teachers go through when conducting action research in their schools and communities (Merriam, 2007). A significant factor in students' learning and achievement is teacher learning. This is reflected throughout the book and the shift in practices that occurred throughout the project among teachers and researchers.

This awareness was integrated into the curriculum through problem solving, group work, research projects, critical-thinking strategies, and PowerPoint presentations. The teachers analyzed their findings and produced themes to showcase critical moments of growth and opportunities for their students. A shift in practice occurs, generating questions into how, why, and what is the impact this has on their classroom and students. Each project was guided by five basic steps: (1) asking a question(s), identifying a problem, or defining an area of exploration; (2) deciding what types of data to collect, how to collect the data, and how often; (3) collecting and analyzing data; (4) describing how the findings could be used and applied; and (5) reporting the findings with relevant participants and beyond (Johnson, 2008).

Trust the Process: Action Research Implementation

How do teachers identify a problem? As you will learn from this book, in order to identify the problem, you need to ask your students and consider their knowledge outside the classroom. In order to identify a problem from your students, you will collect students' FoK. When FoK is successfully incorporated into the classroom, this interrupts the traditional exchange-value process, thus shifting what type of knowledge has value (Rios et al., 2011; Zipin, 2009). Your students are the reason and key to your action research being successful. The teachers identified a problem by investing more into a situation or occurrence they were seeing more often. They asked students and their families to complete a survey, in order to learn about their funds of knowledge. After collecting the survey, the teachers organized the data to show students' FoK. By linking the lesson to students' lives, all the teachers challenged deficit models of ELs and their families (Civil, 2016).

Not Just a Lesson Plan: Curriculum Planning Through Activity Triangle(s)

Now that the problem was identified how did they begin to solve it? The activity triangle is where the teachers begin to plan what their unit or first lesson will look like. As you will continue to see in this book, teachers used the activity to plan each lesson within the unit or one whole lesson, depending on how the teachers favored. Roth and Lee describe the activity triangle as "an integrative roadmap for educational research and practice" (2007, p. 188). Similar to a traditional education plan, activity triangles include a question or focus complete with objectives, or products. The activity triangle goes on to describe subjects, the larger community, rules within the community, and nonmaterial outcomes. These sections help facilitate the organization of the components and help teachers to conceptualize the theories into practice (Appendix A).

Not Teaching "To" but "Through" the Standards: Funds of Knowledge Inventory Table

The funds of knowledge inventory table illustrates how teachers developed content objectives, integrated standards-based practices, leveraged science funds, and contemplated the deeper STEM cultural practices and values at work (see Appendix B for a blank template). While the activity triangle is being created, teachers also fill out an inventory table (Table 1.2). The funds of knowledge inventory table is an organizational tool to assist teachers in addressing the national and state standards (e.g., Common Core and Next Generation Science Standards) while still designing culturally responsive activities grounded in students' mathematics and science funds. Next, you will find an example of how teachers connected mathematics, science, and literacy practices to develop a curriculum that provides an opportunity for students to ask critical questions and develop solutions for community problems. This example was grounded in a unit designed for urban gardening, and in Chapter 6, we show how Cara at Adams school implemented such an activity.

Social Organization of Learning Protocol

The social organization of learning protocol served as an important tool for conceptualizing learning as an intentionally designed social process. A second feature of the protocol is the focus on expanding the linguistic repertoire of students. Thus, the protocol is divided into two sections: (1) the social organization of learning and (2) language practices. When teachers implemented the units, they used protocols (see Appendix C for a blank protocol) to analyze their lessons with their cohort and research assistants. The protocols provided a detailed account of the lesson conducted by the teachers and feedback from the research assistant. For example, the protocol focused attention on spatial configurations, grouping arrangements, discourse practices, mediational tools, assistance strategies, learner identity shifts, and points of disagreement in student talk. Protocols were typically used by teachers to review the lesson from the room setup, materials used, and a reflection of their teaching practices and students.

Observational Field Notes

Teachers used observational field notes to record student behaviors and practices, as well as their reflections and emerging analysis during and after each lesson (see Appendix D for a blank template). Field notes help teachers to plan and adjust their lesson according to their students' needs and the outcomes of the lesson before. Field notes were taken while the video camera was running or when lessons for the project were being conducted. Field notes also help fill in gaps when looking back at the video recordings during the analytical process. The flexibility this project provides in allowing teachers to be curriculum developers is clear

TABLE 1.2 Sample Funds of Knowledge Inventory Table

Standards-Based Practices*	Content Objectives	Funds of Knowledge	STEM Cultural Practices and Values
PROBLEM SOLVING Make sense of problems and persevere in solving them. (CCSS.MP1)	Students will be able to design, plan, present, and take part in the selection of one model to plant.	• Gardening at home • Gardening at school • Negotiate with siblings and classmates • Life cycle of plants	• Problem solving • Perseverance • Confidence • "Reality Check"
MODELLING Model with mathematics. (CCSS.MP4)	Students will be able to create a scaled model of a design using appropriate measurement.	• Sketch • Aesthetics • Conversions	• Planning • Following directions
TOOL USE Use appropriate tools strategically. (CCSS.MP5)	Students will be able to use pencils, paper, rulers, and markers during appropriate steps.	• Different tools have different purposes	• Sequencing • Different tools have different purposes
MEASUREMENT Generate measurement data. (CCSS.3.MD.4)	Students will be able to continuously mark 2–4 intervals.	• Measurement • Inches (whole, half, quarter) • Use of rules • Patterns	• Producing data or information • Articulating generated data
TEXT USE Use text features to determine importance. (CCSs.3.RI.5)	Students will be able to use text features to determine the appropriate steps for planting bulbs.	• Reading nonfiction text features	• Locating important information
COLLABORATION Engage effectively in a range of collaborative discussion. (CCSS.SL.3.1)	Students will be able to share thoughts, ideas, and questions in whole-group, small-group, and partner settings.	• Academic discussions • Social discussions • Family discussions • Turn-taking skills (developing)	• Communicating thoughts, ideas, and questions about the process

QUESTIONING Ask/answer questions about information. (CCSS.SL.3.3)	Students will be able to ask and answer questions related to the plan at hand.	• Casual conversations • Academic conversations	• Questions • Communicating ideas
REPORTING Report on a topic. (CCSS.SL.3.4)	Students will be able to present their small group and to the whole class.	• Class presentations	• Persuading
NARRATIVE Write a narrative based on event using detail and sequence. (CCSS.W.3)	Students will be able to explain difficulties they encountered during the project process. Students will be able to describe the experience of planting their design.	• Class reports • Reading responses • Journaling	• Communicating events • Expressing personal thoughts, ideas, and emotions

* Adapted from Common Core State Standards (CCSS)

TEMPLATE FOR TAKING FIELD NOTES

Date:
Site: Adams
Activity: Focus on Math and Science for Board Game
Participants: Teacher, 21 Girls, 20 Boys
Length of Observation: 10: 15 - 11: 15 a.m.
Field Notes Recording Time: 9:30 p.m.

Summary
Write a one paragraph summary or abstract of the day's events. Include analytic description, such as today was a good example of code-switching.

My goal today was to get the students writing specific questions relating to math and science for their board games. I introduced a chart for them to record their questions to help them get organized. The organization also assists T. with identifying where their connection to math and science is on the game board. I also talked about an article they had read and discussed in Science yesterday about underground communities being built in Japan. I had assumed they had also had homework from this article, but later I found out that about half the class had stayed in music and only the music students had received it for homework - which was just to read the article.

As a whole class I talked about some of the issues related to living underground per the article - again I had assumed they had the articles. But since they didn't, I just tried to bring up the issues hoping they would make some connections between the discussion and the City of Ember. However, as I walked around the classroom and talked with students, few seemed to understand the issues. Working math problems into the game seemed easier for them. Even trying to get them to brainstorm about science ideas in their groups wasn't working.

Narrative
While some of the groups were able to incorporate science and math concepts with efficacy, most of the groups were struggling with trying to get more than 2 or 3 science concepts. Some students weren't participating in any way. I finally suggested that in groups of four, 2 students work on the math and 2 students work on the science.

Questions/Things to follow up with
I want the students to give examples of what they've come up with and for science; they were supposed to be given homework to use the article to write 5 science questions related to The City of Ember. My original question was wondering why the students weren't working at a more efficient rate and wondering why they were struggling. Bev T. suggested I continue to scaffold with them - that the vocabulary and concepts are new for them whereas it's easy for me.

FIGURE 1.2 Field Note Template, Adams' Teachers (Chapter 4)

when looking at their field notes. Teachers are adjusting, adapting, fixing, and re-creating a lesson to fit the needs of their students (Figure 1.2).

Coding Sheet

After each unit was implemented and recorded, there was usually a 3- to 4-week period dedicated for reflection and analysis. During this period, teachers used

1	Time	a. Peer Assistance	b. Funds of Knowledge	c. Multiple Languages /Discourse	d. Questions	e. Tension	f. Third Space	g. Participation Shifts	h. Role Shift	I. Rule Negotation	
2	0:00:00		I	I AAVE							
3	0:02:00		I					I			
4	0:04:00		I			I				I	
5	0:06:00		I								
6	0:08:00		I	I				I		I	(gender)
7	0:10:00	I	I	I				I		I	
8	0:12:00	I	I		I		I	I			Perspective
9	0:14:00							I	I		
10	0:16:00		I					I			
11	0:18:00					I					
12	0:20:00		I					I	I		
13	0:22:00		I	I AAVE							
14	0:24:00							I			
15	0:26:00	I	I					I			
16	0:28:00		I					I	I	I	[illegible]

FIGURE 1.3 Coding Sheet, Adams' Teachers (Chapter 6)

a coding sheet to identify practices within sociocultural domains of learning (see Appendix E for a blank template). They looked closely at specific areas of focus in the study (e.g., IRE discourse patterns, teacher/student talk, mediational tools). They used the coding sheet to tally observable instances of the following: *peer assistance*, *funds of knowledge use*, the use of *multiple languages/discourses*, *questions*, *tension*, episodes of *third space*, *shifts in participation*, learner *role shifts* (expert/novice), and *rule negotiation*. Teachers were then given flexibility in what codes they specifically use in their classroom based on the patterns that arise from coding their pilot or first unit. Teachers then used the coding as data showing areas of improvement, gaps, or further areas of interest they wish they could have studied further (Figure 1.3).

Discourse Analysis and Transcription

The teachers transcribed 2 minutes from three 30- to 60-minute lessons in each unit. Each transcription shows a critical moment caught on camera in their classroom. The video clip can be essential in a teacher's analysis on how to describe the classroom and the shifts that are occurring in their students and practice. As teachers are able to choose the 2 minutes they would like to transcribe, it shows the teacher taking the role as a researcher using data to build themes.

To explain how discourse was analyzed, we must first establish how to define discourse. Gee (2014) defines discourse as stretches of language that make sense to people in a community or in a certain context. There are specific words or phrases that can only be understood within a specific community, for example "PD" in the teacher community most often means "professional development."

```
01 Cara:      What's the first thing you have to do with the ground?
02 Sheldon:   Oh (.) I know!(1 sec) [You
03 Jerry:                           [You water it. Then you put the plant.
04            Then you put then you put the seed.
05 S:         Then you put the soil.
06 Jerry:     You put the dirt.
07 Cara:      Soil? (1 sec) What if there's soil already out there?
08 Sheldon:                          [No::: /that's wrong
09            Ms.C./ I know what you do with it.]
10 SS:        (students raising hands)
11 S:         Dirt.
12 Cara:      Dirt.
13 Sheldon:   I know what you do with it.
```
Transcript Conventions in Appendix F

FIGURE 1.4 Sample Transcript, Adams Cohort (Chapter 6)

In classrooms, it is important that students build knowledge, and one way to measure that growth is through discourse analysis. We used discourse analysis as a metric for how much learners appropriate the object and goals of the activities. Discourse analysis can be used as a form of assessment, especially when it is a clear goal in the classroom (Figure 1.4).

The reports teachers write at the end of each unit help them and the researcher to see their growth in learning and what impact action research is having in their classrooms. Teachers not only get to analyze the change in themselves, but also in their students. Teachers are also able to focus on key concepts or areas in which they wish to improve such as more students talking or less IRE instruction. We provided the following questions for teachers to reflect on at the end of each unit as well as for the final report:

Questions for Unit Reflection and Final Cohort Report

1. Do you see differences from the first to the second video with respect to the protocol (shifts in participation)?
2. Look at modality (shift from uncertainty to certainty) in terms of knowledges students bring to the activity. The move could be from definite to indefinite linguistic features, such as a move from using *may* or *might* to *is*.
3. Have the learning outcomes been achieved? If so, what is the evidence?
4. What would you change/modify based on what you observed and learned?
5. What missed opportunities for expansion did you identify?
6. Are there examples of repair that you noticed?
7. Did the activity system work with respect to math, science, and literacy?
8. What new things emerged?
9. List other aspects of the protocol you would like to discuss.
10. How have your views of action research, sociocultural theory, discourse analysis, identity (i.e., learner, English learners) developed over the course of the semester?

Action Research Timeline

Action Research Course

All teachers began the program by taking a semester-long course, with Professor Razfar and Graduate Assistants, on action research and content integration for ELs, mathematics, and science (Razfar, 2007). The course introduced them to the project's sociocultural theoretical framework through primary research articles. The teachers participated in online discussions, led classroom presentations, conducted fieldwork, and carried out a pilot action research study implementing all the theoretical and discourse analytic tools they would utilize for their yearlong action research.

During the course, each school cohort created an action plan designed to provide participants with practice designing, implementing, and studying an integrated mathematics, science, and literacy unit based on FoK. Participating teachers worked as a cohort to develop a funds of knowledge inventory table, activity triangle, protocol, and field-notes. As a cohort, they analyzed three videos from one teacher's classroom using the coding sheet and wrote a group report of their findings.

Yearlong Action Research Project

In the academic year following the course, each cohort worked with the research team to conduct a yearlong action research project. The process mirrored the one modeled during the action research course with variations in terms of time, space, and depth of content. Each school cohort designed and implemented three thematic units according to the following timeline: (1) Funds of Knowledge inquiry (September); (2) Unit 1 implementation followed by analysis (October–December); (3) Unit 2 implementation followed by analysis (February–April); (4) Unit 3 implementation followed by analysis (May–June). An outline of the action research is shown in Figure 1.5.

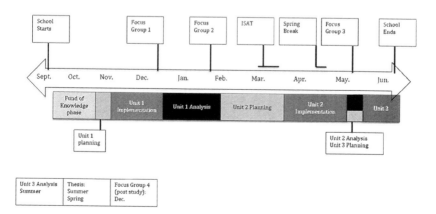

FIGURE 1.5 Action Research Timeline

TABLE 1.3 Integrated Curriculum Units

School Cohort	Unit 1	Unit 2	Unit 3
Adams	Video Games	Community Gardening	Video Games/Community Gardening
Jarman	Microworlds	Levers and Pulleys	Solar Energy
Warner	Technology & Me	Forensics	Forensics
Poplar	Community Awareness	Graffiti/Violence	Community Clean-Up/ Safety

Each cohort of teachers planned and designed three units that were implemented during the year. The unit planning template consisted of three phases: (1) planning; (2) implementing; and (3) analyzing. During the planning phase, the activity triangle and funds of knowledge inventory table were primarily used. During the implementing phase lesson plans, field notes, and coding sheets were used. During the analyzing phase, the entire corpus of data was used to identify, transcribe, and discuss relevant vignettes. Finally, a unit report was produced. For a more detailed template on the unit plan process, see Appendix G. The following table shows the integrated curriculum units designed by the teachers highlighted in this book (Table 1.3).

Teacher Study Groups

The research team met weekly with teachers in study groups to discuss developments in the field, including video recordings from at least three class periods of the unit (one at the beginning, middle, and end). As previously mentioned, the codes were intended as a starting point for discourse analysis, and over time, especially by unit 3, teachers often expanded and/or deleted these codes as they deemed appropriate. Teachers used their summative observation protocols to then identify episodes for more detailed transcription and discourse analysis. After each unit, teachers individually reported emergent themes across their data corpus and addressed key issues regarding content integration, language development, and modifications for subsequent units. After discussing individual reports, each cohort synthesized their collective findings to be shared with the research team.

Final Action Research Report

When completing the action research process, all teachers were impacted by the level of reflection needed to be successful. Teachers have discussed in focus groups and individually about how their teaching changed because of the reflective practices. The teachers in this book often reflected right after a lesson or while the lesson was taking place. These moments helped shape the subsequent lessons. This practice made the unit much more responsive to the students instead of the teachers' goals.

Reflection on their practices, in the form of data collections as well as conversation, helped the teacher–researchers pinpoint areas of improvement. In the first unit, it was clear that as a group they were not utilizing students' funds of knowledge effectively. After realizing this, teachers made it a focus for unit 2. As teachers discussed during focus groups, unit 2 was much more successful. Teachers defined success as more use of nutritional discourse in conversation, students moving for certainty to certainty, and ability to explain content. Teacher researchers connect these successes to their change in approach to include more opportunities for students to use their funds of knowledge to build understanding. Moving forward, these are practices they will use more often to promote confidence and knowledge building through peers.

By using funds of knowledge and having success, teachers also noted the change of focus. The knowledge building was done through peer conversation and input from students. All the teachers structured their classrooms in small-group or large-group discussion with very little teacher direct instruction. The results of these practices were impactful to the teachers. Through data collection, teacher researchers noted that students were using more language and in ways they had not before. Students that felt uncomfortable speaking Spanish were code-switching, or, as we now prefer, *translanguaging* (García, 2009), during a conversation about healthy choices using appropriate vocabulary. Students felt comfortable challenging each other's ideas respectfully, resulting in new knowledge gained. Although teachers noted that they felt it was difficult to relinquish that control, they all noticed the benefits. Teachers were so used to being the knowledge center that it felt awkward to have students explain. However, when the evidence was reviewed, no one could refute the gains made.

Completion of this book should provide teachers a foundation for how to conduct action research in their classroom. It should also provide teachers with an understanding of why there is a need to help ELs through STEM and literacy practices. From this book, teachers should be able to better understand how to conduct research and use data to drive their own practice.

Discussion Questions

1. Language questions:
   i. How do you define language?
   ii. How do you define culture?
2. Tell me about your own experiences as a second language learner. Or if you are not a second language learner, how does that impact how you relate to EL issues? Can you tell me about a time being an EL impacted learning math or science? How have you used a child's primary language in science or math to make learning more accessible?

3. Could you tell me a memorable math or science experience? (Could be positive or negative). When did you feel an affinity or aversion to math and/or science? (Look out for gender issues, EL issues, etc.)
4. How would you define scientific language? How can you help students learn the language of science?
5. How would you define mathematical language? How can you help students learn the language of math?
6. What kinds of errors, linguistic or conceptual, have you experienced with your students? How do you deal with it?
7. What is "standard English"? How important is it to know "standard English" to do science and math?
8. Do you think it is more or less difficult for dialect-speakers and/or second language learners to learn science and/or math? Explain why or why not.
9. How do you feel about students *speaking* in nonstandard English or another language during science and/or math class?
10. How do you feel about students *writing* in nonstandard English or another language in science class?
11. Questions about action research:
    i. What do you see as key issues or challenges in conducting action research?
    ii. How do you feel about working in a cohort? What are some of the challenges or strengths?
12. How does discourse analysis impact how you see yourself? Please provide stories and examples of your own practice.

Additional Resources

1. *English Learning through Mathematics, Science, and Action Research* www.elmsa.org
   Additional specific links to tools and artifacts (protocol, activity triangle, and field note templates)
2. Action Research Projects with a STEM Focus
   https://www.stem.org.uk/resources/collection/3054/action-research-projects
3. NSTA: Action Research for Science Teachers
   https://www.nsta.org/science-teacher/science-teacher-february-2020/action-research-science-teachers
4. NAEYC: Teacher Researcher Resources
   https://www.naeyc.org/resources/pubs/vop/about-teacher-research
5. Integrating Language While Teaching STEM
   https://ell.stanford.edu/sites/default/files/pdf/academic-papers/03-Quinn%20Lee%20Valdes%20Language%20and%20Opportunities%20in%20Science%20FINAL.pdf

Notes

1 *Transforming literacy, science, and math through action research (LSciMAct).* Five-year project funded by Office of English Language Acquisition, U.S. Department of Education. (Award Number T195N070301).
2 *English learning through math, science, and action research (ELMSA).* Five-year grant funded by Office of English Language Acquisition, U.S. Department of Education. (Award Number T365Z110179).

References

Adelman, C. (1993). Kurt Lewin and the origins of action research, *Educational Action Research, 1*(1), 7–24. DOI: 10.1080/0965079930010102

Andrews, D. J. C., Brown, T., Castillo, B. M., Jackson, D., & Vellanki, V. (2019). Beyond damage-centered teacher education: Humanizing pedagogy for teacher educators and preservice teachers. *Teachers College Record, 121*(6), 1–28.

Baquedano-López, P., Solis, J. L., & Kattan, S. (2005). Adaptation: The language of classroom learning. *Linguistics and Education, 16*(1), 1–26.

Bartolomé, L. (1994). Beyond the methods fetish: Toward a humanizing pedagogy. *Harvard Educational Review, 64*(2), 173–195.

Blume, R. (1971). Humanizing teacher education. *The Phi Delta Kappan, 52*(7), 411–415.

Brisk, M. E. (Ed.). (2008). *Language, culture, and community in teacher education.* New York, NY: Erlbaum.

Brown, B. A. (2006). "It isn't no slang that can be said about this stuff": Language, identity, and appropriating science discourse. *Journal of Research in Science Teaching, 43*(1), 96–126.

Carter-Andrews, D. J., & Castillo, B. (2016). Humanizing pedagogy for examinations of race and culture in teacher education. In F. Tuitt, C. Haynes, & S. Stewart (Eds.), *Race, equity and higher education: The continued search for critical and inclusive pedagogies around the globe* (pp. 112–130). Sterling, VA: Stylus Publishing.

Cater, M., Machtmes, K., & Fox, J. (2013). A phenomenological examination of context on adolescent ownership and engagement. *The Qualitative Report, 18*(Art. 31), 1–13.

Cazden, C. B., John, V. P., & Hymes, D. (1972). *Functions of language in the classroom.* New York, NY: Columbia University Press.

Christoph, J. N., & Nystrand, M. (2001). *Taking risks, negotiating relationships: One teacher's transition towards a dialogic classroom.* National Research Center on English Learning and Achievement. CELA Research Report Number 14003.

Civil, M. (2016). STEM learning research through a funds of knowledge lens. *Cultural Studies of Science Education, 11*, 41–59. DOI: 10.1007/s11422-014-9648-2

Campus Compact. (2016). *Carnegie Community Engagement Classification.* Retrieved from https://compact.org/initiatives/engaged-campus-initiative/carnegie-community-engagement-classification/

Cochran-Smith, M., Fieman-Nemser, S., McIntyre, D. J., & Demers, K. E. (Eds.). (2008). *Handbook of research on teacher education: Enduring questions in changing contexts* (3rd ed.). New York, NY: Routledge.

Driscoll, A. (2008). Carnegie's community-engagement classification: Intentions and insights. *Change: The Magazine of Higher Learning, 40*(1), 38–41.

Driscoll, A. (2014). Analysis of the Carnegie classification of community engagement: Patterns and impact on institutions. *New Directions for Institutional Research, 2014*(162), 3–15.

Engeström, Y. (1999). Innovative learning in work teams: Analyzing cycles of knowl-
edge creation in practice. In Y. Engeström, R. Miettinen, & R.-L. Punamäki (Eds.),
Perspectives on activity theory (pp. 377–404). New York, NY: Cambridge University Press.
Freire, P. (1993). *Pedagogy of the oppressed.* New York, NY: Continuum Press.
García, O. (2009). Education, multilingualism and translanguaging in the 21st century. In
A. Mohanty, M. Panda, R. Phillipson, & T. Skutnabb-Kangas (Eds.), *Multilingual educa-
tion for social justice: Globalising the local* (pp. 128–145). New Delhi: Orient Blackswan.
Gee, J. P. (2014). *An introduction to discourse analysis: Theory and method.* New York, NY:
Routledge.
Green, J. L. (1983). Research on teaching as a linguistic process: A state of the art. *Review
of Research in Education, 10*(1), 151–252.
Green, J. L., Camilli, G., & Elmore, P. B. (Eds.). (2012). *Handbook of complementary methods
in education research.* New York, NY: Routledge.
Gupta, K. C. L. (2020). Researcher-teacher collaboration. In Adopting critical content and
language integrated learning (CLIL): Processes, challenges and outcomes. *Trabalhos em
Linguística Aplicada, 59*(1), 42–77.
Gutiérrez, K. D., Baquedano-López, P., Alvarez, H. H., & Chiu, M. M. (1999). Building a
culture of collaboration through hybrid language practices. *Theory into Practice, 38*(2),
87–93.
Gutiérrez, K. D., Rymes, B., & Larson, J. (1995). Script, counterscript, and underlife in
the classroom: James Brown versus Brown v. Board of Education. *Harvard Educational
Review, 65*(3), 445–471.
Hicks, D. (1995). Chapter 2 discourse, learning, and teaching. *Review of Research in
Education, 21*(1), 49–95.
Irizarry, J., & Brown, T. (2013). Humanizing research in dehumanizing spaces: The challenges and opportunities of conducting participatory action research with youth in
schools. In D. Paris & M. Winn (Eds.), *Humanizing research: Decolonizing qualitative
inquiry with youth and communities* (pp. 63–80). Thousand Oaks, CA: SAGE.
Johnson, A. P. (2008). *A short guide to action research* (3rd ed.). Boston, MA: Allyn and Bacon.
Kelly, G. J., & Green, J. (2019). Framing issues of theory and methods for the study of science and engineering education. In G. J. Kelly & J. L. Green (Eds.), *Theory and methods
for sociocultural research in science and engineering education* (pp. 1–28). New York: NY:
Routledge.
Lee, C. D., & Smagorinsky, P. (Eds.). (2000). *Vygotskian perspectives on literacy research:
Constructing meaning through collaborative inquiry. Learning in doing: Social, cognitive, and
computational perspectives.* New York, NY: Cambridge University Press.
Lewin, K. (1946). Action research and minority problems. *Journal of Social Issues, 2*(4),
34–46.
Merriam, S. B. (2007). *Qualitative research and case study applications in education: Revised and
expanded from case study research* (2nd ed.). San Francisco, CA: Jossey-Bass.
Mills, G. E. (2003). *Action research: A guide for the teacher researcher* (2nd ed.). Upper Saddle
River, NJ: Merrill Prentice Hall.
Mills, G. E. (2018). *Action research: A guide for the teacher researcher* (6th ed.). Upper Saddle
River, NJ: Merrill Prentice Hall.
Mirra, N. (2018). *Educating for empathy.* New York, NY: Teachers College Press.
Morales-Doyle, D. (2017). Justice centered science pedagogy: A catalyst for academic
achievement and social transformation. *Science Education, 101*(6), 1034–1060.

Morrell, E. (2006). Toward a bottom up accountability system in urban education: Students as researchers in urban schools. In J. Cammarota, S. Ginwright, & P. Noguera (Eds.), *Beyond resistance! Youth activism and community change* (pp. 111–129). New York, NY: Routledge.

Moschkovich, J. (2007). Examining mathematical discourse practices. *For the Learning of Mathematics, 27*(1), 24–30.

National Research Council. (2014). *Literacy for science: Exploring the intersection of the Next Generation Science Standards and Common Core for ELA Standards: A workshop summary.* Washington, DC: The National Academies Press. https://doi.org/10.17226/18803

Paris, D., & Winn, M. T. (Eds.). (2013). *Humanizing research: Decolonizing qualitative inquiry with youth and communities.* Thousand Oaks, CA: Sage Publications.

Ratner, C. (2002). *Cultural psychology: Theory and methods.* New York, NY: Springer Science & Business Media.

Razfar, A. (2007). *Transforming literacy, science, and math through action research (LSciMAct).* Washington, DC: Grant funded by the U.S. Department of Education.

Razfar, A. (2011). Action research in urban schools: Empowerment, transformation, and challenges. *Teacher Education Quarterly, 38*(4), 25–44.

Razfar, A., Khisty, L., & Chval, K. (2011). Re-mediating second language acquisition: A sociocultural perspective for language development. *Mind, Culture, and Activity, 18*(3), 195–215. DOI: 10.1080/10749030903494427

Razfar, A., & Li, R. (2014, September). *Transforming, literacy, science, and mathematics through action research (LSciMACT): Final evaluation report of national professional development program.* Washington, DC: U.S. Department of Education.

Razfar, A., & Li, R. (2017, October). *English learning through mathematics, science and action research (ELMSA): Final evaluation report of national professional development program.* Washington, DC: U.S. Department of Education.

Reason, P., & Bradbury, H. (2001). Introduction: Inquiry and participation in search of a world worthy of human aspiration. In P. Reason & H. Bradbury (Eds.), *Handbook of action research* (pp. 1–14). London/Thousand Oaks, CA: Sage Publications.

Rex, L. A., & Schiller, L. (2009). *Using discourse analysis to improve classroom interaction.* New York, NY: Routledge.

Rios-Aguilar, C., Kiyama, J. M., Gravitt, M., & Moll, L. C. (2011). Funds of knowledge for the poor and forms of capital for the rich? A capital approach to examining funds of knowledge. *Theory and Research in Education, 9*(2), 163–184.

Rogoff, B., & Chavajay, P. (1995). What's become of research on the cultural basis of cognitive development? *American Psychologist, 50*(10), 859.

Roth, W. M., & Lee, Y. J. (2007). "Vygotsky's neglected legacy": Cultural-historical activity theory. *Review of Educational Research, 77*(2), 186–232.

Sagor, R. (2000). *Guiding school improvement with action research.* Alexandria, VA: Association for Supervision and Curriculum Development.

Sagor, R. (2009). Collaborative action research and school improvement: You can't have one without the other. *Journal of Curriculum and Instruction, 3*(1), 7–14.

Serido, J., Borden, L. M., & Perkins, D. F. (2011). Moving beyond youth voice. *Youth & Society, 43*(1), 44–63.

Shulman, L. S. (1986). Paradigms and research programs in the study of teaching: A contemporary perspective. In M. C. Wittrock (Ed.), *Handbook of research on teaching* (pp. 3–36). New York, NY: Macmillan.

Silberman, C. E. (Ed.). (1973). *The open classroom reader* (Vol. 850). New York, NY: Vintage Books.

Soja, E. W. (1989). *Postmodern geographies: The reassertion of space in critical social theory.* New York, NY: Verso.

Suárez, E. (2020). "Estoy explorando science": Emergent bilingual students problematizing electrical phenomena through translanguaging. *Science Education, 104*(5), 791–826.

Trent, J. (2020, January 31). *Engagement of the highest order: University named "Carnegie Engaged."* Nevada Today, University of Nevada, Reno. Retrieved from https://www.unr.edu/nevada-today/news/2020/carnegie-community-engagement

Wells, G. (2000). Dialogic inquiry in education: Building on the legacy of Vygotsky. In C. D. Lee & P. Smagorinsky (Eds.), *Vygotskian perspectives on literacy research* (pp. 51–84). New York, NY: Cambridge University Press.

Wertsch, J. V. (1998). *Mind as action.* New York, NY: Oxford University Press.

Zipin, L. (2009). Dark funds of knowledge, deep funds of pedagogy: Exploring boundaries between lifeworlds and schools. *Discourse: Studies in the Cultural Politics of Education, 30*(3), 317–331.

2

TEACHING MATH AND SCIENCE THROUGH PLAYGROUND ACTIVISM

Teachers need to show parents and the community that funds of knowledge and native language are important tools for their students' learning. As we engaged in our students' funds, we thought we were only changing the identities of our students to become community activists, but we realized our roles shifted to also become community activists with them. We emerged as leaders.

Karen, Second Grade Teacher, Genesis Elementary

Introduction

At the time of the study, Genesis Elementary was an underachieving school that was placed on academic probation, with 35% of the school population identifying as English learners. Genesis consists of over 875 students with racial demographics of 95% Latinx, 3% African-American/Black, and 2% classified as "Other," with 98% of students qualifying for free or reduced lunch. Although the school adopted a Transitional Bilingual Education program for grades K–4, the teachers, Karen and Abby, self-identified as white, female, English monolinguals. Karen had taught for 5 years with a strong reading background and was teaching second grade. Abby had taught for 4 years as the lead science teacher and was teaching first grade. Both classrooms consisted of students who had transitioned out of a Transitional Bilingual Education (TBE) program but still needed academic language support.

The teachers believed that the fact that their math and science textbooks did not make language or content accessible to their ELs contributed to their school's underachievement. They saw how these textbooks were void of making

DOI: 10.4324/9781351001168-2

real-world connections to their students. The materials did not leverage their students' cultural or linguistic strengths and were not meaningful to them. At the forefront of the teachers' goal was to design a curriculum that would leverage their students' funds of knowledge (FoK) and outside experiences to make meaningful academic connections (González, Moll, & Amanti, 2006). In addition, these science funds would be used to create hybrid spaces of science learning (Barton & Tan, 2009). This chapter represents the story of how Karen and Abby sought to gather, select, and teach mathematics and science content and literacy to ELs. Additionally, we examine how the teachers made FoK align and be centered when planning for unit learning goals, essential questions, lesson objectives, and assessments.

Standards

Science

- Ask questions, make observations, and gather information about a situation people want to change to define a simple problem.
- Simple sketch, drawing, or physical model to illustrate how an object functions as needed to solve a problem.
  (standards adapted from NGSS K-2, ETS1-1, K-2, ETS1-3)

Mathematics

- Organize and display data using pictures, tallies, tables, charts, or bar graphs.
- Describe numerical relationships using variables and patterns.
- Analyze data, draw conclusions, and communicate the result.
  (standards adapted from CISBE 10A.1a, 8A, 10B 1c)

Literacy

- Participate in shared research and writing projects (e.g., explore a number of "how-to" books on a given topic, and use them to write a sequence of instructions).
- With guidance and support from adults, recall information from experiences or gather information from provided sources to answer a question.
  (standards adapted from CCSS ELA-Literacy W.1.7 and W.18)

Language

- English language learners communicate for social and instructional purposes within the school setting.
- English language learners communicate information, ideas, and concepts necessary for academic success in the content area of Language Arts.
- English language learners communicate information, ideas, and concepts necessary for academic success in the content area of Mathematics.
- English language learners communicate information, ideas, and concepts necessary for academic success in the content area of Science.
- English language learners communicate information, ideas, and concepts necessary for academic success in the content area of Social Studies.
  (standards adapted from WIDA Consortium Standards 1–5)

Chapter Objectives

1. Teachers will learn how to design FoK activities that are authentic and meaningful to their students.
2. Teachers will learn how to select and analyze FoK that are aligned to math and science standards.
3. Teachers will learn how FoK can be leveraged to create an integrated math and science lesson to build academic language.

Unit Objectives

1. Students will be able to make observations and draw sketches of a model needed to solve a problem.
2. Students will be able to create, organize, and analyze survey data results to compare findings.
3. Students will be able to mathematically and scientifically communicate with data the need for a playground.

Context: School, Teachers, Students

Genesis is located in an urban public school district with a large population of ELs at risk, consisting of over 875 students with racial demographics of around 95% Latinx, 3% African American/Black, and 2% classified as "Other." Genesis is situated in a predominately Latinx low-income neighborhood with 98% of students qualifying for free or reduced lunch. Although the school adopted a Transitional Bilingual

Education program for grades K–4, the teachers and students were in a monolingual English classroom, where many students transitioned out of the program. When we began working with the teachers at Genesis Elementary School, the school was on academic probation. According to the state report card, the school's reading scores were about 30% compared to the state average of 57%. Additionally, the mathematics scores were about 45% compared to the state average of 59%.

Abby self-identifies as a monolingual, English, Caucasian/white teacher who taught primary grades for 4 years. She holds a science endorsement and is the lead science teacher for first grade. Her classroom consists of 28 students of which she concentrated on four ELs for her action research project. The first student, Alex, is Spanish proficient who has average scores in reading, math, and science. Holly also speaks Spanish as her home language and has low reading, math, and science scores. James is a student who is English and Spanish proficient with high reading scores across math, science, and reading. Finally, Alexis is also English and Spanish proficient with low science, but average math and reading scores. Abby is particularly concerned with science content knowledge and participation for Alex and Holly.

Karen self-identifies as a Caucasian/white, English monolingual teacher who has taught first grade for 3 years. At the time of the study, this was her 4th year teaching, but her first year teaching second grade. Karen has a strong reading background with a bachelors' degree in Elementary Education with a focus on language arts. She is Genesis' lead reading teacher. Many of Karen's students were prior students she had in first grade or Abby's former students. She has 28 students, of which 6 are part of the prior year's gifted program. For her action research, she selected to focus on her student Brock. Brock is an EL, whose home language is Spanish and who she retained when she had him in first grade due to his low achievement. He receives services for speech therapy and has been labeled with attention-deficit/hyperactivity disorder (ADHD). His academic performance is underachieving across reading, math, and science.

Unit Plan: Building a Playground Through Youth Participatory Action Research

Genesis had a large increase in students attending the school, and the administration struggled with how to deal with the overcrowding. Several students would be kept indoors for lunch because there was not enough cafeteria space in the gym. With limited specials classrooms, art and health began to also be held in the general classrooms. Significantly, recess had been indefinitely cancelled for safety reasons as the current play space had caused relatively serious injuries and parent outrage. The students expressed concerns that they were being punished by being held inside the classroom walls for extended periods. The teachers felt they owed their students an outdoor experience but also wanted to learn about their FoK, so they implemented a community walk in order to understand how students interacted with their community. In particular, students saw how a neighboring private school had a beautiful playground and pointed out the inequity, inquiring why their school could not have a playground. Instead, Genesis had an empty cement lot with hazardous cracks. This interaction was a critical moment where teachers learned the importance of playgrounds and recess time from the students' perspectives and understood they are not only something desired, but also a need, necessary for students' livelihood. As a result, teachers and students championed to advocate for a playground at their school.

Youth Participatory Action Research (YPAR) is a groundbreaking critical research methodology that seeks to actively promote youth leadership in participatory action research to address political challenges and the inherent imbalances in conducting research (Cammarota & Fine, 2010). A comprehensive review of YPAR has shown the benefits of developing agency and leadership, academic advancement, as well as positive personal and interpersonal cognitive outcomes (Anyon, Bender, Kennedy, & Dechants, 2018). YPAR is an effective methodology for developing grassroots, community based, and student-led science curriculum (Morales-Doyle & Frausto, 2020). The grassroots science curriculum units developed by the teachers and students at Genesis is an example of moving from teacher-guided and teacher-led participatory action research (PAR) toward student-led youth participatory action research (YPAR).

The unit began with students identifying school leaders and key policy actors and their roles for who they would need to persuade for a playground. They were able to learn about how a policy has come into practice in a school. They began to research steps to solving the issue by bringing in photos of the playground, drawings, and personal experiences. Students also made scientific observations of the current school playlot to argue that the lot was unsafe and practiced technology and engineering skills in science to identify a problem and pose a solution (K-2-ETS1-1). Additionally, students applied statistical and data analysis as they created and implemented surveys to parents, community members, and the local school council to gather results to support their need for a playground. The students shared their survey data with the administration and alderman, and in partnership with Disney and Kaboom organizations, they successfully built a playground (KABOOM!, 2021).

Language Learning Domain: Integrating Mathematics and Science Funds

The mathematics and science standards were demonstrated in the lesson with all language domains of reading, writing, speaking, and listening. However, it was a challenge to make sure that all language domains were balanced in the unit. Initially the teachers were focused on the language domain of speaking and listening. The teachers wanted additional opportunities for students to think independently and talk collaboratively with other students. The teachers began to design lessons by using the perspective of what students would be doing which position, with the teachers as *facilitators* of students' activities. This also informed a different perspective to students' listening skills. Instead of listening to the teacher during the instructional discourse, the students have the chance to *listen to each other*. Students began listening for different purposes. Students were not just listening for teacher directions and explanations of science and mathematics concepts. They were listening to one another's *funds* and made sense of how they were similar or different to their viewpoints on playgrounds. This facilitated deeper and personal mathematics and science learning. In doing so, the teachers were making scientific talk accessible for students because in this example, the students could speak to playground experiences while learning about data analysis.

The teacher also changed the opportunities for students to engage in communicating scientific writing. The students wrote out interview responses from surveys and created science journals to make observations of the playlot. Teachers expanded students' writing to be every day in their journals as opposed to writing once for a final poster assessment. In addition, the teachers thought about scientific reading as more than just interpreting data. The teachers wanted students to familiarize themselves with nonfiction texts, so in their traditional language arts block, they planned to teach students the difference between fiction and nonfiction texts. As a follow-up for independent reading time, students would read nonfiction books. Reading and learning about nonfiction texts prepared students for their whole-class read aloud in unit 2. The teachers relied on materials outside traditional science and math textbooks, such as read-aloud books like *Groovy Gravity* by Rena Korb, to explain the concept of gravity. The book was passed around throughout the unit for students to read on their own as well (Korb, 2007). As a result, the teachers planned to foster reading, listening, oral, and writing communications in math and science.

In the climate of high-stakes assessment and standards-reform, there is a pressing issue on how to apply standards *equitably* to ELs with varying levels of English proficiency. Important to the conversation is equity in access to the resources and outcomes for achievement to ensure ELs reach the standards. In this unit, we noticed that the supports used in the lesson represented the students' dominant culture, as opposed to traditional Eurocentric practices found in packaged curriculum. The supports were drawn from human capital, such as the parents and community members, voicing with the students their needs through survey responses. Many of the survey responses were spoken in Spanish requiring students to translate and leverage their native language for data analysis. We also saw technology supports carried as students used video recorders to create social media footage as a way to advertise to grant organizations to fund their playground. The teachers also created student-friendly graphic organizers such as the survey and data analysis chart to help students leveraging universal design principles with the bold fonts and poster-style presentation. These supports still encouraged academic language development that met students' linguistic proficiency levels while maintaining the rigor of the content standards.

Social Organization of Learning: Becoming Community Activists and Researchers

As teachers created the first unit plan, they thought about the end outcomes. Situated in a sociocultural perspective, they wanted their students to appropriate the identity of a community activist, a researcher, and a team player. They knew that the principles and values of the collective would carry further than the individual. They wanted their students to experience activism so they can empower their civic engagement by using mathematics and science to make claims and persuade the school and alderman committee to change their school. Moreover, the identity of a researcher was vital in being able to draw scientific inquiry and dive into data analysis in mathematics that are found in a researcher.

The Genesis teachers' activity triangle illustrates their unit plan for socially organizing learning around the central question of *how to design and build a playground* (Figure 2.1). The triangle outlines the activity design, the fundamental question that guides the learning process, the *object*, or immediate learning goal of the activity, the *mediational tools* (both material and ideational artifacts) that facilitate movement toward the learning goal, *the subjects* or immediate classroom participants, the *community* or distal participants, *the rules* that establish parameters for participation within the activity system, and *the division of effort*, which establishes roles and responsibilities for each learner toward accomplishing the learning goal, and finally *outcomes*, which are longitudinal effects suggesting a deeper shift in learner identity and consciousness. Outcomes help teachers think about practices and skills that transfer beyond the immediate learning goals or object of the activity.

In this design, Karen, Abby, and Lorena began with a broad question: *How do we design and build a playground?* This question is broad enough to generate robust opportunities for student participation and leveraging their full linguistic and cultural repertoires. It emerged from the funds of knowledge inquiry surveys, *Content Funds Questionnaire* (CFQ) and community walk conducted by the teachers. The *object* of the activity was to socialize learners to engineering practices that would ultimately lead to the appropriation of engineering identity(s). More specifically, the learning goal was situated within the physics content domain of balance, motion, and momentum. The engineering practices included data collection, analysis, presentation, creating graphs, writing surveys, and categorizing information. Other material mediational tools included: *All About Me* activity, a map of students' community walk, Pros and Cons Chart, graphic organizers, and posters. Additional playground-specific survey questions were developed to follow up on initial findings from the CFQ surveys. This

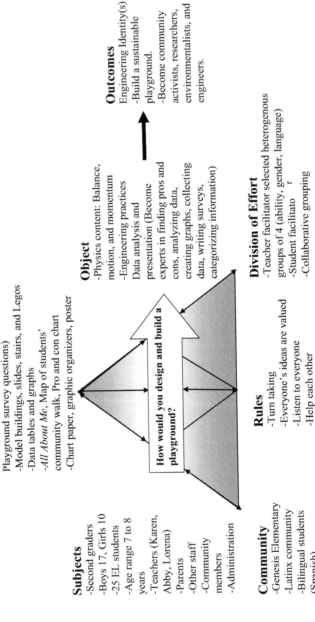

Tools and Artifacts
-Surveys (Content Funds Questions, Playground survey questions)
-Model buildings, slides, stairs, and Legos
-Data tables and graphs
-*All About Me,* Map of students' community walk, Pro and con chart
-Chart paper, graphic organizers, poster

Subjects
-Second graders
-Boys 17, Girls 10
-25 EL students
-Age range 7 to 8 years
-Teachers (Karen, Abby, Lorena)
-Parents
-Other staff
-Community members
-Administration

Object
-Physics content: Balance, motion, and momentum
-Engineering practices
Data analysis and presentation (Become experts in finding pros and cons, analyzing data, creating graphs, collecting data, writing surveys, categorizing information)

How would you design and build a playground?

Outcomes
Engineering Identity(s)
-Build a sustainable playground.
-Become community activists, researchers, environmentalists, and engineers.

Community
-Genesis Elementary
-Latinx community
-Bilingual students (Spanish)
-Families
-Local construction organizations

Rules
-Turn taking
-Everyone's ideas are valued
-Listen to everyone
-Help each other
-Share resources

Division of Effort
-Teacher facilitator selected heterogenous groups of 4 (ability, gender, language)
-Student facilitator
-Collaborative grouping

FIGURE 2.1 Teachers' Activity Triangle

survey led to the incorporation of data tables and graphs as well as playground modeling tools for slides, stairs, buildings, and Legos.

Karen, Abby, and Lorena heterogeneously organized the *subjects*, who were second graders between the ages of 7 and 8 (27 total), English learners (25), evenly split in terms of gender (17 boys, 10 girls), and mostly Latinx. The Genesis Elementary *community* was predominantly working class, Latinx, bilingual (Spanish), and local construction organizations.

The Genesis teachers purposefully designed ways to access community expertise in terms of interacting with local construction experts in building and design. They organized the students into heterogeneous groups of four by ability, gender, and language and explicitly established *rules* for participation, including turn-taking, valuing everybody's ideas, listening, helping, and sharing resources with each other. They designated the *division of effort* to provide students with a framework of how to participate in whole-class discussions as well as small groups. Collaborative grouping norms were established by designating student facilitators. Finally, Kara, Abby, and Lorena outlined transformative longitudinal outcomes for learners such as fostering engineering identity(s), building a sustainable playground, and becoming community activists, environmentalists, and researchers.

All About Me: Designing Curriculum Through Funds of Knowledge

One of the areas the teachers struggled with was trying to figure out what unit theme they would select. They knew it was important that a curriculum reflect students' identities but also were uncertain how math and science standards could be found in students' everyday experiences. In order to accomplish this task, it would require the teachers to purposefully gather math–science funds. We use the term *math–science funds* to articulate funds of knowledge that are aligned to math and science standards. Therefore, teachers knew they had to gather information about students in order to identify which were math–science funds. When the teachers began getting to know their students, they relied on their prior teaching knowledge to design a commonly used traditional *All About Me* worksheet describing their favorite things.

The *All About Me* worksheet focused on eliciting student interests about their favorite subjects, career goals, and favorite things, which led to superficial types of funds. Abby said:

> I just feel like they didn't go deep. They are little first graders. It seemed hard to take my students any deeper than "I cook at home with my mom." Like to get them to really go deep with it, I was disappointed.
>
> (Genesis Final Action Research Report)

The lack of deep funds contributed to the fact the questions were closed-ended, asking students to list interests, rather than share personal narratives. Additionally, the teachers were focusing on in-school knowledge as opposed to meaningful out-of-school experiences. We discovered that the *All About Me* survey did not capture any mathematics–science funds.

Teachers then decided to conduct "Lunch Talks," where they would bring a few students to have lunch with the teacher. The hope was that through informal conversations, teachers could expand on student dialogue from the *All About Me* handout. The teachers focused their discussions on exploring what students were really good at and what they knew a lot about so they could capitalize on students' strengths to teach content. Unfortunately, students did not open up to the teachers. As Karen describes:

> When I asked a few students what they felt they were good at, or what they knew a lot about, two or three just kind of shrugged. I'm not sure if they were being modest, if they didn't understand what I meant, or if they weren't self-aware enough to know what they were good at.
>
> (Genesis Final Action Research Report)

Upon further analysis, we also saw how positionality and power dynamics of the classroom made it difficult for students to talk.

The students were used to a classroom culture of IRE conversations, where the teacher initiated a question, students responded, and the teacher evaluated the answer (Cazden, 2001). In fact, for many students, this was the first time they were asked to have a conversation with the teacher presenting a classroom culture shift and confusion. In other words, students were not used to a classroom culture of initiating discussions by themselves about what is worthwhile in their lives. For a teacher to ask what a student is good at or what a student knows a lot about, it changes the status of what knowledge is significant to be spoken about with teachers. Karen modified the *rules* to the classroom discourse to shift from IRE to conversational discourse for when students interact with teachers (Wells, 1993). However, Karen was unable to provide the *mediational tools* to assist students toward this new type of conversational discourse. Even though it appears that students were partaking in an informal activity of lunch, Karen was unaware that holding the lunch in the official space of the classroom would lead a majority of students to appropriate the official rules of school, which fostered an IRE discourse.

After hosting lunch talks and completing *All About Me* worksheets, the teachers were not close to identifying math–science funds topics for a unit theme. With the support of the research team, Karen and Abby felt it was time for their roles to change. Instead of having students share their funds in the classroom, the teachers would gather student funds in the places they experience it. Being a teacher–ethnographer would require teachers to go outside their comfort zones

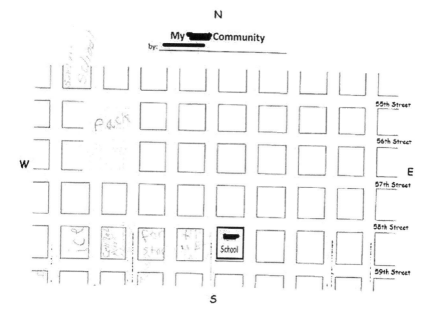

FIGURE 2.2   Map of Students' Community Walk

(i.e., school space) and dive into spaces that were part of the students' life-worlds (i.e., out-of-school space) (Barton & Tan, 2009).

Both Karen and Abby gave the students a handout of the community with a five-block radius from the school as depicted in Figure 2.2. As they walked around the neighborhood students wrote down all the places they go and shared what they do. A critical awareness emerged of where parks are located and not located in their neighborhoods, leading students to question the inequity for why Genesis did not have a playground, but a private school nearby did. Advocating for a playground was a uniting cause for teachers and students, and so they knew it would be a unit theme to keep. Moreover, the more students explained how they played on a playground, teachers could see the mathematical (e.g., geometric shapes on a playground, number sense, and operations for taking turns on a playground) and science engineering connections (e.g., physics on how playground objects work and building a playground). Therefore, they selected playgrounds as the unit theme.

What we learned from this experience is that designing a funds of knowledge activity requires a student-centered approach. It is important that teachers prompt students to ask questions and inquire about their community experiences. The goal is to have students not just share about their life, but also to problem pose and inquire. Students should be prompted to think critically and analyze their life experiences as a social problem. In doing so, teachers can use mathematics and science to solve the issue. Notice how topics about students' interests did not generate a problem. It is the role of the teacher to guide an inquiry to how the world works or what to change about the world. The question of "Why doesn't Genesis have a playground?" opens up the possibilities of an essential question that is explored through a mathematics and science lens. Moreover, the teacher must build a classroom culture that breaks the IRE discourse to one that is truly conversational with a shared teacher and student voice in order to elicit meaningful funds. Teachers need to be aware of how in-school ways to access funds will privilege school-dominant discourses, while out-of-school places will leverage student-centered experiences. Therefore, deep funds are elicited when teachers embody ethnographic tools, like community walks, to understand students' meaning and perspectives, as opposed to in-school contexts that are removed from their life-worlds. Finally, selecting a unit theme is not a neutral topic. The topic we choose will either invite or marginalize students to the conversation. Commercialized curriculums often select topics that are directly found in the standards. For instance, in science, we see weather, space, or animal units. These topics center on the standard rather than on the student creating barriers for a child to access because of their experiences to see science in weather, space, or animal connections. However, teaching mathematics and science through a central focus of a playground invited all students to participate. In doing so, we are not superficially inserting students' lives into content topics, but grounding students' lives at the center to show them the content, thereby making meaning stronger for the students.

"Should Genesis Have a Playground?" Aligning FoK to Mathematics and Science Standards

The goal of the first unit was to build solidarity and buy-in amongst key policy stakeholders and administration to understand that a playground is a need for their students. The teachers created an essential question asking, "Should Genesis have a playground?" In order to answer this question, the students would need to engage in the scientific and engineering design practices of *"Ask questions, make observations, and gather information about a situation people want to change to define a simple problem"* (adapted from Science Standards). The teachers created survey questions with students as a way to gather data and define the problem. The survey questions were *(1) What grade are you in? (2) Should we have a playground? (3) Why should or shouldn't we have a playground? (4) What kind(s) of things should we have on our playground? (5) What is wrong with the "playlot" that we have? (6) How often do you go to a playground each week?* The survey questions were administered by the students to school staff, community members, and parents.

Students also were to develop a *simple sketch, drawing, or physical model to illustrate how an object functions as needed to solve a problem* (adapted from Science Standards). Several students drew the picture of the play lot and discussed the cause and effect of safety issues from the hazardous cement. Additionally, students engaged in mathematical data and statistical standards to *collect, organize, and display data using pictures, tallies, tables, charts, or bar graphs, and arranging data into logical patterns* (adapted from Science Standards). The students examined their survey results and created a data chart tallying each person's response as depicted in the section "parent data chart." Moreover, they quantified and created a graph for the survey results on how many times people went to a playground. They also gathered qualitative data to write significant quotes that explain what the quantitative data meant as shown in the "interview quote" section. Students displayed these findings on a poster to communicate their findings as a way to *compare observations from individuals and groups* from science and mathematics standards.

What we learn here is the importance for teachers to incorporate ways to solve the playground problem using potential solutions from mathematics and science. By engaging in FoK as a problem-based process, the teachers had the opportunity to see where FoK could exist. So, the teachers could take a fund, like playgrounds, and make it mathematical and scientific. The topic of playgrounds in and of itself didn't appear mathematical or scientific, but when the teachers situated playgrounds as a problem with solutions that involved using mathematics and science, the end result was science and mathematics funds. The result of the community walk provided an initial direction to the teachers' understanding of how students' identities could be applied to mathematics and science funds. The community walk was important because this was the first teacher awareness that students' funds can lead to mathematics and science standards. The teachers were able to include content that went beyond mandated textbooks and build mathematics and science practices around students' funds. Furthermore, the community walk activity, in conjunction with learning about problematic playground funds, opened the door for teachers to continue to learn further those types of funds that were rooted in problem-based funds, which were masked under the larger problem of Genesis needing a playground.

Building the Playground: Family and Community Engagement

As the teachers acquired information about their students' funds of knowledge, they expanded in how they viewed student learning. For instance, the teachers initially thought the purpose of playgrounds was entertainment or interest based. However, they discovered that when the school banned recess, it had a negative impact on student self-esteem and identity as students. Playgrounds are an integral part of "being a student" and "being a member of a school community." Without a playground, the sense of community was largely missing. It was also connected to how students viewed classroom management, recess, and being a successful learner. Students asked the teachers, "Are we bad kids because we can't have recess … it's the bad kids that are the worst students." After hearing this, the teachers came together to create the Genesis Playground Committee (GPC), which consisted of students, parents, community members, and local school council leaders, who aimed to bring awareness and write grants to advocate for a playground. We saw a shift to collective responsibility where students led in the fund raising efforts by developing after-school events such as movie nights. For the teachers, this was monumental because this was the first time they engaged in activism work driven by students. The GPC was fortunate to have their grant accepted by Kaboom & Disney partnership. The grant supplied the materials, and the initiatives consisted of local community members, school staff, and families to come together for 5 hours and physically build the playground in teams. The alderman and the local news appeared to celebrate the event (*Local Students Win Dream Playground from Kaboom! and Disney*, 2013). We learned that engaging in funds of knowledge and student inquiry can enhance family engagement. Often many schools struggle with how to promote family engagement; however, what we see here is that when students are at the center and have the opportunity to lead, they are the greatest champions to recruit their families' involvement in schools.

Conclusion

Realizing that their current scripted curriculum did not consider ELs funds, the teachers developed their own FoK curriculum, with the intent to privilege students' cultural-linguistic resources for mathematics and science. In this case study, a FoK curriculum explores a social problem, grounded in students' funds, which becomes the curriculum theme. Additionally, a FoK curriculum aims to create fluid boundaries between ELs' language and cultural practices with mathematics and science. In doing so, ELs contextualize and make meaning of mathematics and science derived from their familiar everyday practices.

The playground project demonstrated the transformative possibilities of student-led initiatives. It further shifts the epistemological expertise of youth in conducting research. It illustrated how youth can resist systemic forms of oppression by engaging in critical and collective inquiry, reflection, and ultimately action (Cammarota & Fine, 2010). Involving youth in leadership roles and positioning them to have greater responsibility for their learning has been shown to have multiple benefits and represents a paradigm shift in curriculum design (Anyon et al., 2018; Foster-Fishman, Law, Lichty, & Aoun, 2010).

Mathematics, science, and STEM fields more broadly, in particular, empower youth to move from passive social critique toward developing pragmatic solutions (Yang, 2009). For communities who have been historically marginalized from STEM education, YPAR provides a tangible path toward liberation from systemic oppression by opening opportunities in STEM fields that have immediate material consequences. With smart technologies becoming ubiquitous in young people's lives, actualizing equity change in real time and space is no longer a pipe dream but a reality that needs to be designed and implemented. The "food revolution" in Oakland is an example of how youth leveraged smart technology to lead such an effort (Akom, Shah, Nakai, & Cruz, 2016). Grassroots YPAR methodologies as demonstrated by the Genesis teachers and students will undoubtedly have longitudinal impact not only on them but also on their communities for years to come (Morales-Doyle & Frausto, 2020). Through engaging families and communities, a more profound collective ethos and energy is generated. When we consciously design integrated social, cultural, racial, linguistic, and disciplinary spaces, it inevitably leads to an alchemical transformation that produces greater harmony, balance, and a state of collective equilibrium (Torre, 2005).

Discussion Questions

1. How do you define teaching for social justice? In what ways did the teachers teach for social justice? Name the barriers and opportunities for you to teach with a social justice lens.
2. Write a rebuttal statement to someone who believes that it is not the responsibility of mathematics and science educators to teach literacy to their students.
3. Design a funds of knowledge activity that you could do to gather your students' funds. How could you make sure that you are eliciting mathematics and science funds in your activity?

Additional Resources

1. TEACH Math discusses how you can take your students on a community walk to learn about mathematics in your neighborhood. It is complete with lesson plans and student work samples. Visit https://teachmath.info/activity-1-community-walk/
2. Edutopia describes teachers' perspectives on ethnography tools, such as home visits, to build relationship and academic learning. Visit https://www.edutopia.org/blog/family-engagement-works-parent-teacher-home-visits-anne-obrien
3. Teaching Tolerance gives examples for enacting activism and community action work at your school. Visit https://www.tolerance.org/magazine/teaching-as-activism-teaching-as-care

References

Akom, A., Shah, A., Nakai, A., & Cruz, T. (2016). Youth participatory action research (YPAR) 2.0: How technological innovation and digital organizing sparked a food revolution in East Oakland. *International Journal of Qualitative Studies in Education*, *29*(10), 1287–1307.

Anyon, Y., Bender, K., Kennedy, H., & Dechants, J. (2018). A systematic review of youth participatory action research (YPAR) in the United States: Methodologies, youth outcomes, and future directions. *Health Education & Behavior, 45*(6), 865–878.

Barton, A. C., & Tan, E. (2009). Funds of knowledge and discourses and hybrid space. *Journal of Research in Science Teaching: The Official Journal of the National Association for Research in Science Teaching, 46*(1), 50–73.

Cammarota, J., & Fine, M. (Eds.). (2010). *Revolutionizing education: Youth participatory action research in motion.* New York, NY: Routledge.

Cazden, C. B. (2001). *Classroom discourse: The language of teaching and learning* (2nd ed.). Portsmouth, NH: Heinemann.

Foster-Fishman, P. G., Law, K. M., Lichty, L. F., & Aoun, C. (2010). Youth ReACT for social change: A method for youth participatory action research. *American Journal of Community Psychology, 46*(1), 67–83.

González, N., Moll, L. C., & Amanti, C. (Eds.). (2006). *Funds of knowledge: Theorizing practices in households, communities, and classrooms.* New York, NY: Routledge.

KABOOM! (2021, January 17). *KABOOM! works nationally to achieve playspace equity.* https://kaboom.org/

Korb, R. (2007). *Groovy gravity* (B. Reibeling, Illus.). Minneapolis, MN: Magic Wagon Publishing.

Local students win dream playground from Kaboom! and Disney. (2013, May 2). *Eyewitness News ABC 7.* https://abc7.com/archive/9088440/

Morales-Doyle, D., & Frausto, A. (2020). Youth participatory science: A grassroots science curriculum framework. *Educational Action Research, 29*(1), 1–19.

Torre, M. E. (2005). The alchemy of integrated spaces: Youth participation in research collectives of difference. In L. Weis & M. Fine (Eds.), *Beyond silenced voices: Class, race, and gender in United States schools* (pp. 251–266). New York: State University of New York Press.

Wells, G. (1993). Reevaluating the IRF sequence: A proposal for the articulation of theories of activity and discourse for the analysis of teaching and learning in the classroom. *Linguistics and Education, 5*(1), 1–37.

Yang, K. W. (2009). Mathematics, critical literacy, and youth participatory action research. *New Directions for Youth Development, 2009*(123), 99–118.

3

COMMUNITY RENEWABLE ENERGY

Designing Solar Panels Through Science-Funds of Knowledge

I think it helped them to connect their school work with home, which a lot of times school is school and home is home. [The unit] helped students to make the connection to solar energy in our neighborhood. Asking students to make connections outside of the school, helped give them a specific interest in science.

Lola, Fifth-Grade Transitional Bilingual Teacher

Introduction

This chapter presents a science unit in a fifth-grade transitional bilingual classroom in which the bilingual classroom teacher and a special education teacher developed extension activities based on the FOSS Solar Energy science kit. The Full Option Science System (FOSS) science kits are the standard "off the shelf" curriculum that is mandated by the district. While it is designed to provide all the necessary components related to the science content, in this case solar energy, it does not provide methods, tools, or strategies for making connections to students' lives or communities. They conducted the research in Lola's bilingual Spanish classroom of 29 students. Dana identified as a monolingual special education teacher who taught middle school students, but as part of their university coursework she planned, cotaught lessons, and analyzed data with Lola. This was a fifth-grade science lesson on solar energy and covered topics related to engineering design.

DOI: 10.4324/9781351001168-3

Standards

Science

- Define a simple design problem reflecting a need or a want that includes specified criteria for success and constraints on materials, time, or cost.
- Generate and compare multiple possible solutions to a problem based on how well each is likely to meet the criteria and constraints of the problem.

(standards adapted from NGSS 3-5-ETS1-1, 3-5-ETS1-2)

Mathematics

- Calculate the number of cells per solar panel and the energy produced by each cell.
- Calculate the maximum watts per hour created by a solar panel set at the optimal tilt.

(standard adapted from CCSS.5.NBT.A.1)

Literacy

- Review the key ideas expressed, and draw conclusions in light of information and knowledge gained from the discussions.
- Draw on information from multiple print or digital sources, demonstrating the ability to locate an answer to a question quickly or to solve a problem efficiently.
- Write informative/explanatory texts to examine a topic and convey ideas and information clearly.

(standards adapted from CCSS ELA-Literacy SL.5.1.D, RI.5.7, W.5.2)

Language

- English learners communicate information, ideas, and concepts necessary for academic success in the content area of language arts.
- English learners communicate information, ideas, and concepts necessary for academic success in the content area of mathematics.
- English learners communicate information, ideas, and concepts necessary for academic success in the content area of science.
- English learners communicate information, ideas, and concepts necessary for academic success in the content area of social studies.

(standards adapted from WIDA Consortium Standards 2–5)

Chapter Objectives

1. Teachers will be able to leverage science-funds of knowledge.
2. Teachers will be able to have students use their full linguistic repertoire.
3. Teachers will be able to mediate opportunities for student interaction to explain their reasoning and solve problems.
4. Teachers will be able to incorporate concepts of solar energy into community projects.

Unit Objectives

1. Become aware of the potential of solar energy, an inexhaustible source, as an alternative energy source to fossil fuels, a nonrenewable source.
2. Acquire vocabulary associated with solar energy and energy transfer.

Context: School, Teachers, Students

Jarman Elementary School is located in a large urban city in a historically immigrant neighborhood with an enrollment of 328. Of the student population, 94% are classified as low-income. The population of the school is 92% Latinx, 6% African-American/Black, and 2% Multiracial/Ethnic. Of these students, 49% are considered ELs and are eligible for the school's transitional bilingual programs. The majority of the students at the school have Spanish as their first language, and 98% of students receive free and reduced school lunch. Most of the students at Jarman live in the neighborhood surrounding the school and walk to school.

Lola graduated from a top-tier elementary education program and immediately began teaching at Jarman the subsequent fall. She began our action research program at the start of her 7th year and completed her Masters and Bilingual/ ESL certification in 2 years. She was certified to teach in Spanish. Dana was a more recent graduate and had already completed a Masters degree in Special Education prior to enrolling in our action research Masters program. She earned her bachelor of arts in photography at a large public research university and worked in graphic design for several years before deciding to enter the teaching profession. She was a relatively new teacher (2 years) at Jarman and was eager to join the action research Masters program. She saw it as an opportunity for professional development. As a middle school special education teacher, she worked with both resource and inclusion students and completed her ESL endorsement.

Both Lola and Dana conducted action research in Lola's fifth-grade classroom of 29 students. The class consisted of 15 boys and 14 girls. Four students received special education services. Twenty-eight of the students in the classroom were from Latinx backgrounds, and one student was African-American. Twenty-one percent of the students were enrolled in the school's transitional bilingual program at the time of the study. Most students in the classroom were English learners; however, not all students participated in the school's bilingual program.

Unit 3 Plan: From "Curriculum Fidelity" to Transformation

While planning for the spring, the teachers had already conducted two FOSS units with minimal success being culturally responsive and leveraging students' funds of knowledge. Their analysis of the videos and subsequent conversations revealed to them that even though they were well intentioned in organizing peer groups, the conversations somehow defaulted to being teacher centered. The fall unit was about *Microworlds* and microorganisms, and the winter unit was about levers and pulleys. However, in both cases, Lola and Dana were strictly focused on "curriculum fidelity" and less on building scientific discourse through community connections and student agency. Early in the project, Lola and Dana regularly used the phrase "fidelity to the curriculum" to describe their teaching and learning goals. When our research team probed them to explain what this meant, they said, "we want all the students to have the same water sample, so they all get the same results." Variation was viewed as deviation from the mandated script. Student initiative and agency was viewed as disturbing the curricular flow. For example, while considering water samples for conducting microbial tests, they missed opportunities to have students bring in samples from their homes and communities because they feared they might lose control of the curriculum. Lola and Dana reflected on this process stating, "We resolved to step back and release control of the extension activities to allow students more ownership of the projects as shown in our focus group interview conducted at the end of unit 2." (Jarman Final Action Research Report). They reflected on the challenges of "curriculum fidelity," releasing control of the project, and moving from directors to facilitators (lines 1–12):

```
01 Lola:   I also try to step back and let them have control over the projects
02 Dana:   The first one was [not like that]
03 Lola:   Yeah, the first one was like okay we are all going to do this
04         and the second one it was a lot to step back and have six
05         different teams with six projects going on at the same time and
06         there is always that one group I feel like I have to go over and
07         help out and see them try it out and see what can happen. Most of
08         the groups did excellent.
09 Dana:   Yeah, they came up with something that fit the project. Some of
10         the groups took it further than others took it.
11 Lola:   And some just needed a little or a few questions to get their
12         thoughts going it worked out well.
```

(Jarman Focus Group #4 Transcript)

They further noted, at the start of the transcript (line 1), Lola recognized that it was a challenge to step back and let students have control over the projects. The transfer of power to the students was not immediate. In lines 3 through 8, she commented that it was increasingly difficult to manage six groups, each with different projects. She identified the internal struggle of feeling the need to "help out," which often meant taking control back from the group. Dana reflected on the students' ability to succeed to varying degrees (9–10) and showed an acceptance of the different ways students may complete the project. However, in lines 11–12, Lola continued to express a need to guide students' projects by asking questions, which she interpreted as getting "their thoughts going" (Final Action Research Report).

As part of their action research the teachers designed a 3- to 4-weeks extension activity that built off of the FOSS curriculum on Solar Energy. These kits were a self-contained boxed unit that included everything needed for teaching the science module. The modules were structured to be implemented within a quarter, or 10 weeks of instruction. The kits provided hands-on investigations. In planning the activity, they took into consideration their large English learner population and designed activities that would support their learning needs. The "Solar Energy" unit naturally lent itself to a multitude of extension projects. In order to maintain a balance between the mandated goals of the curriculum and being responsive to students' ideas, the teachers narrowed the focus of their extension activities. They decided the goal of their extension project was to have the students develop a way to incorporate solar energy to benefit the community. This guideline allowed students to be creative and implement the concepts of solar energy they learned about from the science kit.

Language Learning Domain: Multiple Language Use and Translanguaging

Working in small groups allowed students to use language fluidly in a way they were most comfortable. Students benefited from being able to translanguage, using English and Spanish to assist in understanding scientific discourse (García, 2009; Karlsson, Larsson, & Jakobsson, 2019). Likewise, the project reinforced the notion that English learner students benefit from multiple opportunities to talk with their peers in unofficial or less formal school spaces (Farnsworth, 2012). Although the students shared the same L1 of Spanish, English was the dominant language in the group. Spanish was used to clarify, comment, and carry on side conversations; however, when students used only Spanish to give suggestions, their ideas were not always voiced and at times were ignored. Verbal and nonverbal communication contributed to shared understandings.

Social Organization of Learning Science Through Solar Science Talks

During the action research project, the teachers varied the student groups as a way to facilitate discussion and allowed students to generate discussion, build meaning making, and practice scientific discourse. *Science Talks* were incorporated into the first unit of study (Gallas, 1995). These talks were purposefully designed to guide students through scientific discourse practices such as summarizing and paraphrasing ideas generated through group discussion. Science talks have been found to be particularly effective with EL students (Ernst-Slavit & Pratt, 2017). Initially, the teachers' goal was to challenge student thinking and expand their ideas. The first attempt was to introduce science talks with the whole class of

TABLE 3.1 Teachers' Description of Focal Students

Names	Alex	Maria	Lupe	Marco
EL Status	EL (newcomer)	EL	EL	Transitioned
ESL Standardized Proficiency (English Language and Content)	Beginner	Intermediate	Intermediate	Advanced
Participation	Low	High	Low	High
Personality Type	Introvert (quiet)	Extrovert (outspoken, natural leadership skills)	Introvert (quiet, hard-working student)	Extrovert (leader, high-achieving student)
Language Fluency (Spanish)	High	High	High	Low

29 students. The teachers found that not all students were comfortable talking during the whole-class discussion. They put students into smaller groups to complete the solar energy extension project. Groups were heterogeneous and selected based upon multiple factors, including students' interests and funds of knowledge, compatibility, and English proficiency levels. This type of grouping allowed students to draw upon both languages to discuss scientific topics. Students actively contributed their ideas and questions related to solar energy. Table 3.1 provides the teachers' description of the unit's focal students.

In this unit, the teachers found a balance of offering guidance to the students while still giving them choice and control over their projects. Students were self-motivated to finish the projects and worked outside of school to complete tasks assigned by their group. This was a stark comparison to the videos from the first unit, where students waited for their directions, and when the teachers left the group, students stopped working. Dana and Lola found as they gave up control, the students took more ownership of the projects, and their roles shifted from the experts to facilitators. They are rarely present in the videos and only briefly enter the group to check in with students. Students rarely asked for help during the construction of their solar energy projects, except when they needed extra materials. Throughout the unit, students actively showed leadership within their group and continued to move the projects forward.

The Jarman teachers' activity triangle illustrates their unit plan for socially organizing learning around the object of how solar energy application can help the community (Figure 3.1). The triangle outlines the activity design, the fundamental question that guides the learning process; the *object*, or immediate learning goal of the activity; the *mediational tools* (both material and ideational artifacts) that facilitate movement toward the learning goal; *the subjects* or immediate classroom

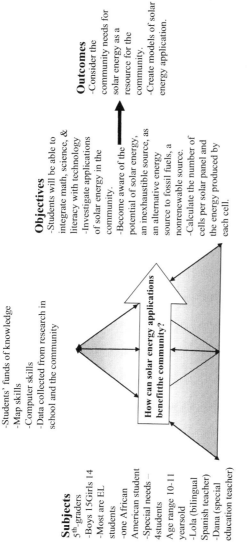

Tools and Artifacts
-FOSS Solar Energy science kit
-*Science Talks*
-Students' funds of knowledge
-Map skills
-Computer skills
-Data collected from research in school and the community

Objectives
-Students will be able to integrate math, science, & literacy with technology
-Investigate applications of solar energy in the community.
-Become aware of the potential of solar energy, an inexhaustible source, as an alternative energy source to fossil fuels, a nonrenewable source.
-Calculate the number of cells per solar panel and the energy produced by each cell.

Outcomes
-Consider the community needs for solar energy as a resource for the community.
-Create models of solar energy application.

How can solar energy applications benefit the community?

Subjects
5th-graders
-Boys 15Girls 14
-Most are EL students
-one African American student
-Special needs — 4students
Age range 10-11 yearsold
-Lola (bilingual Spanish teacher)
-Dana (special education teacher)

Rules
-take turns
-rotate leadership and expert roles
-peer interaction
-peer assistance
-teacher facilitates with questions

Division of Effort
-Teacher selected groups of 4 studentsbased on heterogenicity of students' interests and funds of knowledge, compatibility, and English proficiency
-Teacher whole group instruction
-Student-centered activities
-Small groupdiscussions

Community
-Jarman Elementary School
-Mexican neighborhood
-Students from Pre-K to 8th grade
-Bilingual students (Spanish)

FIGURE 3.1 Jarman Teachers' Activity Triangle

participants; the *community* or distal participants; *the rules* that establish parameters for participation within the activity system; *the division of effort*, which establishes roles and responsibilities for each learner toward accomplishing the learning goal; and finally *outcomes*, which are longitudinal effects suggesting a deeper shift in learner identity and consciousness. Outcomes help teachers think about practices and skills that transfer beyond the immediate learning goals or object of the activity.

In this design, Lola and Dana begin with a broad question: *How can solar energy applications benefit the community?* This question is broad enough to generate robust opportunities for student participation and leveraging their full linguistic and cultural repertoires. The *object* of the activity system was threefold: (1) explore concepts of mathematics, science, and literacy in solar technology; (2) become aware of the potential of solar energy, an inexhaustible source, as an alternative energy source to fossil fuels, a nonrenewable source; and (3) calculate the number of cells per solar panel and the energy produced by each cell. The mediational tools included: FOSS Solar Energy science kit; Science Talks; students' funds of knowledge, map and computer skills; and data collected from research in school and the community. The *subjects* were 15 boys and 14 girls with most English learners in Lola and Dana's fifth-grade bilingual classroom. The classroom was situated within the broader Latinx and Mexican community consisting of bilingual Spanish speakers as well as a few African-American/Black families. Lola and Dana explicitly and implicitly established discourse rules and expectations such as turn-taking, rotating leadership and expert roles, peer interaction and assistance, and teachers facilitate small-group work with questions. The *division of effort* consisted of teacher-selected groups (four students) based on heterogeneity of student interests and funds of knowledge, compatibility, English language proficiency, teacher-led whole-group mini-lessons, and student-centered activities and discussions. Finally, projected longitudinal *outcomes* for the activity included considering the community needs for solar energy and creating models of solar energy as a resource for the community.

Requiring that the solar invention must benefit the community created tension. Through discussions in the groups, students' ideas developed into meaningful projects. At first students wanted to make solar-powered cell phones and video games, but challenging them to benefit others led students to design solar energy projects that would help their families and members of their community. One group of students chose to add solar panels to a laundromat to make it less expensive for people in the community to do their laundry. This highlighted a factor in the community that the teachers had not considered; however, it was an important concern for the students, most of whom use the laundromat regularly. Realizations such as this made an impact on the teachers and allowed them to have a better understanding of their students' experiences.

Once students identified the focus of their extension activities, the teachers realized students would be more successful if they were more knowledgeable about technology. Watching the videos and reflecting on the unit, the teachers identified how students struggled with technology skills such as emailing and accessing information online. Students had the ideas for solar energy projects, but struggled to execute them. To address these needs the teachers scaffolded mini-lessons to provide technology skills. The first mini-lesson was a slideshow of solar inventions to frontload knowledge and create a shared understanding about ways in which solar energy can be implemented. This included solar panels on a calculator, a local fire station, and a hospital (Figure 3.2).

The next mini-lesson focused on computer skills, such as how to use Google Maps to locate a satellite and street view of locations in the neighborhood (Figure 3.3). They also explained how to use the district email and look up online articles related to solar energy. Through mini-lessons like these, the students were able to gain and demonstrate the skills needed to complete their community

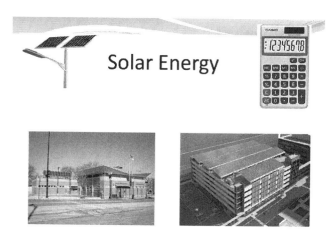

FIGURE 3.2   Examples of Solar Energy

FIGURE 3.3   Using Google Maps for Satellite Imaging of Neighborhood

solar inventions. The unit developed a balance between the mandated science curriculum and the students' funds of knowledge. As such, the teachers adjusted their level of support to move students forward.

Science-Funds of Knowledge: Designing Solar Energy Panels

At the beginning of the project, Dana and Lola created and administered a funds of knowledge survey about the students' families and backgrounds (Rios-Aguilar, 2010). The survey questions were in English and Spanish and intentionally open-ended to identify and target connections to the science and mathematics curriculum. The questions included information about family activities and occupations. The teachers read the survey with the students to be sure they understood each question. Students completed the survey at home. In class, they discussed the findings and tallied the results, which included: How many students and their families speak Spanish, cook meals at home, and use tools to help fix things around the house. They also learned about family members' jobs and categorized them. This process allowed students to see connections to each other and to also make connections to areas they might have overlooked when they completed the survey. The teachers carefully analyzed the survey data for information that would help create connections to the science kit.

The teachers launched the unit with a class discussion about solar energy and examined how students used their funds of knowledge in the classroom. After the discussion students were given homework assignments to interview their families about what they knew about the given topic. Students reported back the next day, and they added the information to the class knowledge chart. To continue to draw on their students' funds of knowledge, Lola and Dana incorporated images from the community that the students were familiar with to elicit further conversations and possible inquiry project questions.

From the beginning of the unit, the students drew on their knowledge of solar energy both in school and in the community. Students made reference to the solar-powered calculators used in the classrooms and solar panels on buildings in the neighborhood. In discussions and planning for creating their solar energy application in the community, the student displayed knowledge of how solar panels worked. The students' projects all organized the solar panels on the same side of the building facing the same direction toward the sun, or they made the panels adjustable to follow the sun. Students were knowledgeable about their community and what businesses and community organizations their families used. By allowing students opportunities to work in collaborative groups, the teachers continued to allow students' funds of knowledge to emerge.

Mediating Multiple Language Use

In this transcript taken from unit 3, lesson 2 (3.2), the students used their funds of knowledge to build a realistic solar panel model. The group of students discussed how to construct an expressway sign. Marco had an understanding of the attributes. The teachers noticed how he used English with gestures to explain his concept to the group. Although he did not use the word *sign*, his gestures helped the group understand that he was talking about the large signs on the expressway.

```
01 Marco:   You know how on the expressways they put it like this?
02          (models shape of large signs on expressways)
03 Maria:   [No tengo el tuyo Marco. Aca no es el tuyo] {I don't have
04          yours Marco. Yours is not over there.}
05 Alex:    How?
06 Maria:   Mira este estea, de Alex. {Look at this, its Alex's}
07 Alex:    [I don't get it.]
```

When Alex didn't understand the idea. Marco continued to explain and used gestures to make his ideas clear.

```
08 Marco:   Um. You know those thingys that say slow down or whatever?
09          Um. Next right to Indiana or next right out. Like that
10          (gestures the shape of an expressway sign to the students).
```

Alex tried to give Marco directives about how to construct the signs. He used gestures to further clarify his ideas, however his suggestion were ignored.

```
11 Alex:    Glue them like that. (holding popsicle sticks in the air)
12 Marco:   [No.]
```

After Marco responded negatively to Alex's request, Alex finally picked up on the concept and was able to expand on it.

```
13 Alex:    Okay like you know those things like miles ahead?
```

The students have a concept of how to build an expressway sign on their solar energy model. They have references to their knowledge and experience of the many expressways around the city. This is clear because they both made a specific reference to what the signs said on the local expressways.

The transcript also shows the importance of English learner students interacting to facilitate learning. In their interaction with each other, the students were able to make meaning and come to an understanding. Even though both students had sufficient knowledge of English, as evident by their English proficiency (see Table 3.1), they still had difficulty explaining their ideas to each other in English. Their conversation relied heavily on gestures and hand motions and never used the word "sign" to describe their solar energy idea. Later on Dana interacted with the group and said the word "sign," and the group then began to use "sign" to describe what they created. Further along in the transcript 3.2, Marco, Alex, and Lupe use their funds of knowledge to resolve structural issues with the sign's construction.

```
14 Maria:   Porque no cortamos un poco de ese si ya lo ponemos al
15          arriba con uno de estas? (gestures towards foam board) {Why
16          don't we cut a little of this and then we can put it on top
17          with one of these?}
18 Marco:   [Make it right here.] It's like
```

```
19 Alex:   Like that
20 Marco:  Make it one cuz if you put too many it's gonna fall
21         (gestures and claps hands)
22 Maria:  Ya que {It's that}. There's nothing to support it. Just a
23         piece of aluminum foil.
24 Marco:  Oh. Good thing I got that one (picks up a scrap of foam board).
```

Marco continued to speak in English with gestures to express his ideas (lines 18, 20). Both Marco and Maria gave Alex advice about the structure of the sign he was trying to construct. The teachers noticed that Marco did not use the word "weight," which was what he was referring to when he said "if you put too many it's gonna fall." This demonstrated how he drew on his past experiences to guide the construction of a traffic sign. Maria began to talk in Spanish and then switched to English as the conversation with Marco and Alex continued in English. Maria also showed her understanding of the properties of aluminum foil and the need to have a structure to support it in lines 22–23.

Throughout the project the teachers noticed the ways students used language to demonstrate their scientific understandings. Working in small groups allowed students to use language in a way they were most comfortable. Students benefited from being able to use English and Spanish to assist in understanding or explaining certain concepts. The project reinforced the notion that English learner students benefit from multiple opportunities to talk with their peers informally. The design of the project allowed the space for students to clarify meanings, take on leadership roles, and become experts within the group, something that may not always be possible in the whole-class setting. Dana and Lola also saw that students' language was not equal in the small groups. Although the students shared the same L1 of Spanish, English was the dominant language in the group. Spanish was used to clarify, comment, and carry on side conversations; however, when students used only Spanish to give suggestions, their ideas were not always voiced and at times were ignored. In traditional assessments and lessons, EL students may fall into the category of having insufficient English skills or background knowledge; however, through inquiry projects students are able to demonstrate the information they know. The students had multiple opportunities to draw from their funds of knowledge and in turn became the experts on their solar energy topics.

The teachers' activities were organized to mediate opportunities for student interaction, and students were able to access a fuller range of their linguistic repertoire by drawing on multiple languages to explain their reasoning and solve problems. The teachers' summative coding of video 3.4 (Unit 3, 4th Transcript) revealed how the use of multiple languages was prevalent (see Figure 3.4). This section is an example of how multiple languages and discourses were used for the first 17 minutes, interspersed with questions, and a number of participation shifts where novice learners assumed more expert roles in the dialogue.

The Jarman teachers also used the comment column to provide additional details about this episode. For example, Alex took on a greater role by answering

Video 3.4

Time	a. Peer Assistance	b. Funds of Knowledge	c. Multiple Languages/ Discourses	d. Questions	e. Tension	f. Third Space	g. Participation Shifts	h. Role Shift	i. Rule Negotation	
1.00			I							
2.00			I				I			
3.00			I				I			
4.00			I	I						Alex answers
5.00			I							Alex consults with Marco
6.00			I							SIGN PLACMENT CODE SWITCHING
7.00			I	I						
8.00			I	I						WORK TOGETHER TO PUT UP SIGN
9.00		I	I				I			
10.00			I				I			
11.00			I							
12.00			I							Alex gives directions
13.00			I							
14.00			I							
15.00			I							
16.00			I							SIGN AGGREEMENT
17.00			I							

FIGURE 3.4 Coding Sheet

questions, consulting his peers, and giving directions. The teachers selected this vignette for more detailed transcription and used it as evidence of how students engaged in purposeful translanguaging. In this episode, Maria and Lupe worked together to construct a solar-powered traffic sign. Alex tried to direct them to put the sign where he wanted on the model. Lupe, who had not transitioned to conversational English, continued to speak mostly in Spanish. Lupe's conversation with Maria was in Spanish, as they were the group members building the sign:

```
01 Alex:   No, no se ponen allí. {No, don't put it there} Not the side, the
02         middle.(motions with hands to form a column coming up from the
03         middle of the expressway model)
04 Maria:  Aquí? {Here} In the middle? (motions with hands to create two
05         columns coming up from either side of the expressway)
06 Alex:   Aquí {Here} in the middle.(repeats gesture of column in middle)
07 Maria:  Okay, okay okay.(Ignores advice and puts sign along the side of
08         the expressway)
09 Alex:   Allí no, allí no. {Not there, not there}
10 Maria:  Aquí Lupe, vamos a poner el. {Here Lupe, we are going to
11         put it}(continues to ignore Alex and directs her conversation
12         towards Lupe)
13 Alex:   No, aquí por aquí.{No, here right here}(Gestures where he wants
14         the sign)
15 Maria:  That's why: Aquí y va a quedar aquí.{Here and it will stay here}
16         (Defiantly makes the final decision about sign placement.)
```

In lines 1–3, Alex emphatically directed Maria to place the solar-powered sign in the middle of the road, and he persisted with several attempts using Spanish and English and gestures to show placement of the sign (e.g., lines 6, 9, 13). Maria did not agree with Alex's idea and suggested an alternative placement with a limited explanation (lines 7, 10, 15). This transcript along with annotations was done by the teachers to show how multiple languages mediated peer interactions in purposeful ways. The teachers reported that students often chose to use English during whole-group discussions; however, when placed in small groups, they were more likely to use multiple languages to have science talks (Morton, 2012). They explained, "within the small group context, students were comfortable with both languages; however, most times the students' L1 was used as a clarifier. Students would use Spanish to further explain their ideas or words they were uncertain of" (Final Action Research Report).

All the students presented their community solar projects. Models included a high school with solar panels, a bus with solar panels, a hospital with solar panels on the windows and roof, a laundromat with solar panels, a restaurant with solar panels, and a library with solar panels. The focal EL students presented an expressway with solar panel signs.

Conclusion

At the beginning of the project, Lola and Dana struggled with "curriculum fidelity" and "releasing control." In their final action research report, they discussed their initial trepidation with unpredictability and uncertainty:

In unit 1, we could not envision releasing control to allow students to develop and implement different projects. The uncertainty and unpredictability of the path the projects would take created uncertainty for us.

(Final Action Research Report)

Releasing control and becoming comfortable with uncertainty is a fundamental pillar of action research (Razfar, 2011). Furthermore, positioning students to assume greater responsibility for their learning as well as being encouraged to take on scientific identities are key features of integrated and social constructivist learning (Barak, 2017). This also requires teachers to trust their own professional expertise and let go of disabling fidelity to scripted curriculum. They noted this shift occurring as a result of discourse analysis and study groups in between units:

During unit 2 we allowed students complete control over their projects, however in retrospect, we did not provide them enough structure. Rather than gradually releasing control and practicing how to negotiate the group setting, students were immediately given a group and expected to perform.

(Final Action Research Report)

Sometimes in the quest to foster greater student agency and student-centered curriculum, teachers shortchange their own role as curriculum designers and facilitators. In particular, students need the critical dimension of designing sustainable activities over time with critical supports and mediational tools. They learn that, from a sociocultural perspective, learning is a shift in the mediational tools as learners shift from novice to expert learner identities. In preparing for the final solar energy unit, they discuss the importance of providing their students with better guidance, problem-solving strategies, and mediation tools:

By the third unit we found the balance of offering guidance to the students while still giving them voice and control over their projects. We found as we gave up control, the students took more ownership of the projects and our roles shifted from the experts to facilitators. We observed this shift in the unit 3 videos.

(Final Action Research Report)

They noted this shift in their analysis of the final unit, "they (Lola and Dana) were rarely present in the videos and only briefly to check in with students." While they were invisible on the videos, their presence was integral to the design of the activity system, the leveraging of scientific-funds, and balancing curricular innovation with fidelity to the mandated curriculum. Clearly, the nature of student participation shifted, and their movement toward greater self-regulation was demonstrable through the solar energy unit:

Throughout the third unit students actively show leadership within their group and continue to move the project forward. Students rarely sought help from us during the construction of their projects, when they did it was usually because they needed extra materials. Students were self-motivated to finish the projects and worked outside of school to complete tasks assigned by their group. In comparison to the videos from the first unit, where students waited for our directions and when we left the group productivity stopped.

(Final Action Research Report)

Through using discourse analysis, the teachers were able to enact these changes. Discourse analysis has been a key professional development tool for improving classroom interactions and learning (Rex & Schiller, 2010). The teachers shifted their role to facilitators, which led to independent work from students. They used meaningful connections to students' funds of knowledge to plan the solar energy unit, including how they implemented mini-lessons to frontload technology and preassess students' prior knowledge of the content. Group work provided meaningful interactions for EL students to use multiple languages and make sense of their ideas. Expanding students' repertoires of practice is more than just an instructional strategy for emergent bilinguals, it is a fundamental aspect of academic, scientific, and researcher cultural practices (Molle & Lee, 2017). The activity theory triangle mediates teachers' ability to design curriculum that is sensitive to the nuances of collaboration (Lave & Chaiklin, 1993). For example, heterogeneous grouping of learners based on linguistic and disciplinary expertise as well as culturally responsive mediational tools promotes more dynamic opportunities for academic and literacy development. It makes dynamic role shifts in learning and movement from novice to expert learner identities more possible (Razfar, Khisty, & Chval, 2011). Thus, discourse analysis helped the Jarman teachers empirically verify the critical role of multiple language use in peer and teacher assistance toward achieving the learning goal of the activity.

Discourse analysis not only made teachers aware of the nuances of moment-to-moment learning in the classroom, but it also helped them see opportunities to leverage science funds toward addressing larger issues of environmental justice and developing climate literacy. By exploring real-life energy problems and seeking solutions, elementary students can authentically experience the relevance of science to their lives (Merritt, Bowers, & Rimm-Kaufman, 2019; Nussbaum, 2013). More importantly, by engaging in participatory action research, they can envision and experience their own vital role in fostering environmental justice.

Energy and climate literacy has never been more critical as our world encounters the real consequences of global warming, climate change, and the rapid depletion of natural resources. Energy conservation and environmental justice are values and practices that Lola, Dana, and their students appropriated. Their integrated curriculum was not only aligned with curricular standards, but it also prepared them for leadership in renewable energy initiatives at the local and global levels. The Jarman teachers demonstrated that participatory action research does not come at the expense of rigor and achievement. In fact, community-based action research transforms scripted and mandated curricular activities into more rigorous and relevant science activities that have impact well beyond the classroom (Balazs & Morello-Frosch, 2013).

Discussion Questions

1. How can students use multiple languages as a resource to facilitate science talks in small groups?
2. How can teachers use students' funds of knowledge to develop science extension projects?
3. What are some other ways students and teachers address issues of environmental justice and global warming?

Additional Resources

1. *FOSS (Full Option Science System) Modules*
   https://www.fossweb.com/delegate/ssi-wdf-ucm-webContent?dDoc-Name=D1474047
2. Hands-On Science and Literacy Activities about Solar Energy
   https://beyondpenguins.ehe.osu.edu/issue/energy-and-the-polar-environ-ment/hands-on-science-and-literacy-activities-about-solar-energy
3. *Science Buddies:* Experiment with Solar Power
   https://www.sciencebuddies.org/science-fair-projects/project-ideas/experiment-with-solar-power
4. *Sun Power Source:* Solar Projects for Kids
   https://www.sunpowersource.com/solar-projects-for-kids/

References

Barak, M. (2017). Science teacher education in the twenty-first century: A pedagogical framework for technology-integrated social constructivism. *Research in Science Education, 47*(2), 283–303.

Balazs, C. L., & Morello-Frosch, R. (2013). The three Rs: How community-based participatory research strengthens the rigor, relevance, and reach of science. *Environmental Justice, 6*(1), 9–16. DOI: 10.1089/env.2012.0017

Ernst-Slavit, G., & Pratt, K. L. (2017). Teacher questions: Learning the discourse of science in a linguistically diverse elementary classroom. *Linguistics and Education, 40*(1), 1–10.

Farnsworth, M. (2012). Who's coming to my party? Peer talk as a bridge to oral language proficiency. *Anthropology & Education Quarterly, 43*(3), 253–270.

Gallas, K. (1995). *Talking their way into science: Hearing children's questions and theories, responding with curricula.* New York, NY: Teachers College Press.

García, O. (2009). *Bilingual education in the 21st century: A global perspective.* Malden, MA: Wiley/Blackwell.

Karlsson, A., Larsson, P. N., & Jakobsson, A. (2019). Multilingual students' use of translanguaging in science classrooms. *International Journal of Science Education, 41*(15), 2049–2069.

Lave, J., & Chaiklin, S. (Eds.). (1993). *Understanding practice: Perspectives on activity and context.* Cambridge, UK: Cambridge University Press.

Merritt, E. G., Bowers, N., & Rimm-Kaufman, S. E. (2019). Making connections: Elementary students' ideas about electricity and energy resources. *Renewable Energy, 138,* 1078–1086.

Molle, D., & Lee, N. (2017). Opportunities for academic language and literacy development for emergent bilingual students during group work. *International Journal of Bilingual Education and Bilingualism, 20*(5), 584–601.

Morton, T. (2012). Classroom talk, conceptual change and teacher reflection in bilingual science teaching. *Teaching and Teacher Education, 28*(1), 101–110.

Nussbaum, M. M. (2013). Embedding issues of environmental justice in the mainstream curriculum. *Environmental Justice, 6*(1), 34–40.

Razfar, A. (2011). Action research in urban schools: Empowerment, transformation, and challenges. *Teacher Education Quarterly, 38*(4), 25–44.

Razfar, A. Khisty, L. L., & Chval, K. (2011). Re-mediating second language acquisition: A sociocultural perspective for language development. *Mind, Culture, and Activity, 18*(3), 195–215. DOI: 10.1080/10749030903494427

Rex, L. A., & Schiller, L. (2010). *Using discourse analysis to improve classroom interaction.* New York, NY: Routledge.

Rios-Aguilar, C. (2010). Measuring funds of knowledge: Contributions to Latina/o students' academic and nonacademic outcomes. *Teachers College Record, 112*(8), 2209–2257.

4
PREPARING THE NEXT GENERATION OF CITY PLANNERS AND TECH-SAVVY TEACHERS

Using video games as part of our curriculum changed the way we saw our role. Letting go of control, we were able to facilitate the collective expertise of students and teachers. We came to understand and value students' knowledge of video games and the learning principles embedded in the games. During the project, we saw that video games offered ELs opportunities to use problem-solving skills and academic discourse to make connections to their funds of knowledge. We seized these moments to redesign the activities.

Susan, Eva, and Cara (Adams Elementary Teachers)

Introduction

About 10 years ago, when we first entered Susan, Eva, and Cara's rooms, there were no keyboards, smart boards, smart phones, or Internet service. Most educators and administrators were averse to using technology in the classroom. They viewed technology, especially video games, as antithetical to learning and development. However, the children were fully engaged in playing and learning through video games outside of school. At the time, it was hard to imagine a technologically integrated classroom where playing video games for the purpose of academic achievement and STEM learning would be acceptable let alone normative. However, in the span of a decade, what we and the Adams teachers began as a "strange," "unusual," and even "detrimental" action research project has now become a standard for learning and development. The global

DOI: 10.4324/9781351001168-4

pandemic of 2020 has rapidly mainstreamed the leveraging of digital literacies across the globe, and today's urban planners are quite literally the *SimCity* generation that began at around the time we first stepped foot into Adams Elementary. Those children playing games in their homes at the time when we began our action research partnerships are today's city planners who "found their calling" through playing *SimCity* and playing imaginary roles and identities (Roy, 2019).

This chapter presents a combined seventh–eighth-grade class in which a language arts teacher created thematic units using video games and covered topics related to engineering design.

Susan conducted the research in her general education classroom with 34 students. She used transcript data to analyze student talk in small groups. Role shifts and participation shifts were common findings in this unit, particularly in the small-group interactions playing *SimCity*. Susan selected and changed groupings throughout the school year to observe changes in student discourse and shifts in participation roles. She found that the activities promoted multiple discourses, and EL students used Spanish as a linguistic resource.

Standards

Science (Engineering and Technology)

- Define the criteria and constraints of a design problem with sufficient precision to ensure a successful solution, taking into account relevant scientific principles and potential impacts on people and the natural environment that may limit possible solutions.
                    (standards adapted from NGSS MS-ETS1-1)

Mathematics

- Formulate questions, design data collection methods, gather and analyze data, and communicate findings.
- Estimate; make and use measurements of objects, quantities, and relationships; and determine acceptable levels of accuracy.
- Select and use appropriate technology, instruments, and formulas to solve problems, interpret results, and communicate findings
                    (standards adapted from ISBE MS-10B, MS-7C)

Literacy

- Use the language arts to acquire, assess, and communicate information.
- Locate, organize, and use information from various sources to answer questions, solve problems, and communicate ideas.
- Analyze and evaluate information acquired from various sources.
                    (standards adapted from CCSS ELA-Literacy LS-5A, LS-5B)

Language

- English learners communicate information, ideas, and concepts necessary for academic success in the content area of language arts.
- English learners communicate information, ideas, and concepts necessary for academic success in the content area of mathematics.
- English learners communicate information, ideas, and concepts necessary for academic success in the content area of science.
- English learners communicate information, ideas, and concepts necessary for academic success in the content area of social studies.
                    (standards adapted from WIDA Consortium Standards 2–5)

Chapter Objectives

1. Teachers will be able to leverage science and mathematics funds of knowledge.
2. Teachers will be able to mediate opportunities for student interaction to explain their reasoning and solve problems.
3. Teachers will be able to have students use their linguistic repertoire.
4. Teachers will be able to have students use technology and video games to solve real design problems.

Unit Objectives

1. Use video games to solve design problems.
2. Acquire vocabulary associated with problem solving and concepts of design.

Context: School, Teacher, and Students

Adams Elementary is a small urban, public K–8 community elementary school with 269 students. It's a community school with a mathematics and science magnet program. Adams saw a substantial increase in reading and mathematics standardized scores with a ranked schoolwide reading proficiency of 70% and a ranked schoolwide mathematics proficiency of 82%. The neighborhood has undergone significant transformation due to gentrification leading to decreased enrollment. Latinx make up 82.5% of the enrollment, 24.2% of the student population identified as English Learners (ELs) and 95.9% as low income (School Report Card).

Susan is a self-identified female, European-American who taught a combined seventh–eighth-grade language arts class. She was a Mennonite missionary in Central Africa in the 1990s for 10 years. She has a mainstream classroom with some ELs. She was in her 11th year of teaching when she began doing action research. Her classroom community was predominantly Latinx with 34 students in total. There were 10 eighth graders; six boys and 4 girls. The seventh graders were a total of 24 with 10 boys and 14 girls. Two students were Caucasian/white, and one was Caucasian/white and Japanese; one student spoke exclusively English, and the Caucasian/Japanese student studied Japanese. The other Caucasian/white student's primary language was Romanian. Six students were from Puerto Rico, while the rest were from Mexico and spoke Spanish at varying proficiencies. Spanish was the primary language spoken at home for 14 students. All of these students were in the bilingual program at some time in their education, and 5 students were receiving ESL pullout services.

Susan's Focal Group

Three students in the group spoke Spanish at home. Sonia was a seventh grader of Mexican heritage who was finishing her 2nd year of English language services. Grace was also of Mexican heritage and in seventh grade, in her 4th year of English language pullout services by the ESL teacher. Sonia and Grace are academically stronger in mathematics than in reading and language arts. In sixth grade, Sonia was in the 90th percentile for mathematics, while her reading score was in the 36th percentile. Grace's mathematics score was in the 73rd percentile while her reading score was in the 56th percentile for sixth grade. Iris's first language is also Spanish. She scored in the 90th percentile for both reading and mathematics (Table 4.1).

Unit Plan: Developing "Smart" Urban Planners Through Science-Funds of Knowledge

Susan designed several activities in literacy, mathematics, and science for the purpose of learning about students' science and mathematics funds of knowledge. During classroom conversations, she discovered that all the students played video games on a daily basis either alone, with each other, or with family. They reported

TABLE 4.1 Teachers' Description of Focal English Learners (ELs)

Names	Sonia	Grace	Iris
EL Status	EL	EL	Transitioned
Standardized Math	High	High	Exceeds
Standardized Reading (English)	Below Average	Average	High
Participation	Low	Low	High
Personality Type	Introvert (quiet)	Introvert (quiet)	Extrovert (outspoken)
Language Fluency (Spanish)	High	High	High

spending more time playing video games than doing homework. Along with the other cohort teachers, she reflected on their initial impressions to use video games in the curriculum:

> When we began this process we could not imagine how to use video games as learning tools in the classroom. Initially, we believed that video games were too violent and more for entertainment than for learning and being actively involved. Yet, we wondered what attributes of video games engaged our students and why they were so passionate about video games.
>
> (Final Action Research Report)

Susan had her doubts about using video games in the classroom and even wondered what others would say. As part of the action research project she read *Good Video Games, Good Learning* (Gee, 2007) and came to value learning principles built into video games. The text provided 25 essential principles for reimagining video games in the context of school-based learning. Susan resonated with all of them and in particular emphasized the identity and multiple routes principles in her final action research report. First, the *identity principle* involves taking on and playing with identities in such a way that the learner has real choices. Second, through the *multiple routes principle*, gamers learn through their mistakes; learners can take risks in a space where real-world consequences are lowered. Susan appropriated these principles and established practices that would expand learning opportunities. It was essential that students explicitly knew that not only can they make errors, but also that taking risks and even failing were essential to their development. Those risks may not have the same impact as dying within a game, but the tension and frustration can be just as high. She recognized how video games provide opportunities to use spoken and written language for different purposes. Susan had students discussing, writing, and presenting how and why video games engaged them. She noted that when students talked about video games, there was a vibrant exchange of discourse amongst students, even talking over each other.

She developed unit activities based on these questions and evaluated each unit to determine what direction she would take in the next unit. Susan used video games to design three curricular units throughout the school year. Because the school did not have gaming systems or software to play the games, the students brought their own personal systems and games from home. The university research team provided additional technological supports including laptops, games, and cameras to record synchronous game play.

Susan noted being surprised by the high level of excitement that students showed when exploring any topic related to video games, including assisting her as a novice gamer. She said, "Since we did not have the systems or games, the students brought their own personal systems and games from home." It was a journey filled with trepidation, anxiety, but also potential and possibility, "I love the idea of taking ideas that we learned, about video games, the learning principles and applying that to the classroom and our instruction." Like all journeys into unchartered waters there is a struggle between "knowing where I'm going and what I want" and the best methods for reaching there. It also meant significantly letting go of control and letting the students embrace their expertise.

The objective was to explore concepts of mathematics, science, and literacy that students recognized when playing video games. Susan had students work in teams to analyze the games, create posters, and persuade the other students to vote for their video game. The winners got to play their game (e.g., *Guitar Hero*) in the classroom.

Upon completion of Unit 1, Susan, Eva, and Cara reflected on their struggles with the video game unit. In fact, while noting the increased enthusiasm and engagement of the students, they also felt uneasy about losing control and, more important, the lack of connection to mathematics and science. It was clear that a completely student-centered selection process led to games that were more entertainment and less adaptable to the mathematics and science objectives of their class. Games like *Guitar Hero*, *Rock Bank*, and *Happy Feet* (Table 4.2), were not readily compatible with mathematics and science content. This made the teachers question "too much" student autonomy. Eva said, "Maybe we shouldn't give so much democracy," with Susan and Cara nodding in agreement. While the goals of student autonomy, agency, and empowerment were ideals they aspired to, in practice it seemed to come at the cost of teacher identity and unsuitable

TABLE 4.2 Unit 1 Video Games Selected by Students

Game	Rock Band	Guitar Hero	Happy Feet
Console	Wii	PlayStation II	PlayStation I
Susan	X	X	
Eva	X	X	X
Cara			X

content. When asked after the unit, what they would do differently, they said, "We would know the games better." In other words, without teacher knowledge and expertise of the content or process, in this case the video games, the teacher's role is fundamentally compromised.

The teachers felt unable to properly design, organize, and mediate toward the learning goals. Thus, there was little purposeful peer-to-peer interaction and a lack of collective cohesion. Roles were not defined, rules were unclear, mediation was lacking, and the purpose of the activity was not coherent. Teachers play a vital role in socially organizing and designing learning, and this can't be done without some degree of content expertise. More critically, it can't be done without expertise in how to socially organize learning. As a result, student agency and autonomy, without a collective direction and design led by teachers, descends into individualistic, disorganized chaos and lacking purpose. For example, Susan stated, "All they see is that they want to have fun with video games and socialize with their friends—that's all they care about." This is an extremely uncomfortable and perhaps untenable space for a teacher. Empowering students doesn't mean disempowering teachers, especially their critical role in socially organizing learning. This was a significant realization for all the teachers after reflecting upon Unit 1.

As the teachers planned for Unit 2, there was a growing sense that they needed to pull back and reassert their control of the curriculum, but also develop better strategies to leverage mathematics and science funds. Video games were put on hold. In the second unit, Susan designed a thematic unit about community and environmental sustainability, a theme that reflected student interests, experiences, and problems. She transitioned from playing video games to having the students create their own game boards and design energy-efficient homes (Figure 4.1). Unlike the first unit, she created more of a teacher-guided curriculum in advance. Based on the community theme, the class read the book *The City of Ember* (DuPrau, 2003). Students worked in groups to create a board game incorporating mathematics, science, and literacy. Susan also planned field trips to Frank Lloyd Wright's Robie House and the "Smart Home" at the Museum of Science and Industry, where students were able to experience firsthand how homes were built with values inherent in the design and to see an example of a home built with environmentally friendly and energy-efficient materials. A resident artist from the Frank Lloyd Wright Society assisted students in drafting, designing, and building an energy efficient home starting from blueprints to their own 3-D model (Figure 4.2).

This process was critical to developing the teachers' content expertise and having an eye for video games that were compatible with their learning objectives. It was clear that the second unit helped Susan, Eva, and Cara develop better content knowledge and pedagogical strategies within the domains of engineering design, modeling, and urban planning. The teachers and students together learned about environmental sustainability, and this process led them to a genre

FIGURE 4.1 Designing Games and Cities

FIGURE 4.2 3-D Model of a City

TABLE 4.3 Unit 3 Video Games Selected by Teachers

Game	SimCity4	MySims	Dora the Explorer
Console	PlayStation	Wii	Nintendo DS
Susan	X		
Eva		X	
Cara			X

of video games that would both leverage science and mathematics funds as well achieve the learning goals of the mandated curriculum.

The teachers meticulously analyzed the videos of Unit 2. Their coding sheets helped reveal the nature of participation. At the end of Unit 2, Susan commented about her struggles, "I don't see the students using funds of knowledge and not really seeing them, even though they are doing their board games and talking about community, I just don't see them really engaged" (Unit 2 Discourse Study Group). Eva and Cara agreed, and this process led to the selection of urban planning and simulation games like *SimCity4*, *MySims*, and *Dora the Explorer* (Table 4.3).

This is where Susan had an epiphany, "I think bringing in these video games is going to help, building a model city is going to help, so I went to the students and suggested *SimCity4*, and they're all excited about it" (Unit 2 Discourse Study Group). She talked with her students about planning and building their own city with *SimCity4*, "and they got really excited." This was a powerful synergistic moment for all the teachers. A moment where student, teacher, and state-mandated voices spoke together in harmony.

Unit 3: *SimCity4* and the Return to Video Games

The third unit integrated and connected the first unit of video games and the second unit of community. Susan selected the video game *SimCity4*, a city-building simulation game, as part of the community curriculum (Figure 4.3). *SimCity4* places players in the role of a mayor, with the task to populate and develop tracts of lands into cities, while fulfilling the needs of fellow Sims that live in the city. Players can zone different areas of land as commercial, industrial, or residential development, as well as build and maintain public services, transportation, and utilities. To develop a successful city, players must manage its finances, environment, and quality of life for its residents. These were all aspects students had to manage working together in small groups.

Susan thoughtfully planned supports in the groups so that English learners were grouped with fully English proficient speakers, and all groups had a video game expert. She planned the unit to develop new academic concepts based on

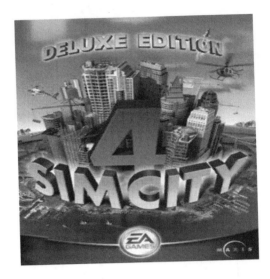

FIGURE 4.3 *SimCity4*

FIGURE 4.4 Focal Students Playing *SimCity4*

students' previous knowledge from units 1 and 2. By seeing familiar knowledge domains as resources, and not obstacles, over a period of time, she related mathematics and science concepts to students' previous experiences. Role shifts and participation shifts were common findings in this unit, particularly in the small-group interactions playing *SimCity4* (Figure 4.4).

Language Learning Domain: Speaking, Writing, and Translanguaging

The unit incorporated multiple content areas and included the four language domains with a focus on speaking and writing in small groups. Susan examined how students communicated in Spanish and English and the role of translanguaging in small-group interactions. Through her analysis, she became aware of the importance of nurturing students' home language in the classroom.

Social Organization of Learning

Susan's activity triangle illustrates her unit plan for socially organizing learning around the object of how video games can help us simulate real design problems (Figure 4.5). The triangle outlines the activity design, the fundamental question that guides the learning process; the *object*, or immediate learning goal of the activity; the *mediational tools* (both material and ideational artifacts) that facilitate movement toward the learning goal; *the subjects*, or immediate classroom participants; the *community* or distal participants; *the rules* that establish parameters for participation within the activity system; and *the division of effort*, which establishes roles and responsibilities for each learner toward accomplishing the learning goal, and finally *outcomes*, which are longitudinal effects suggesting a deeper shift in learner identity and consciousness. Outcomes help teachers think about practices and skills that transfer beyond the immediate learning goals or object of the activity.

In this design, Susan begins with a broad question: *How do video games help us to simulate real design problems?* This question is broad enough to generate robust opportunities for student participation and leveraging their full linguistic and cultural repertoires. The *object* of the activity system was threefold: (1) explore concepts of mathematics, science, and literacy in video games; (2) use technology and video games to simulate real design problems; and (3) use literature to learn about environmental sustainability. The mediational tools include video games such as *SimCity4*, gaming systems, laptop computers, board games, posters, the book *The City of Ember*, field trips to the Robie House and Museum of Science and Industry, and Spanish. The *subjects* were 16 boys and 18 girls with 5 English learners in Susan's combined seventh- and eighth-grade language arts and social sciences classroom. The classroom is situated within the broader Ukrainian and Latinx community consisting of 14 bilingual Spanish and 1 Romanian speaker as well as African-American/Black, biracial families. Susan explicitly and implicitly established discourse rules and expectations such as turn-taking, rotating leadership and expert roles, peer interaction, listening to others while they speak, not to talk while the teacher is speaking, and be respectful. The *division of effort* consisted of teacher-selected groups (4 students) based on heterogeneity of gender, language ability, and video game expertise (from novice to expert), whole-group instruction, and student-centered activities. Finally, projected longitudinal

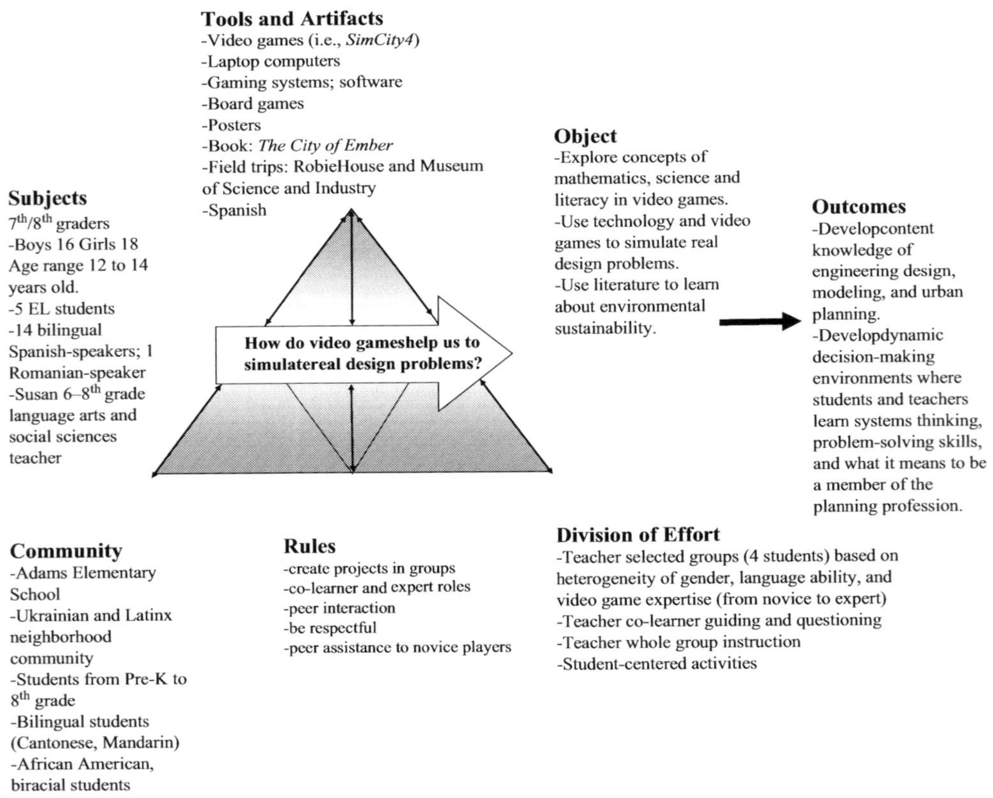

Tools and Artifacts
-Video games (i.e., *SimCity4*)
-Laptop computers
-Gaming systems; software
-Board games
-Posters
-Book: *The City of Ember*
-Field trips: RobieHouse and Museum of Science and Industry
-Spanish

Object
-Explore concepts of mathematics, science and literacy in video games.
-Use technology and video games to simulate real design problems.
-Use literature to learn about environmental sustainability.

Outcomes
-Develop content knowledge of engineering design, modeling, and urban planning.
-Develop dynamic decision-making environments where students and teachers learn systems thinking, problem-solving skills, and what it means to be a member of the planning profession.

How do video games help us to simulate real design problems?

Subjects
7th/8th graders
-Boys 16 Girls 18
Age range 12 to 14 years old.
-5 EL students
-14 bilingual Spanish-speakers; 1 Romanian-speaker
-Susan 6–8th grade language arts and social sciences teacher

Community
-Adams Elementary School
-Ukrainian and Latinx neighborhood community
-Students from Pre-K to 8th grade
-Bilingual students (Cantonese, Mandarin)
-African American, biracial students

Rules
-create projects in groups
-co-learner and expert roles
-peer interaction
-be respectful
-peer assistance to novice players

Division of Effort
-Teacher selected groups (4 students) based on heterogeneity of gender, language ability, and video game expertise (from novice to expert)
-Teacher co-learner guiding and questioning
-Teacher whole group instruction
-Student-centered activities

FIGURE 4.5 Activity Triangle

outcomes for the activity included appropriating video game expert identity as well as applying scientific practices within the planning profession.

Video Game, Group Work, and Expertise

Susan selected and changed groupings throughout the school year to observe changes in student discourse. At first she found it difficult to engage ELs in whole-class and small-group discussions, but found that the activities promoted multiple discourses (Gee, 2007), and in most cases students used Spanish as a linguistic resource. She looked at how students communicated in Spanish and English and the role of translanguaging in small-group interactions (García, 2009), and through this she became aware of the importance of nurturing students' linguistic resources.

> As teachers who did not speak Spanish we found students were able to make academic connections when they used their home language. We believe teachers need to provide opportunities for small group discussion where students can draw on all their linguistic resources.
>
> (Final Action Research Report)

Learning as Shift in Participation and Learner Roles

Planning the *SimCity4* video game groups, Susan selected students with different academic and language abilities as well as personality dispositions to encourage the use of Spanish in the groups. The three Spanish bilingual students had been in the same group for most of the year. Arthur was one of the high performers and "experts" in the class. He was also an expert in video games and in particular *SimCity4*. Susan added Arthur to the group in order to create greater opportunities for peer mediation and dynamic interactions. While he was not considered fully proficient in Spanish, he valued its use. In fact, his Spanish use was sometimes corrected by the three bilingual students in this frame (Table 4.4).

TABLE 4.4 Adding Arthur

Names	Sonia	Grace	Iris	Arthur
EL Status	EL	EL	Transitioned	None
Standardized Math	High	High	High	High
Standardized Reading (English)	Low	Average	High	High
Participation	Low	Low	High	High
Personality Type	Introvert (quiet)	Introvert (quiet)	Extrovert (outspoken)	Extrovert (articulate, respectful)
Language Fluency (Spanish)	High	High	High	Low

The following three episodes illustrate how regrouping and the addition of Arthur shifted the nature of participation, discourse, and learner identities for all.

Initial "Static" Learner Identities

At the beginning of the activity, Arthur was positioned as the expert by the other members, given his reputation in the classroom (Figure 4.6). He offered suggestions and recommendations and explained the rules of the game. He controlled the laptop computer and delegated it according to the task at hand. He attempted to encourage others to participate, but they deferred to him as novice learners, and he remained firmly in control of the game as the expert. He directed the others by designating roles and responsibilities. He assigned Sonia the laptop computer; Iris asked him questions after being the expert and group leader in previous interactions. While Sonia had the laptop computer, she directed all her questions to Arthur. Grace hesitantly attempted to take the laptop computer but didn't. Arthur also took the laptop computer from Sonia to show the others how to put solar panels on homes. The initial learner identities were static and top-down with Arthur as expert and Iris, Grace, and Sonia being novices who deferred to him.

Key
Black = Static learner identity
Circle Size = Proportion of contribution
Arrows = Computer movement
Red X = Failed attempt to retrieve computer

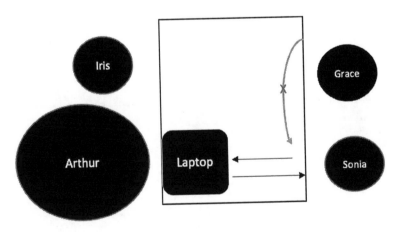

FIGURE 4.6 Initial Learner Identity (Episode 1)

As seen in the transcript on the first day playing *SimCity4*, the three girls drew on his expertise. Susan noticed that even though Arthur was the video game expert, he still allowed and encouraged the others, and they relied on his support.

```
01 Arthur:   (Arthur gives the laptop to Sonia) What do I do?
02 Iris:     Can we [inaudible] no we need to put in electricity into the
03           homes?
04 Arthur:   We are.
05 Sonia:    How?
06 Arthur:   The environment is starting to go down a bit.
07 Iris:     Cause we have pollution / that's why / that's what I didn't
08           want to happen.
09 Arthur:   Well do you want me to show you that one place to make a bunch of
10           windmills. (.) (Arthur in Spanish)
```

Arthur facilitated the group by giving the other three students control over the laptop computer (line 1). He pointed out in line 6 a measurement on the game that shows the rating for the environment that is decreasing due to pollution in the city. He also offered the suggestion to add windmills as a solution to the pollution problem (lines 11–22).

```
11 Sonia:    Okay. What do I do now? (gesturing with her hand as if to say tell
12           me)
13 Grace:    Eh don't be mean to each other (gesturing with her hand)
14 Arthur:   (laughing)
15 Sonia:    Okay, help me.
16 Iris:     I don't know how to play this game.
17 Grace:    (speaks in Spanish and reaches for keyboard)
18 Iris:     Where is the electricity? How do we put electricity into people's
19           homes?
20 Grace:    [inaudible] Electricity↑:::
21 Arthur:   Do you want to make a (.) a small
22 Iris:     No let's [inaudible] how do we put electricity in people's homes?
```

Sonia, Grace, and Iris acknowledged they were novices to the game and asked for Arthur's assistance as they learn to play it (11, 15, 16, 18). Arthur begins to make a recommendation in line 21 when Iris asks again (line 22) about how to get electricity in the homes.

```
23 Arthur:   I want/I want to do the (.) uhm the time to be farther so that we
24           can do like uhm solar (.) [solar] (puts head down) gas plant
25           (makes a sound to put down idea)
26 Sonia:    Okay so how do I do (3 sec) [Iris]
27 Iris:     [I need a break]  (5 sec) Ask Arthur. He knows how.
28 Arthur:   (softly) I win. (softly again) I win. (loudly) I win.
29           (Arthur takes keyboard from Sonia)
30 Sonia:    (Speaks to Iris in Spanish)
```

Arthur used *"I" want, I win* which demonstrated his dominant and somewhat authoritative role as "expert" (lines 23, 28). Arthur strongly encouraged using solar power as opposed to building a power plant for the city (23–25). As he tried to figure out how to do this, the other students become frustrated (26–27). Arthur took the laptop computer from Sonia and tried to put solar panels on the homes (28). Again Susan noted that Sonia spoke to Iris in Spanish (30), but did not have someone write what was said.

```
31 Iris:    (watching game) oops! O:::h OO::::h
32 Arthur:  You/ah, that's the requirements of the solar pl/plant
33 Iris:    Why?
34 Arthur:  We don't have the right requirement for it.
35 Iris:    Why?
36 Arthur:  We need 3,000 people (.) to build a solar plant.
37 Iris:    How many?
38 Arthur:  Three thousand.
39 Iris:    People
40 Sonia:   (high voices) Who::::a, Ooo::::h (and they lean away from the
41          screen)
42 Arthur:  Thirty thousand for hydrogen.
```

Because they were unfamiliar with the rules, Arthur explained to the group that they need more people living in the city to build a solar power plant (34, 36). To provide a comparison, he explained that to build a hydrogen plant requires ten times the amount of people as the solar plant (line 42).

Transitioning Learner Identities Episode 2

Throughout the unit, Susan studied the EL students' verbal and nonverbal participation. Sonia and Grace's roles shifted from peripheral, silent, and passive participatory roles to central, expressive, and active roles. One way they demonstrated this was through becoming more assertive in controlling the laptop computer. Susan noted this in her coding sheet as a shift in participation with the laptop computer toward them. Susan used the coding sheet to mark the students' participation. From the first to the fourth transcript in the *SimCity4* unit, the EL students' verbal participation shifted from 22% to 60%. In episode 2 (lines 1–26), Grace initiated several failed attempts to control the laptop computer (Figure 4.7).

The following vignette further illustrates how Grace, Sonia, and Iris's learner identities started transitioning from novice to expert learners. They shifted through nonverbal actions as well as verbal participation. In the following lines, the discourse among the group became more contested. Grace and Sonia became more engaged after having a reputation for being quiet and passive. Arthur became somewhat frustrated as his epistemological authority was challenged. Grace reached for the keyboard (line 1) and claimed that her position on taxes was correct all along "I told you guys" (line 4), which was taken up by Iris (lines 5, 7), and Arthur became frustrated with being wrong and wanted to "destroy

Key
Gray = Transitioning learner identity
Circle Size = Proportion of contribution
Arrows = Computer movement
X = Failed attempt to retrieve computer

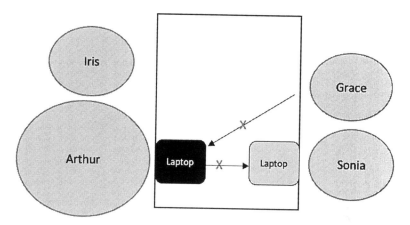

FIGURE 4.7 Transitioning Learner Identity (Episode 2)

the city" (line 8). Sonia, Iris, and Grace, calmly reassert control as they consider alternatives (lines 9–11):

```
01 Grace:    (reaches for the keyboard)
02 Iris:     Arthur, no. I'm going to cry.
03 Sonia:    Iris.
04 Grace:    See the taxes. I told you guys to leave the taxes alone.
05 Iris:     (points to screen) Raise the taxes. (2sec)
06 Grace:    (laughs)
07 Iris:     It's telling us to raise them.
08 Arthur:   Destroy the city.
09 Sonia:    No::
10 Iris:     You know what we should have done [like] fifty percent taxes.
11 Grace:                                                             [No]
```

Arthur's frustration continued as he relinquished control of the laptop to Sonia (line 12) and mockingly told the group to "raise taxes as high as they'll go" (lines 12–13). Iris countered with "they'll [the workers] go on strike," and Sonia responded in Spanish, "Donde era (Where was it?)" (line 16):

```
12 Arthur:   (Gives laptop to Sonia). You know what (.) raise taxes as high
13           as they'll go.
14 Sonia:    (controlling the keyboard)
15 Iris:     They'll go on strike.
16 Sonia:    ¿Donde era? (Where was it?)
```

Arthur attempted to regain control by taking back the keyboard, but Sonia rejected this attempt (line 18). He continued his mocking tone about "raising taxes" (lines 19–21), and Iris was disturbed with Arthur's stance (line 22):

```
17 Arthur:   (takes control of keyboard) There (pointing)
18 Sonia:    No::::
19 Arthur:   Raise taxes as high as they'll go. (2 sec)
20 Sonia:    No::::::::: (2 sec)
21 Arthur:   See how high they'll go. (3 sec)
22 Iris:     Painful
```

Sonia and Iris's outspoken participation was a dramatic shift from the first two units, During the first two units their verbal participation was limited. They assumed "silent" roles such as making posters or taking notes while the other students talked, guided, and made decisions. This illustrates a shift in participation in that the EL students not only talked more, but also took on active gamer design roles. Sonia took control of the laptop computer and explicitly initiated conversation with Arthur and Iris about taxation.

This dialogue was highly contested and evolved into true scientific discourse characterized by inquiry and evidence. Initially Arthur was unwilling to legitimize Sonia's proposal and mocked her proposal to raise taxes. However, the dialogue that followed consisted of scientific practices such as marshalling evidence to support claims and navigating disagreement through communication. This happened with Iris pointing to the screen and citing evidence from the mayor's office (lines 5, 7). By the end of the episode, one of the "shyest" EL students, Grace, took the floor (lines 23–26). She demonstrated a collective, vested interest in what happens (line 23) to "our city" (line 25) and the importance of taking action (line 26):

```
23 Grace:    What if something [happens]
24 Arthur:   Cause                           [Twenty percent]
25 Grace:    If something happens to our city it's all you guyers fault.
26           we weren't doing nothing. [We put it right.]
```

Episode 2 shows how Sonia and Grace transitioned from novice learner roles to expert identities within this activity.

Dynamic Learner Identities Episode 3

By episode 3 of this vignette, we observed dynamic learner identities and movement toward expert learner roles. The discourse structure had become more egalitarian and shifted toward greater collaboration (Figure 4.8, overlapping circles). The laptop computer circulated more freely, and the dialogue was contested yet collaborative as they collectively moved toward the learning object of

Key
White = Dynamic learner identity
Circle size = Proportion of contribution
Overlappin gcircles = Dynamic participation roles
Arrows = Computer movement

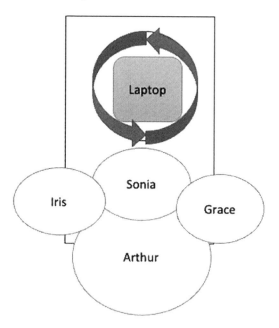

FIGURE 4.8 Shift in Learner Identity (Episode 3)

the project. The laptop computer and its positioning within the interaction significantly mediated more dynamic learning. Sonia assumed a greater leadership role by taking the laptop computer and guiding the conversation (Figure 4.8).

They continued their debate from episode 2 on how to best solve the problem of taxation. In this episode, Grace and Sonia turned the laptop computer toward themselves to lead the conversation. As each participant made claims, they supported it with evidence by pointing to the screen (lines 1–11). Arthur continued to blame Sonia, Grace, and Iris for the declining state of the city through rapid expansion (lines 3, 5, 7, 10). The students used the game's panel view, which includes information such as the city's budget, jobs, and mayor's rating, to make decisions. Arthur referred to the green bar being all the way at the bottom, which indicates the mayor's rating is declining (10–11).

```
01 Sonia:    Okay okay yo soy aqui. (I am here.) (takes control of the laptop)
02 Grace:    No::
03 Arthur:   I thought it was going to be easier.
04 Iris:     You're lying to me.
```

```
05 Arthur:   Cause you guys made it big.
06 Iris:     How'd we make it big?
07 Arthur:   You guys wanted to expand everything.
08 Grace:    No we didn't. (2sec)
09 Iris:     Okay they're asking for more houses.
10 Arthur:   (pointing to screen) Look at th::at! (.) Look at that! The green
11           bar's all the way at the bottom.
```

Arthur and Iris continued to debate as each points to the screen to assert their claim (lines 12–17). Iris defended their decision to build more houses and expand the city to make more money, which will fix the city's debt (12–13). As Arthur voiced his displeasure (line 16), Grace took the computer and turned it toward herself and Sonia (line 17).

```
12 Iris:     But look at look at (points to screen). We made more money (.)
13           We earned always more. It's because of the taxes, that's why.
14 Grace:    No. (inaudible)
15 Iris:     No.
16 Arthur:   You screwed up the city.
17 Grace:    (turns computer towards herself and Sonia)
```

Focal Group's Reflection on Learning Through Collaborative Tension

At the end of the unit, Susan saw how the students' participation changed in group, and she also noted that the activity may have impacted the frequency and quality of their participation while playing video games. During the end-of-the-year class presentations, she asked them what they liked about the unit. All of them agreed that it was fun playing video games for a classroom assignment. Susan specifically asked Sonia what she liked, and she stated that she liked learning how to play the game and gained confidence toward the end of the game. During a study group meeting (SG #12), Susan talked about a writing activity she used to help students reflect on the obstacles or tension they experienced while playing *SimCity4* in their groups:

> And what they wrote about, which I found interesting again was that when they were doing groups, they said that when we got to the point of tension, we had to come up with new ideas. Many of the students talked about that. They said we disagreed and then new ideas came. And they talked about that in their writing.

The students, themselves, demonstrated an understanding of the role tension can play in creating new knowledge. They identified discursive tension and contested meaning-making points toward an opportunity to create a third space where new ideas could be mediated (Razfar, 2013). For example, Sonia's reflection (Figure 4.9) demonstrated how the game created a learning environment that encouraged failure through real-life problem solving. The group worked together (mirror), trying out their ideas (light bulb), and learning from their

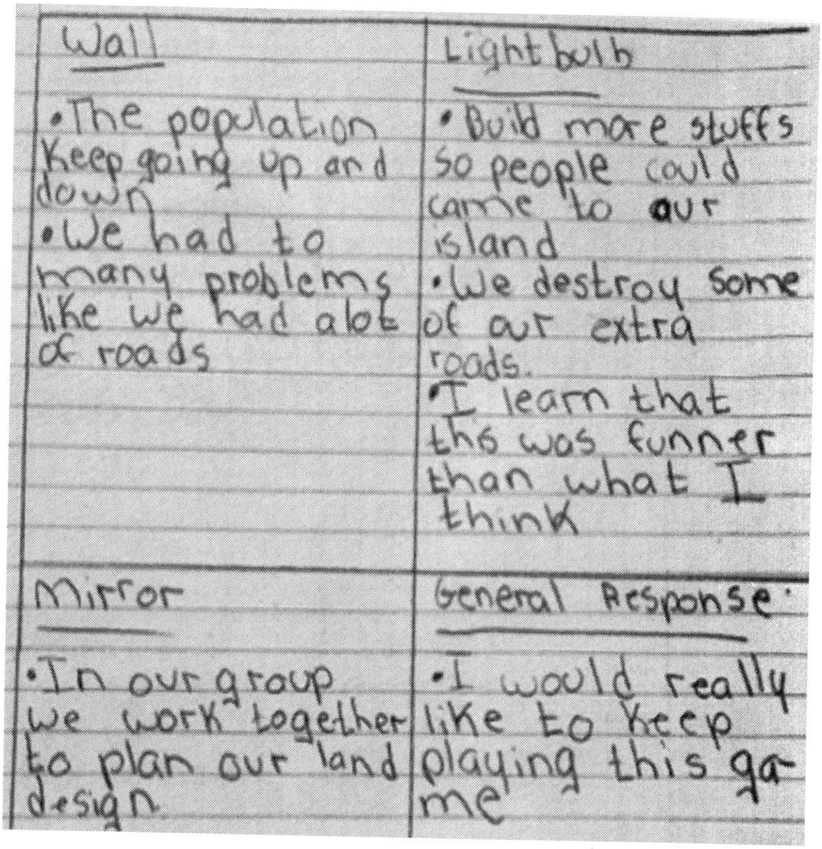

Wall	Light bulb
•The population keep going up and down •We had to many problems like we had a lot of roads	•Build more stuffs so people could came to our island •We destroy some of our extra roads. •I learn that this was funner than what I think
Mirror	General Response:
•In our group we work together to plan our land design	•I would really like to keep playing this game

FIGURE 4.9 Sonia's Written Reflection of *SimCity4*

mistakes (wall). Although the activity was filled with tension, as previously demonstrated, Sonia showed an interest in continuing to play and learn with her peers (general).

The District Walk-Through: Teachers as Advocates and Curriculum Experts

To become "more complete members" of their community, the teachers had to redefine their roles within a community that appeared to be moving in one direction as they were moving in another. They had to move from being one type of teacher to being another one. This was difficult to do when what they were trying to do was not valued or respected by their community *writ large*. They recognized that in comparison to the other LSciMAct Program school cohorts, their group benefited from having a supportive administration that, at the time of the research, gave them autonomy in their classrooms and encouraged them to conduct action research. But, even within this supportive environment, the teachers recognized that what they were being asked to do by the program, and what they would begin to champion and see as their work as teachers, had been misinterpreted and misrepresented by education reform advocates as less than rigorous and inappropriate for nonmainstream students.

As part of a district walk-through, the assistant principal, principal, and an administrator from the central office walked into her classroom unannounced as the students played the video game. Susan recalled feeling panicked when she talked with the principal later in the day:

> The principal said I didn't have any idea what you were doing there. I was so afraid [the central office administrator] would say something, but when she went out, she said I am so impressed that I could finally see *student discourse* instead of [just] teacher discourse. I said okay. There is one person that's thinking (laughs). She could understand what I'm doing.
>
> (Focus Group #4)

Susan's fears were alleviated, and she found support and validation in the administrator's comments, but the fear was real. With increased pressure on teachers to raise test scores and teach prescribed curriculum and now with new teacher evaluation measures tied to student performance, the fears are even greater today than they were a decade ago. At the end of the action research project, when she was asked how the project had informed her teaching, Susan became philosophical and contextualized her changed practices within the landscape of education.

> This kind of teaching is not perceived in a positive way. It is much more because it is so much more flexible and open and it has to flow; it's very threatening to people. They [teachers and administrators] don't understand it. I think they've always been puzzled at how I get the scores but I do. And I'm puzzled too, to tell you the truth. (laughs) Because it's not as structured as most people would think it should be or would expect it to be.
>
> (Focus Group #4)

In redefining themselves as teachers and in redefining what it meant to teach, the teachers had, in fact, created tension within their professional community as it appeared to them. It was a tension that they felt, believing that what they were doing in the classroom could be misinterpreted and used against them and knowing that stronger trends within education perceived what they were doing as inappropriate even as it met with success. It failed the litmus test of accountability and objectivity even as it proved successful.

Tension, contestation, and joint meaning-making in the third space were an intentional aspect of our action research process. Activities, such as *SimCity 4*, were strategically designed with multiple mediational means and heterogeneous groups to create learning opportunities through episodes of third space. When teachers consciously and strategically design activities with the explicit purpose of generating third space episodes, learners can challenge dominant perspectives and use nondominant mediational tools without fear (Razfar, 2013). These third space vignettes expand the range of possibilities when it comes to assessing student learning when they access their life-worlds and use multimodal means of communication (Wiseman, 2011).

Conclusion

Using video games as part of the curriculum changed the way Susan saw her role. Letting go of control, she was able to facilitate the collective expertise of students and teachers. She came to understand and value students' knowledge of video games and the learning principles embedded in the games. During the project, she saw that video games offered ELs opportunities to use problem-solving skills and academic discourse to make connections to their funds of knowledge. She seized these moments to design activities to examine the ways ELs participated and used multiple discourses. She encouraged students to use their full linguistic repertoire in which students communicated in Spanish and English and used translanguaging in small-group interactions, even though she did not speak Spanish. Ultimately this led to shifts in student participation.

The COVID-19 global pandemic has fundamentally changed the role of digital literacies in classrooms, and design games like *SimCity* have an integral role in STEM education (Roy, 2019). *SimCity 4* as a simulation game now must be taken seriously as a powerful mediational tool for developing dynamic decision-making environments where students and teachers learn systems thinking, problem-solving skills, and what it means to be a member of the planning profession (Gaber, 2007). More importantly, it cannot be used as a one-size-fits-all activity and must be adapted and honed by teacher researchers (Razfar et al., 2015). Research now confirms what our team of teachers learned through action research, that the cognitive benefits of simulation games far outweigh the perceived shortcomings (Aguilar et al., 2019; Wouters, van Nimwegen, van Oostendorp, & van der Spek, 2013). More important, we learned that the technological, curricular, and content expertise as well as the support of the administration are essential to successful learning outcomes through video games. While today's wisdom is often yesterday's ignorance, this chapter is the story of curriculum design, technology integration, and contrarian thinking led by teachers and university partners who believed in what students were doing in their homes and communities.

Additional Resources

1. Research Brief and Video Clips of Video Games in the Math Classroom (National Council of Teachers of Mathematics) https://www.nctm.org/Research-and-Advocacy/Research-Brief-and-Clips/Video-Games-in-the-Math-Classroom/

2. Video Games to Help Make Teaching Math Fun
https://interestingengineering.com/7-video-games-to-help-make-teaching-math-fun
3. The Science Game Center offers games with science content
https://www.sciencegamecenter.org

Discussion Questions

1. How can student video game expertise be used to teach mathematics, science, and literacy?
2. How would you advocate for digital literacies with your administration and district?
3. How can teachers strategically group students in terms of their activity roles in order to optimize participation shifts and learning outcomes?

References

Aguilar, J., Díaz, F., Altamiranda, J., Cordero, J., Chavez, D., & Gutierrez, J. (2019). Metropolis: Emergence in a serious game to enhance the participation in smart city urban planning. *Journal of the Knowledge Economy, 86*(211), 1–24.

DuPrau, J. (2003). *City of Ember.* New York, NY: Random House.

Gaber, J. (2007). Simulating planning: SimCity as a pedagogical tool. *Journal of Planning Education and Research, 27*(2), 113–121. DOI: 10.1177/0739456X07305791

García, O. (2009). Education, multilingualism and translanguaging in the 21st century. In A. Mohanty, M. Panda, R. Phillipson, & T. Skutnabb-Kangas (Eds.), *Multilingual education for social justice: Globalising the local* (pp. 128–145). New Delhi: Orient Blackswan.

Gee, J. (2007). *Good video games, good learning.* New York, NY: Peter Lang.

Razfar, A. (2013). Multilingual mathematics: Learning through contested spaces of meaning making. *International Multilingual Research Journal, 7*(3), 175–196.

Razfar, A., Troiano, B., Nasir, A., Yang, E., Rumenapp, J. C., & Torres, Z. (2015). Teachers' language ideologies in classroom practices: Using English learners' linguistic capital to socially re-organize learning. In P. Smith (Ed.), *Handbook of research on cross-cultural approaches to language and literacy development* (pp. 261–298). Hershey, PA: IGI Global Publications.

Roy, J. (2019, March 5). Must reads: From video game to day job: How "SimCity" inspired a generation of city planners. *Los Angeles Times.* https://www.latimes.com/business/technology/la-fi-tn-simcity-inspired-urban-planners-20190305-story.html

Wiseman, A. (2011). Powerful students, powerful words: Writing and learning in a poetry workshop. *Literacy, 2*(45), 70–77.

Wouters, P., van Nimwegen, C., van Oostendorp, H., & van der Spek, E. (2013). A meta-analysis of the cognitive and motivational effects of serious games. *Journal of Educational Psychology, 105*(2), 249–265.

5

FROM IRE TO CONVERSATIONAL

Shifting Classroom Discourse Through Community-Based Forensics Expertise

A [colleague] was nice enough to get us a forensic investigator who came in and that tied the whole unit together. And he talked about crimes in the neighborhood and he brought in tools that investigators used to solve crimes, and that was the technology piece.

Allison, Sixth-Grade Teacher

Introduction

This chapter presents a science unit in a sixth-grade classroom in which the teacher attempts to open up opportunities for student-led discussion while applying concepts from the scientific method to a mystery simulation. Allison was a veteran teacher of Chinese heritage, similar to many of her students. While she did not speak a Chinese language on a regular basis, she often encouraged students to use their own languages in discussions. Students were encouraged to collect, analyze, and synthesize data to build a cohesive, evidence-based argument. Throughout the lesson, particular students shifted in their participation, using multiple languages and modalities. During classroom discussions, students drew on their own funds of knowledge, which the teacher then used to expand the learning environment. In particular, one bilingual student, Min Hin, shifted into a position of leadership while articulating her reasoning in Mandarin. She also took on a new identity as she produced a written record from the group discussion. The content standards, along with specific language objectives, were coaligned to allow the lesson to flow from science practices to real-world applications.

DOI: 10.4324/9781351001168-5

Standards

Science

- Analyze and interpret data on the properties of substances before and after the substances interact to determine if a chemical reaction has occurred.
- Develop a model to generate data for iterative testing and modification of a proposed object, tool, or process such that an optimal design can be achieved.
- Define the criteria and constraints of a design problem with sufficient precision to ensure a successful solution, taking into account relevant scientific principles and potential impacts on people and the natural environment that may limit possible solutions.
- Gather and make sense of information to describe that synthetic materials come from natural resources and impact society.

(standards adapted from NGSS MS-PS1-2, MS-ETS1-4, MS-ETS1-1, MS-PS1-3)

Mathematics

- Reason abstractly and quantitatively.
- Use ratio and rate reasoning to solve real-world and mathematical problems.
- Summarize numerical data sets in relation to their context.

(standards adapted from Math CCSS MP.2, RP.A.3, SP.B.5)

Literacy

- Cite specific textual evidence to support analysis of science and technical texts, attending to the precise details of explanations or descriptions.
- Integrate quantitative or technical information expressed in words in a text with a version of that information expressed visually (e.g., graph).

(standards adapted from CCSS ELA-Literacy RST.6-8.1, RST.6-8.7)

Language

- English language learners communicate for social and instructional purposes within the school setting.
- English learners communicate information, ideas, and concepts necessary for academic success in the content area of language arts.
- English learners communicate information, ideas, and concepts necessary for academic success in the content area of mathematics.
- English learners communicate information, ideas, and concepts necessary for academic success in the content area of science.
- English learners communicate information, ideas, and concepts necessary for academic success in the content area of social studies.

(standards adapted from WIDA Consortium Standards 1–5)

Chapter Objectives

1. Teachers will be able to leverage science funds of knowledge.
2. Teachers will be able to become aware of their own discursive patterns and move toward more conversational patterns.
3. Teachers will be able create an applied science program.

Unit Objectives

1. Students will be able to test evidence against a control, synthesize multiple data sources, and draw reasonable conclusions from data.
2. Students will be able to create an argument based on scientific evidence.
3. Students will be able to connect social phenomena in the community (e.g., crime and punishment) with applied science.

Context: Teacher, Students, and School

Allison, a veteran teacher of nearly 30 years, worked in a high-performing public elementary school. Though she identified as monolingual, she had grown up in a multilingual household. Her parents had immigrated to the United States from Hong Kong. She had taken up her current teaching post in a school with a large population of Chinese-American students in a locally identified "Chinatown." The school was marked as a multilingual space and included a transitional bilingual program. In 2011, Warner included 704 students, 93% of whom were Asian (most of whom were from families who had immigrated from Cantonese and Taishan regions of China), 6% African-American/Black and 1% from other racial groups. Twenty-six percent of the students were identified as bilingual or requiring bilingual services, and 95% had free or reduced lunch. In Allison's sixth-grade classroom, 11 students had been identified as ELs and were designated as receiving ESL services. Some had recently immigrated from China, while others had transitioned from the bilingual program housed within the school. One student, Min Hin, had been identified as a focal student for Allison's research. She had noticed that she was "quiet" and often called her "shy" but placed her in groups with other Mandarin speakers to facilitate her conversing. Indeed, early in the year, she relied heavily on three students in her group to respond in whole-group contexts, and the other students often had to draw her into the conversation while the group was being video-recorded. Wei Sheng, the student who emerged as the leader in the group, often facilitated Min Hin's involvement. Over the course of the year, she transformed both in spoken and written conversation, in part because of strategic pedagogical decisions made by Allison.

Unit Plan: From "Very IRE!" to Expanded Opportunities for Student-Talk

Allison focused a great deal of time on student interaction throughout her action research. Prior to the action research, she identified her discourse style as "strict." Prior to the study, she claimed that she was "very IRE!" meaning that she always followed a traditional teacher-centered script where teachers initiate questions (I), students are selected to respond (R), and the teacher evaluates (E) the correctness of the response (Cazden, 2001). Classroom discourse was introduced in the first introductory course designed for the project. This was a course led by the project director, Aria Razfar, and graduate assistant at the time, Ambareen Nasir. During the course, teachers designed a pilot project that simulated the major components of the action research project they would be doing over the next 2 years: funds of knowledge inquiry, unit design, discourse analysis, and a final group report. Given the compressed schedule, only one teacher from each cohort volunteered to have their unit implementation video-recorded by the university research team. Allison enthusiastically volunteered, given she was the most experienced teacher of the group (26 years), so our research team video-recorded three sessions of her pilot project.

After the first analytic session, to her own chagrin, it became clear that her discourse pattern was extremely teacher-centered. Each video-recorded session was analyzed independently by all of the members of her cohort in 1-minute increments. Each of the members of her cohort independently noted a strict IRE pattern in Allison's classroom discourse pattern. She was surprised by the degree and amount of teacher-centered discourse. She had never seen herself that way. She imagined her class to be much more valuing student voice, student-centered, and conversational discourse. It was a moment of clarity for her after 26 years of teaching. Allison was comfortable sharing the group's observation of her unit with the entire action research class.

In her final report two years later, she recalled the pivotal classroom discussion of the pilot study in Professor Razfar's action research course. The contrast between what she thought she was doing and what she saw were so diametrically opposed and vividly clear that the professor and Allison could not help but laugh out loud at what was happening. She noted in her final report how Professor Razfar was laughing and calling her "stoic" and "scary" at how teacher-centered she was. While it was all in gist and fun, this interaction left an enduring impression on Allison. She was determined to make a change from strict IRE to conversational discourse. She wanted to mediate an environment that was more egalitarian and valued student agency. For a teacher of her stature and experience, this was a critical reminder and demonstration for the other members of the class that learning is a lifelong process and that "you can teach an old dog new tricks."

Because Allison was so open and willing to make herself vulnerable early on, her action research goal in terms of herself was clear. She realized that she tended to control the classroom space by prompting and regulating student responses to teacher-posed questions. She rarely deviated from the IRE pattern, and she was eager to reorganize learning in her classroom. While she used science inquiry in her classroom, in the form of the Full Option Science System (FOSS) curriculum (Full Option Science System [FOSS], 2020), she said she didn't give students ample time for peer interaction. Allison's comfort with making herself vulnerable was critical not only to her own development but also for the other teachers within her cohort and the rest participating in the action research project.

Over the first two units, Allison attempted to reorganize the classroom space and practices to include more opportunities for student-to-student talk as well as the space to allow the use of multiple languages. In particular, she organized groups to allow bilingual students to work in English and Mandarin or English and Cantonese. As the third unit approached, she included an experiential learning activity that she used each year. The unit featured a missing person mystery in which students acted as both detectives and forensic scientists—collecting evidence, testing it using the scientific method, and interpreting it—to solve the mystery. During this activity, students communicated in dynamic ways—without teacher mediation. This experience was then integrated into a new lesson about crime and technology in which students interacted in small groups and presented to the whole class. As students considered the social phenomena of crime and punishment in relation to their own community, Allison noticed that they were drawing on deep-situated community experiences and funds of knowledge. She used these funds of knowledge to plan a new lesson, inviting a crime scene detective from a local police district to share his experiences. In this way, Allison leveraged funds of knowledge while strategically interlacing content objectives into the new ways to foster student interaction.

During Allison's final science unit of each year, she customarily built on science skills of observation and description through a crime scene investigation simulation entitled "The Mystery of Felix" (*GEMS: Mystery Festival–Lawrence Hall of Science*, 2021). This simulation gives students the opportunity to employ science skills to gather evidence, build arguments, and come to conclusions. The narrative of this simulation is built around a missing person and calls for a crime scene to be set up in the corner of a classroom. The crime scene includes a silhouette of a body on the ground with various items in disarray (Figure 5.1). Variations of the simulation may include hairs, fingernails, blood splatters, and chemicals to allow students to collect evidence and test against known samples.

FIGURE 5.1 Crime Scene Artifacts

In addition to evidence from the crime scene itself, four character suspects had written testimony that was posted in the classroom. While the crime scene unit was an attempt to end the school year on an enjoyable note, it also delves into essential aspects of a strong science curriculum.

Forensics is an applied field of science, leveraging scientific concepts and knowledge in criminology. Popularized in crime dramas such as CSI, investigators collect, test, and interpret evidence. They also propose theories or models of that data that can then be used to support a particular conclusion. Thus, this forensic simulation pulled together several concepts from the sixth-grade science curriculum such as testing against a control, observational strategies, documentation, and several others. To thread in other classroom objectives, such as language objectives, teamwork was encouraged to emphasize the social and linguistic nature of doing science.

Language Learning Domain: Multiple Language Use with Mandarin and English

Allison's intentional focus on organizing small groups in a way that allowed students to draw on their widest communicative repertoires to build group discussions facilitated participation from students who often did not speak up in the classroom. Whereas most students in the class spoke Cantonese and English, and English was the medium of whole class instruction, in the small-group with Min Hin students could facilitate collaboration in both English and Mandarin. Allison also distributed the labor in the groups in a way to allow students to take up new learner and leadership roles, as with Min Hin moving into the recorder/writer role. While the shifts in small-group discussions were fairly easy for Allison to plan for through the use of multiple languages, it was her attempts at organizing classroom discussion that benefited from various iterations of planning, implementing plans, and analyzing instruction that allowed changes in whole-class discussions. The small-group discussions often played a role in organizing ideas and building scientific arguments through multiple languages that would later be shared in English in whole-class discussion. In this way, multiple languages were used to facilitate the meaning making of the group, while the IRE structures were simultaneously peeled away.

Social Organization of Learning: Using Forensics to Solve Crimes

Allison's activity triangle illustrates her unit plan for socially organizing learning around the object of how forensic technology can help us solve crimes in the community (Figure 5.2). The triangle outlines the activity design; the fundamental question that guides the learning process; the *object*, or immediate learning goal of the activity; the *mediational tools* (both material and ideational artifacts)

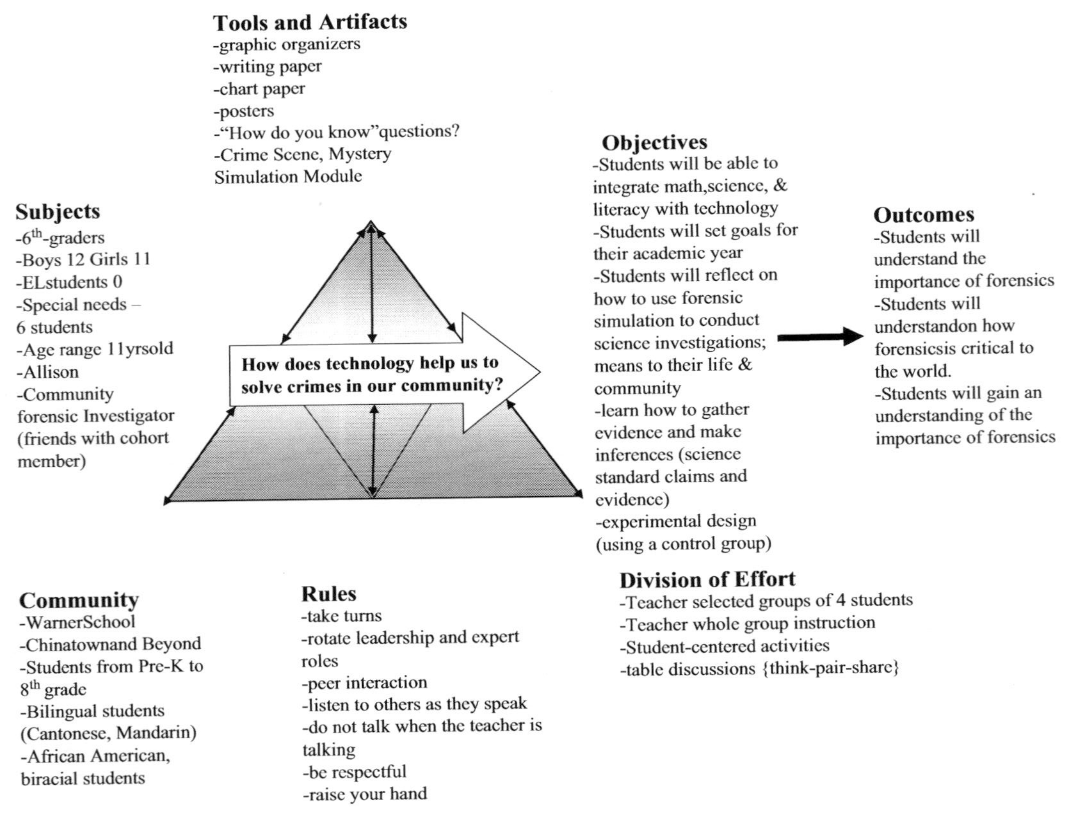

Tools and Artifacts
-graphic organizers
-writing paper
-chart paper
-posters
-"How do you know"questions?
-Crime Scene, Mystery Simulation Module

How does technology help us to solve crimes in our community?

Objectives
-Students will be able to integrate math,science, & literacy with technology
-Students will set goals for their academic year
-Students will reflect on how to use forensic simulation to conduct science investigations; means to their life & community
-learn how to gather evidence and make inferences (science standard claims and evidence)
-experimental design (using a control group)

Outcomes
-Students will understand the importance of forensics
-Students will understandon how forensicsis critical to the world.
-Students will gain an understanding of the importance of forensics

Subjects
-6th graders
-Boys 12 Girls 11
-ELstudents 0
-Special needs – 6 students
-Age range 11yrsold
-Allison
-Community forensic Investigator (friends with cohort member)

Rules
-take turns
-rotate leadership and expert roles
-peer interaction
-listen to others as they speak
-do not talk when the teacher is talking
-be respectful
-raise your hand

Community
-WarnerSchool
-Chinatownand Beyond
-Students from Pre-K to 8th grade
-Bilingual students (Cantonese, Mandarin)
-African American, biracial students

Division of Effort
-Teacher selected groups of 4 students
-Teacher whole group instruction
-Student-centered activities
-table discussions {think-pair-share}

FIGURE 5.2 Allison's Activity Triangle

that facilitate movement toward the learning goal; *the subjects* or immediate classroom participants; the *community* or distal participants; *the rules* that establish parameters for participation within the activity system; *the division of effort*, which establishes roles and responsibilities for each learner toward accomplishing the learning goal; and finally *outcomes*, which are longitudinal effects suggesting a deeper shift in learner identity and consciousness. Outcomes help teachers think about practices and skills that transfer beyond the immediate learning goals or object of the activity.

In this design, Allison begins with a broad question: *How does technology help us to solve crimes in our community?* This question is broad enough to generate robust opportunities for student participation and leveraging their full linguistic and cultural repertoires. The *object* of the activity system was threefold: (1) integrate mathematics, science, and literacy with technology; (2) reflect on how to use forensic simulation to conduct science investigations (i.e., gathering evidence, making inferences); and (3) develop experimental design principles such as using control and experimental groups. The mediational tools include *Crime Scene Mystery Simulation Module*, "how do you know" questions, crime scene artifacts, posters, and graphic organizers. The simulation centered around solving a murder mystery by using scientific concepts such as evidence gathering, data analysis, and interpretation. The *subjects* were 12 boys and 11 girls with 6 special-needs students, 20 English learners, and 3 African-American students all in Allison's sixth-grade classroom. The classroom is situated within the broader Chinatown community consisting of bilingual and multilingual (Cantonese, Mandarin, Taishan, and English) speakers as well as African-American and biracial families. Allison explicitly established discourse rules and expectations such as turn-taking, rotating leadership and expert roles, peer interaction, listening to others while they speak, not to talk while the teacher is speaking, and be respectful. The *division of effort* consisted of teacher-selected groups (4 students) based on heterogeneity of gender, language ability, and learner identity (from novice to expert), whole-group instruction, student-centered activities, and table discussions (think–pair–share). Finally, projected longitudinal *outcomes* for the activity included appropriating forensic expert identity as well as applying scientific practices within the community.

The unit list of activities demonstrates an integration across the curriculum, allowing for a more dynamic and cohesive unit that allowed for a broad interpretation of scientific evidence within a social and cultural setting (Table 5.1).

The teachers at Warner didn't specifically use a social organization of learning protocol, but they discussed at length the social organization of learning in meetings, field notes, and their own analytical documents. As seen earlier, threaded throughout the final unit was an attempt to shift the organization from teacher centered to student-centered. This was a goal from very early on in Allison's research. In fact, when she wrote her thesis about her research, she indicated that one of her main goals was to "relinquish the authoritarian regime after 26 years

TABLE 5.1 Unit 3 Activity Plan by Day

Day	Description
1	Introduce the "crime scene" to the students as they read along about what happened to Felix. Predict what they think might have happened to Felix (i.e., disappeared, murdered, faked his murder). They will observe the crime science by groups and sketch the crime scene. They will read about the four suspects involved and start to gather evidence based on their alibis.
2	Discuss what they know about crimes. Brainstorm what kind of questions they would like to ask their parents about crime in their community. In groups, they will come up with several questions. They will survey their parents about crime in their community.
3	Students will report on what they found out about crime in their community. The class will generate a tally mark chart on what types of crimes were committed and how many crimes were committed in the community (i.e., robbery, kidnapping, personal inquiries, breaking and entering homes and cars). They will each make a line graph and chart the results.
4	Students discuss what places around their community have the most crime. They will discuss what types of crime might be committed in their school.
5	Students begin the investigation of the crime scene "Who Killed Felix?" They will test using chromatography and fingerprinting as their first experiments for the crime. Students will write their results on their investigating sheet and log in their science journals.
6	Students will investigate using the pH factor experiment. One of the crimes committed was that the victim, Felix, drank from a cup of Coca-Cola with a substance in it. Students will determine who drank from the tainted cup and continue to gather more evidence. Also, they will burn fibers (string and wool pieces) to compare and deduce what type of fiber was in the crime scene.
7	Students will complete a graphic organizer based on the experiments and clues they have gathered as evidence.
8	Students will analyze different handwritings from the suspects of the crime scene. Someone wrote a mystery note, and it was signed by one of the suspects. Can they compare and contrast different handwriting? Did Vera (suspect) really write the note? If not, who did?
9	Students will look at different types of fibers left on the suspects' clothing (grass, dog hair, wool pieces, human hair). Students will compare and contrast the different types of fibers and match them to the crime scene.
10	Students will look at the various experiments completed so far and start to piece together the evidence that leads to the suspect(s).
11	PowerPoint on DNA will be shown to the students. They will learn about how DNA is unique in everyone. It is the blueprint of each individual. Then, they will look at DNA strands and match them to the DNA on the comb from the crime scene.
12	Students will experiment with using different mystery white powders. They will discover what type of mystery white powder was on the shoe of several of the suspects from the crime scene. They will compare and contrast cornstarch, sugar, baking soda, and flour powders.

(Continued)

TABLE 5.1 (Continued)

Day	Description
13	PowerPoint shown on *what is a crime scene?* How does an investigator use evidence to conclude and solve a case? Footprints and fingerprints will be shown that were in the crime scene. Students will match the footprints and fingerprints of several suspects to the scene of the crime.
14	Students write a letter requesting for an expert forensic investigator from the police department. The students will ask questions and discuss with the investigator crime in the neighborhood. *How does technology play a role in solving crimes in the neighborhood?*
*15	Students will meet with guest speaker, Mr. Chris from the forensics investigation unit. He will bring in technology that is used to help solve crimes. He will discuss how investigators go about compiling evidence to solve crimes. He will display some of the technology used to aid him when investigating. He will answer questions for the students. The students will have conversations with him about forensic science. This will hopefully connect how much technology is used in solving crimes and why it is important in our everyday lives.

* Culminating Activity

of teaching." Her understanding that the classroom was set up in a way that organized her as the sole authority was the beginning of a shift in her own teaching. That awareness occurred early on when she began to look at interactional data from the classroom.

Awareness for Allison occurred in at least three different phases. In the first phase, she, like every social actor, operates under assumed norms of social practice. That is, the teacher is generally viewed as the holder of knowledge, language is assumed to be a conveyor of knowledge, and students are assumed to be a receptor of knowledge. This manifests, often, in the classroom as autonomous literacies such as discrete worksheets and individual activities as well as a strict IRE/F interactional structure (Wells, 1993).

The second phase of awareness began to occur early on when Allison reflected on the language use in the classroom, specifically through the use of discourse analytic tools. Through her analysis of transcripts, Allison immediately became aware that the everyday social norms she was guided by said something. They were part of a hidden curriculum that taught students that they have little voice and agency (Brodie, 2013). This recognition allowed Allison to experiment with different interactional styles like reorganizing small groups to facilitate translanguaging interactions and to reposition students like Min Hin into leadership roles. In one class period, Allison attempted to spatially reorganize the classroom in a circle to allow students to talk with one another (Figure 5.3). This allowed for more interaction among students while Allison attempted to release control of the linguistic authorization. Of course, as with any learning process, this led

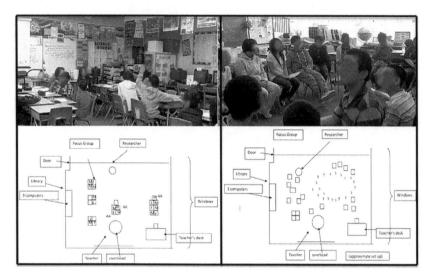

FIGURE 5.3 Spatial Reorganization of the Classroom

to some successes and many failures, but the important thing here is that Allison intentionally manipulated the social organization—via discourse—to reshape the social relationships. Analyzing classroom discourse made her aware of the pragmatic functions of language.

The final phase of awareness emerged when Allison recognized the connection between social position and language. By reconceptualizing language as a relationship building tool rather than a conveyor of knowledge, she was able to make informed decisions about the social organization. Rather than operating under the general social norms with which she was familiar—as she did early on—or attempting to manipulate solely the structures of the classroom and hope the language changed—as she did via the classroom reorganization—she developed a way to talk about the relationship between language and social position. This development of a language to talk about language use in the classroom was the third level of awareness. It allowed Allison to not only attempt to control the discursive structure vis-à-vis her own power and control, but also helped her to deconstruct her own agency and allow students more autonomy. It also allows, even requires, teachers to view student identity in new ways (Rumenapp, 2016a). This final phase coincided with her use of funds of knowledge in the third unit.

Thus, what occurred with Allison's own learning took place through the analysis of classroom discourse. By first challenging the everyday social norms we experience through using a research tool like discourse analysis and then through making actual attempts to change those norms (with proper evaluation after), Allison used her action research to become aware of the relationship between language and social organization.

The Linguistic Organization of Applying Science in a Crime Investigation

Students in Allison's classroom were encouraged to complete this activity through using broad communicative repertoires. Min Hin and her group were no exception. After gathering evidence from the crime scene, the group began to test their evidence against known samples to build a case against the character responsible for Felix's disappearance. During their rotations to specific lab stations, they collected and compared fingerprint evidence, conducted smell tests for certain chemicals, and also conducted a litmus test. As she implemented the different tests, Min Hin flourished in her participation through the scientific practices. For example, while her group was discussing a particular set of evidence and attempting to come to a conclusion about who committed the crime, Min Hin walked over to a board that contained a written testimony from suspects in English. She read through a statement and returned to her group. In nearly a minute, she argued her point in Mandarin, prompting another bilingual student to say "CAN YOU SPEAK ENGLISH?" She continued in Mandarin, and other students responded in both Mandarin and English. This transcript was created by Allison to analyze the group dynamics, she did not have the transcript translated. In the transcript, Jeanne and Alfredo are suspects from the mystery.

```
01 Min Hin:    (speaking Chinese) Laughing
02 Wei Sheng:  I know another one. I know another one. I think the brown felt
03             pen. The brown stain was Gene's. So Jeanne might take the brown
04             felt pen. Vera might hate Jeanne and…Jeanne and Alfredo have
05             a brown pen. Huh?
06 Min Hin:    (Laughing. Speaking Chinese. Motion with hands)
07 Pengfei:    I know that. Why do they hate Kendra?
08 Wei Sheng:  Maybe Gene's dog might bite Vera.
09 Min Hin:    Maybe… the dog bite.
10 Yaozu:      Sounds like lady.
11 Pengfei:    Let's write it down first.
12 Min Hin:    Maybe…(talking Chinese for about 1 min)
13 Pengfei:    CAN YOU SPEAK ENGLISH? (Yelling)
14 Wei Sheng:  (speaking Chinese)
15 Wei Sheng:  So, he was sleeping so I saw what happened.
16 Min Hin:    (speaking Chinese)(pointing to YN paper and turns the pages.)
16 Pengfei:    Ok, now what?
```

In this moment, Min Hin took up a leadership role in her group, contesting the insistence to use English for a task that easily could be completed in Mandarin. As Allison reflected on this, she began to challenge her own assumptions of Min Hin as "quiet" and "shy." Indeed, she did use both English and Mandarin as she listened to her classmates' points, as she read through written testimony, and as she occasionally wrote notes in English. Her use of Mandarin, in this episode, and specifically the decision to ignore the student who told her to speak English, demonstrates the importance for science to be conducted in meaningful ways, drawing on multiple resources. This shift was one moment that Min Hin shifted into a leadership role, though she was not often viewed in this way. All students can take up these roles if the activities are meaningful and allow each student to exercise their own expertises. All of the students could speak Mandarin and English at various degrees of proficiency.

Learning Funds of Knowledge to Address Social Problems

The following week, after the Felix mystery, Allison attempted to transition from the science unit. Students had been particularly interested in crime and technology, so Allison continued her unit of how social phenomenon like crime relates to the development of technologies. To begin the unit, she organized a small-group activity in which she encouraged students to engage in a critical-thinking activity that brought up issues of crime that afflicted the Chinese community and what punishments they would associate with it. As with all of her action research, Allison was strategically trying to encourage conversation among students, as well as provide opportunities for writing. In this case Min Hin was the designated note taker for the group to require her to write and summarize ideas. By integrating the unit on crime after the Felix mystery, Allison was able to situate students to think through the implications of science in their daily lives.

As students discussed crimes they knew about, they also recommended punishments, thus integrating ethics and cultural perceptions of crime. Allison had attempted activities like this frequently, allowing students to discuss social issues in groups, in an attempt to not only accomplish curricular goals, but also to allow students to draw on their own backgrounds, life experiences, and especially funds of knowledge. In this particular discussion, students began to reveal personal experiences of witnessing or being a victim of a crime. For example, Wei Sheng's family owned a store in Chinatown and recounted a time when it had been broken into. Another student discussed a potential home robbery. Students expressed concern, anxiety, and empathy around the issue of crime in the community, even as they discussed the potential punishments for these crimes. Allison was attempting to draw out emotional responses as well to discuss how crime affects people in the community. At least five students had experiences or had a family member who had experienced a robbery.

Experiencing crime, itself, is not a fund of knowledge, it is an experience. However, the response of families and communities to crime does reveal the cultural practices and strategies of navigating life in this particular community. When students discussed specific crimes that happened to their family, Allison asked what their family's response was. Some students explained how their family felt or reacted. These reactions, the practices learned in the family or community, as well as the practices of protecting a family from crime are funds of knowledge. Students in the class had developed particular knowledge(s) through these family experiences. Wei Sheng, for example, the student whose family store had been broken into, clearly had seen how the family copes with such a violation. He was not the only student in the class whose family had a gift shop either. These community resources, brought into the classroom, demonstrate a deeper connection between the classroom and life. The science unit was beginning to become real to students, as they discussed police involvement and wondered why catching criminals was so difficult. The notion of criminality and solving crimes was not just a classroom simulation but had real tangible connections to the life experiences and situated epistemologies of students.

During this activity on the third day of the unit, Min Hin began to take up more of an interactive role, facilitated, in part, by Wei Sheng. Allison, in an attempt to give Min Hin more of a leadership role in her group, asked her to be the recorder, writing the notes from the group. As seen from the figure (Figure 5.4), Min Hin began recording notes from two criminal episodes and

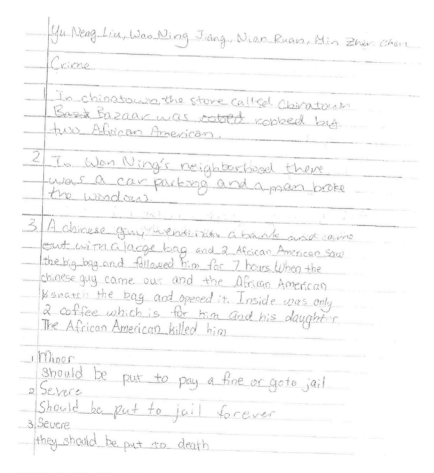

FIGURE 5.4 Min Hin and Wei Sheng's Notes

two punishments. After Allison announced that they needed to finish up to move into a group discussion, Min Hin passed the paper to Wei Sheng, who quickly finished writing episode number three and the third punishment. This was a new way of interacting in the group for Min Hin.

It is important to note that several unintended consequences emerged in this activity that Allison did not follow up on. In particular, as seen earlier, the students in this group noted the race of suspected criminals in two scenarios. During classroom talk, race was never mentioned. This is important due to the social factors of the neighborhood. Chinatown is situated across train tracks from what, at the time, was a well-known and quite large low-income housing project. Racism in Chinatown was salient. Several news reports and interviews have documented tensions between African Americans and Asian Americans in the neighborhood. There were three African-American students in the classroom, and this may be a reason that race was not overtly mentioned in the class discussion, but the writing revealed that crime was *raced* in writing. Allison did not follow up on this or challenge the *racing* in writing nor in discussion.

Race and language, in all its forms, are inextricably linked and has in recent years come to be known as *raciolinguistics* (Alim, Rickford, & Ball, 2016; Rosa, 2019). This phenomena has become even more visible in the Asian-American context especially during the global pandemic of 2020 with the rise of hate crimes against their communities (Gover, Harper, & Langton, 2020). As Rosa argues,

> I argue that the co-naturalization of language and race is a key feature of modern governance, such that languages are perceived as racially embodied and race is perceived as linguistically intelligible, which results in the over-determination of racial embodiment and communicative practice—hence the notion of looking like a language and sounding like a race. Thus, race, language, and governance must be analyzed collectively.
>
> (Rosa, 2019, p. 2)

The topics of forensics and crime needs to be understood in the context of anti-Asian racism globally and anti-Asian-American racism in the United States. Asians and Asian Americans have often been stereotyped as "perpetual foreigners" (Ng, Lee, & Pak, 2007), and this can especially be seen in Chinatown in which the community is designated largely as a tourist areas that is ethnicized or raced, commodified, and politicized (Rumenapp, 2013). Historically, Chinese immigrants to the United States have been met with blatant racism, poor living conditions, hard labor, sex trafficking, and immigration policies oriented at subjugation and exclusion rather than inclusion (Chang, 2003). While there was great diversity in the student population at Warner—especially in relation to linguistic and immigration backgrounds—the default assumption was homogeneity, though this was contested by students in the classroom (Rumenapp, 2016b).

These markers and markets of "otherness" have not only led to real-life crime in neighborhoods—some experienced by Allison's students—but also a deep sense of exclusion from a fair criminal justice system. How could a government that authorized the *Chinese Exclusion Act* or engaged in Japanese internment (Executive Order 9066) have a neutral and fair police force in Asian-American communities (Chinese Exclusion Act, 1882; Roosevelt, 1942)? These questions invariably require critical examination, especially in the context of a forensics unit.

Another unintended consequence of this activity was that students became visibly disturbed. It was clear that several had experienced trauma, and this discussion gave them space to talk about it. For example, one student recounted how her uncle was robbed and a gun was held to his head. These traumatic experiences emerging in the classroom could have lasting consequences.

The crime scene activity and follow-up conversation on crime represented a shift in Allison's classroom. Students seemed to take more ownership of their argumentation. Allison noted that while students were sharing out to the full group, they began to speak more openly than during other similar instances.

> So for example, [one student] who doesn't speak much in my room was saying that their car was robbed. So she started to give the full account of how the police came and how they were so upset because then, um, their car was gone, but then a week later their car came back and was all stripped and they were devastated and, well, it meant a lot to her to share with us about her experiences. And then other kids started piping up like "My car was robbed too!" It just snowballed and it meant a lot to them and they would speak up and there was much more discourse and I was more in the background. Believe it or not.
>
> (Final Focus Group)

Allison, noticing that the application of scientific practices in a simulation drew on students' background knowledge and related to specific funds of knowledge in the community, brought this up in her teacher–researcher meeting. One of her colleagues offered to contact a friend who was a crime scene investigator for a local police district. A week later, the investigator came in to talk with students and demonstrate different types of evidence collection. Just as the students had conducted the crime scene unit, they asked about different evidence that was gathered.

While the investigator discussed gathering physical evidence and testing from the perspective of a field practitioner, Allison encouraged students to make connections to their own scientific testing from the Felix simulation. The detective used several different materials to discuss scientific and legal concepts like cross contamination, chain of evidence, documentation, and scientific testing. Allison referred back to their simulation and other concepts in her class. They also made connections to specific crimes they knew of locally. This practical application of science, connected to students' experiences and generated from their own interests, demonstrated how Allison used her own awareness of funds of knowledge to develop a curriculum that was responsive to students.

Conclusion

Allison and her colleagues engaged in deep study of their own classrooms. In particular, Allison studied students' funds of knowledge to create meaningful learning units and attempted to challenge the discourse patterns of the classroom. Indeed, Allison and her colleagues associated the school with being "well behaved" and "high performing" and other tropes associated with the "Model Minority" stereotype (Lee, 2009). The study of classroom discourse required teachers to move beyond some of these stereotypes and change the way they perceived student identity (Rumenapp, 2016a). The model minority stereotype misunderstands Asian and Asian heritage students as "passive," "shy," or simply "well behaved," when in reality, the discourse of the classroom has been organized to keep them silent. Allison's shift from IRE to a more instructional conversation structure allowed students to take up more agentive and dynamic roles. After more than 25 years of teaching, Allison chose to undergo transformation by closely studying the discursive patterns in her classroom. Her shift to relinquishing control over the IRE discursive pattern allowed her to establish solidarity with and among students (Rumenapp, 2013).

While it must be celebrated that Allison's transformation of her classroom opened up the opportunity for more conversational discourse among students in multiple languages, it should also be recognized that conversation should be coupled with critical discourse. As can be seen, students, like Min Hin, were provided opportunities to shift into leadership roles through Allison's intentional reorganization of the classroom. However, this unit, focused on the role of science in the criminal justice system, builds on a long history of criminalizing U.S. Chinatowns as well as racial tensions that existed in the contemporary space of this "Chinatown." U.S. framing of "Chinatowns" have largely focused on othering residents as "forever foreign to American sensibilities" (Wong, 1995, p. 4) and casting the communities as tourist destinations (Santos et al., 2008). Additionally, Chinatowns have been associated with crime historically (Anderson, 1987) and in pop-culture—reflect on any scene in contemporary movies (e.g., *Rush Hour*, *Men in Black 3*). While the students in Allison's classroom brought up real incidents of crime in the neighborhood, this trope was not lost. Though Allison drew on students' own experiences with crime, this was an opportunity to analyze the broader questions of criminality and its intersection with race.

Additionally, around the time of this lesson, there had been growing tension around race. In the writing sample shown earlier (Figure 5.4) the students "race" the crimes by pointing out that the perpetrators were African American (this is explicit in #1 and #3), and the victims were Chinese (this is assumed in #1 and #2, but is explicit in #3). This "racing" of the crimes extends a common racial thread that was common at the time. The intersection of race, language, and discourse needs to be foregrounded in teacher professional development (Alim, Rickford, & Ball, 2016; Rosa, 2019). While racial tensions have ebbed and flowed in the Asian-American contexts and was relatively mild when Allison was teaching, the current racial climate calls for more overt and explicit raciolinguistic analysis (Gover et al., 2020).

Given the overpolicing and criminalizing of Black communities, a lesson that intersects science and the criminal justice system would benefit from a critical framing that foregrounds racial and linguistic justice (Baker-Bell, 2020; Razfar, Rumenapp, & Torres, 2020). Third space theory provides a valuable framework for navigating racial and cultural tensions that inevitably arise in classroom conversations (Gutiérrez, Rymes, & Larson, 1995). Throughout the history of our action research project, some teachers more overtly foregrounded third space as a way to build curricular activities that navigated racial tensions in their classrooms and the broader community (Razfar, Troiano, Allebach, & Koustas, in press). Typically when our teachers first encountered or elicited funds of knowledge related to gang and/or police activities, they were reluctant to use these "dark funds" of knowledge as part of their action research (Razfar & Nasir, 2019). We learned that engaging such issues, while often difficult and uncomfortable, can become valuable learning opportunities when teachers play a lead role in designing mediational tools for navigating those tensions.

Although we did not see any evidence of Allison drawing on third space theory to mediate issues of racial differences and tensions in her classroom, especially as it relates to policing in communities of color, forensic sciences are not neutral. The application of forensics and other crime scene technologies, especially in communities of color, cannot afford to be ambiguous about the role of race and need to be explicit about how they add to structured inequalities (Skinner, 2020). Leveraging scientific practices from community spaces must be mindful of social, political, racial, and historical contexts of those technologies. In Allison's classroom, three of the students were Black, and presenting science as a neutral tool in the hands of a friendly government agent further erases the historical violence of policing in their communities. In addition, her Black colleagues, including the school's principal, who were also participants in our action research project were clearly impacted by these issues. We will probe this issue further in Chapter 8.

The emerging field of forensic linguistics where the intersection of language and scientific methods intersect is another potential connection for this type of curriculum. In addition, the use of technology to unpack meaning is another key component. This unit brings together science content, technology, and dynamic language learning through the topic of forensics. In fact, a broader disciplinary connection can be made to the growing prominence of forensic linguistics. Forensic linguistics, particularly discourse analysis, has been applied in intellectual property disputes, plagiarism, dubious claims of authorship, and contextualizing scattered electronic messages (Coulthard & Johnson, 2007). While forensic linguistics has historically been applied to law enforcement, courtrooms, and judicial contexts, there is growing interest in the implications of discourse analysis for legal education (Udina, 2017). Allison's unit points to the possibility of how this area could be further leveraged in K–12 educational settings by integrating science, language, and technology (Dewdrop, 2016). This further confirms the importance of discourse analysis in teaching and teacher development as we move beyond linguistic code and focus on learning as shifts in meaning-making.

Discussion Questions

1. How can students' funds of knowledge be leveraged to shift discourse patterns in the classroom?
2. In what ways can community-based sciences, such as local forensic resources, be leveraged to teach scientific concepts in the classroom?
3. How might teachers organize and leverage students' linguistic repertoires to build collaborative problem-solving teams?

Additional Resources

1. ACS Chemistry for Life | Forensics Chemistry
   https://www.acs.org/content/acs/en/education/students/highschool/chemistryclubs/activities/forensics.html
2. NOVA Teachers | Forensics Classroom Activities
   https://www.pbs.org/wgbh/nova/education/resources/subj_04_03.html
3. Forensics Classroom
   http://www.forensic-classroom.com/
4. Forensics Linguistics
   https://www.cambridgeenglish.org/learning-english/activities-for-learners/c1r001-forensic-linguistics

References

Alim, H. S., Rickford, J. R., & Ball, A. F. (2016). *Raciolinguistics: How language shapes our ideas about race.* New York, NY: Oxford University Press.

Anderson, K. J. (1987). The idea of Chinatown: The power of place and institutional practice in the making of a racial category. *Annals of the Association of American Geographers,* 77(4), 580–598.

Baker-Bell, A. (2020). *Linguistic justice: Black language, literacy, identity, and pedagogy.* New York, NY: Routledge.

Brodie, K. (2013). Hidden curriculum. In J. Ainsworth (Ed.), *Sociology of education: An a-to-z guide* (Vol. 1, pp. 352–353). Thousand Oaks, CA: SAGE Publications.

Cazden, C. B. (2001). *Classroom discourse: The language of teaching and learning* (2nd ed.). Portsmouth, NH: Heinemann.

Chang, I. (2003). *The Chinese in America: A narrative history.* New York, NY: Viking Adult.

Chinese Exclusion Act. (1882). *Harvard university library open collections program.* Accessed December 18, 2020, http://ocp.hul.harvard.edu/immigration/exclusion.html Retrieved from https://www.loc.gov/law/help/statutes-at-large/47th-congress/session-1/c47s1ch126.pdf

Coulthard, M., & Johnson, A. (2007). *An introduction to forensic linguistics: Language in evidence* (pp. 162–163). Oxford, UK: Routledge.

Dewdrop. (2016, December 12). *What is forensic linguistics? Language matters!* Retrieved from https://lama.hypotheses.org/70

Full Option Science System (FOSS). (2020, February 20). Full Option Science System (FOSS). Retrieved from https://fossnextgeneration.com/

GEMS: Mystery Festival–Lawrence Hall of Science. (2021, February 5). Lawrence Hall of Science. Retrieved from https://store.lawrencehallofscience.org/Item/gems-mystery-festival

Gover, A. R., Harper, S. B., & Langton, L. (2020). Anti-Asian hate crime during the COVID-19 pandemic: Exploring the reproduction of inequality. *American Journal Criminal Justice, 45,* 647–667. DOI: 10.1007/s12103-020-09545-1

Gutiérrez, K. D., Rymes, B., & Larson, J. (1995). Script, counterscript, and underlife in the classroom: James Brown versus Brown v. Board of Education. *Harvard Educational Review, 65*(3), 445–471.

Lee, S. (2009). *Unraveling the model minority stereotype: Listening to Asian American youth* (2nd ed.). New York, NY: Teachers College Press.

Ng, J. C., Lee, S. S., & Pak, Y. K. (2007). *Asian American education: Acculturation, literacy development, and learning. Research on the education of Asian Pacific Americans.* Charlotte, NC: Information Age.

Razfar, A., & Nasir, A. (2019). Repositioning English learners' funds of knowledge for scientific practices. *Theory Into Practice, 58*(3), 226–235.

Razfar, A., Rumenapp, J. C., & Torres, Z. (2020). Administrating language: The language ideological voices of urban school administrators in urban education. *Urban Education.* Retrieved from https://doi.org/10.1177/0042085920959136

Razfar, A., Troiano, B., Allebach, B., & Koustas, D. (in press). From languishing to languaging in the third space: Teachers applying linguistics to mediate language and STEM learning. In T. B. Peele-Eady (Ed.), *Integrating home and heritage languages in schools: Pedagogy and promise.* New York, NY: NCTE/Routledge Research Series.

Rosa, J. (2019). *Looking like a language, sounding like a race: Raciolinguistic ideologies and the learning of Latinidad.* New York, NY: Oxford University Press.

Roosevelt, F. (1942, February 19). *Executive order 9066.* U.S. National Archives & Records Administration. Retrieved December 18, 2020.

Rumenapp, J. C. (2013). *RE-positioning English learners in teacher development: A language ideologies approach to urban education* [Doctoral dissertation, University of Illinois at Chicago].

Rumenapp, J. C. (2016a). Analyzing discourse analysis: Teachers' views of classroom discourse and student identity. *Linguistics and Education, 35,* 26–36.

Rumenapp, J. C. (2016b). (Re)positioning the "Chinatown" default: Constructing hybrid identities in elementary classrooms. In W. Ma & G. Li (Eds.), *Chinese-heritage students in North American schools: Understanding hearts and minds beyond test scores* (pp. 137–152). New York, NY: Routledge.

Santos, C. A., Belhassen, Y., & Caton, K. (2008). Reimagining Chinatown: An analysis of tourism discourse. *Tourism Management, 29*(5), 1002–1012.

Skinner, D. (2020). Race, racism and identification in the era of technosecurity. *Science as Culture, 29*(1), 77–99.

Udina, N. (2017). Forensic linguistics implications for legal education: Creating the e-textbook on language and law. *Procedia-Social and Behavioral Sciences, 237,* 1337–1340.

Wells, G. (1993). Reevaluating the IRF sequence: A proposal for the articulation of theories of activity and discourse for the analysis of teaching and learning in the classroom. *Linguistics and Education, 5*(1), 1–37.

Wong, K. (1995). Chinatown: Conflicting images, contested terrain. *Melus, 20*(1), 3–15.

6
FROM WESLANDIA TO URBAN GARDENING

Shifting Teacher Language Ideologies Through Ecological Science and Third Space

> At the beginning, I felt I needed to be the leader. By the end, my participa-
> tion shifted in that I gave up some control and provided more opportunities
> for students to share their expertise while I facilitated.... I had misjudged
> them at the beginning and I had made comments; which I am sorry and I
> do apologize. I just didn't think that they were going to be capable of it. I
> was really impressed with them. I think they really enjoyed it.
>
> Cara, Second-Grade Teacher

Introduction

This chapter presents a second-grade class in which an elementary teacher created a gardening unit. Cara conducted the action research in her general education second-grade classroom. She planned the lessons with her cohort as part of
a community unit. Cara's deficit view of city kids' gardening knowledge transforms as the project develops. She did not believe city kids were capable of such
projects. Guerilla gardening is a new area that has grown in recent years. In his
TED talk, Los Angeles activist Ron Finely (2013) said, "You're changing an ecosystem when you put in a garden. We are part of that ecosystem so that garden is a
part of us." We recommend integrating this body of work with teacher researchers. Expertise shifts from the teacher to the students as she allows space for them
to share their home experiences.

DOI: 10.4324/9781351001168-6

Standards

Science

- Plan and conduct an investigation to determine if plants need sunlight and water to grow.
  (standards adapted from NGSS 2-LS2-1)

Mathematics

- Reason abstractly and quantitatively.
  (standards adapted from CCSS 2-LS2-1, 2-LS4-1)

Literacy

- Participate in shared research and writing projects (e.g., read a number of books on a single topic to produce a report; record science observations).
- Recall information from experiences or gather information from provided sources to answer a question.
- Describe how characters in a story respond to major events and challenges.
- Describe the overall structure of a story, including describing how the beginning introduces the story and the ending concludes the action.
  (standards adapted from CCSS ELA-Literacy
  W.2.7, W.2.8, RL.2.3, RL.2.5)

Language

- English learners communicate information, ideas, and concepts necessary for academic success in the content area of language arts.
- English learners communicate information, ideas, and concepts necessary for academic success in the content area of mathematics.
- English learners communicate information, ideas, and concepts necessary for academic success in the content area of science.
  (standards adapted from WIDA Consortium Standards 2, 3, 4)

Chapter Objectives

1. Teachers will be able to leverage science and mathematics funds of knowledge.
2. Teachers will be able to mediate opportunities for student interaction.
3. Teachers will be able to integrate literature into science learning.

Unit Objectives

1. Make predictions about growing seeds in soil and sand.
2. Acquire vocabulary associated with planting seeds.

Context: Teacher, Student, and School

Adams Elementary is a small urban, public K–8 community elementary school with 269 students. Adams Elementary School is a community school with a math and science magnet program. Adams saw a substantial increase in reading and math standardized scores with a ranked schoolwide reading proficiency of 70% and a ranked schoolwide math proficiency of 82%. The neighborhood has changed during the time of the study due to gentrification. Consequently, enrollment has decreased significantly. Latinx make up 82.5% of the enrollment, 24.2% of the student population identified as English learners and 95.9% as low income (School Report Card).

Cara is a self-identified female European American who taught second grade. The year of the action research was her 2nd year teaching. She was born in Chicago to parents that emigrated from Serbia, and her first language is Serbian. She conducted action research in her second-grade classroom of 26 students. The class consisted of 15 girls and 11 boys. Five were African American; the majority were Latinx. All the students received free lunch. Six students were pulled out for bilingual services, and one was not pulled out because the families signed a release form. About four families only spoke Spanish at home. Many of the families came from Puerto Rico and Mexico. Most of the students have known each other since preschool or kindergarten; this created deep bonds among the students. Some of the students did not live in the neighborhood, which made socialization outside of school difficult for many of the children. There are some students, however, who lived near each other and played outside of school. Because many parents worked two jobs or nights, socialization outside of the school was difficult. Three African-American male students were bussed to Adams as part of the NCLB Act.

Table 6.1 provides the teacher's description of the focal students. Sheldon is African American and was chosen because he spoke African American Vernacular English and also received speech therapy services for stuttering. He was bused to

TABLE 6.1 Teacher's Description of Focal Students

Names	Isabela	Crystal	Ian	Sheldon
EL Status	EL (3rd year)	EL (4th year)	None	None
Standardized Mathematics	Average	Average	Average	Low
Standardized Reading (English)	Average	High	Average	Average
Participation	Low	High	Average	High
Personality Type	Introvert (quiet and focused)	Extrovert (verbally assertive)	Introvert (lacks confidence)	Extrovert (needs support)
Language Fluency (Spanish)	High	High	Low	None
Language/Dialect Fluency (AAL)	None	None	None	High

Adams from a predominantly African-American neighborhood. Prior to starting the action research project, he was not able to work independently and needed support from the teacher. Ian is Latinx but did not speak Spanish at home. Crystal and Isabela are Latinx born in the United States and speak Spanish at home. Isabela rarely spoke in class, using one-word responses. Cara wanted to see how she would interact with others, if there would be a change in her ability to work with others.

Unit Plan

"City Kids" Can't Grow Plants

When Cara began the gardening unit, she did not think "city kids" would have experience growing plants. For Cara, gardening, farming, and any sort of agricultural activity were not city activities but rather located in rural areas. In Cara's classroom there were two distinct communities: the local Latinx neighborhood community and the three Black kids who were bussed in from a predominantly Black part of the city. At the time, many of the schools in this part of the city were closed down due to being classified as "failing schools." Like many school closures, it was a policy that disproportionately and systematically impacted Black neighborhoods and communities (Lipman & Haines, 2007; Woestehoff, 2016). Sheldon was one of the three Black kids who were bussed into Cara's classroom, and at the beginning of the year, her views of him can be summarized in the following exchange between Susan and Cara. After Susan points out to Cara, "you're not listening to him [Sheldon]," Cara responds (lines 1–12):

```
01 Cara:    He [Sheldon] gets so much attention ALL THE TIME and he (pause)
02          even though this [Action Research Project], usually it's just
03          other attention. This time it's academic. I mean he is like
04          trying to explain, usually it's just he wants (pause) do you
05          know what I mean like? The focus to be on him whether he's
06          banging into something and (pause) I don't know? (longer pause)
07          so I don't know I would have to re-watch it and kind of pay
08          more attention. You know, like whatever it might be, you have
09          to work with your partner or your table mates and help each
10          other and he doesn't even want to try to initiate the work on
11          his own first to see if he can do it. He's always just like, "I
12          need help, I need help."
```

[Study Group Meeting, During Unit 2]

In this video analysis session, Cara's response to her more senior colleague and action research partner is filled with hedging practices, which points to status as a new teacher and her struggle to reposition him as a learner in her classroom. Perhaps the most revealing moment comes in lines 6 and 7, when she says, "I don't know? so I don't know I would have to re-watch it and kind of pay more attention." This was a key moment of reflection for Cara in her movement toward reimaging and repositioning Sheldon as an expert. Sheldon was no longer aimlessly "banging into something" (line 6) just seeking "attention ALL THE TIME" (line 1), but an individual learner whose context had to be intimately understood in order to create viable learning opportunities.

"I Can Do That?" Repositioning African American Language for STEM Learning

After the second unit, the teachers were analyzing their units and trying to establish themes to focus on in their analysis. One of the major themes was the use of multiple languages and discourses to mediate student participation. For Cara, this was a great dilemma in terms of what counts as language. After all, Susan and Eva had clear examples of their Latinx students code-switching, code-meshing, and translanguaging with Spanish and Spanglish. While their students were languaging in a variety of ways, Cara couldn't clearly see multiple languages and/or discourses being used. In addition, Susan and Eva's students were formally recognized as "English learners" so they were entitled to institutional support systems. Cara didn't have English learners using multiple languages, but she did have speakers of so-called nonstandard varieties.

This is where the role of the university-based research team became visibly important for mediating a more egalitarian language ideological stance and, more important, leveraging it for STEM learning (Razfar et al., 2015). Language ideologies refer to our beliefs and attitudes about the nature, function, and purpose of language in everyday discourse practices (Schieffelin, Woolard, & Kroskrity, 1998). It specifically draws our attention to how everyday language use is infused with value judgments, status, and differentiation in power along multiple epistemic, gender, racial, linguistic, socioeconomic, and sociocultural categories (Irvine & Gal, 2000 in Kroskrity, 2000). More recently, scholars have also focused on how our beliefs, attitudes, and values about language practices are fundamentally racialized (Alim, Rickford, & Ball, 2016; Flores & Rosa, 2015; Rickford, 2016). Raciolinguistics speaks to the fundamental role of how language shapes our ideas about race and vice versa (Rickford, 2016). Language ideologies and raciolinguistics provide a critical lens for analyzing racialized language use and beliefs through everyday micro interactions while connecting it to broader macro historical and institutional forces. Our action research project and university research team drew on these perspectives to mediate conversations about nondominant languages such as African American Language (AAL) or Black Language (BL). The naming of the languages and discourses used in historically African-American communities is something educators struggle with (Razfar, Rumenapp, & Torres, 2020). We prefer AAL or Black Language (BL) because they foreground the linguistic sovereignty of African-American and Black communities; however, we are also mindful that other terms such as African American Vernacular English (AAVE) were also widely used at the time we worked with the Adams teachers.

The following exchange comes from a study group following Unit 2, where we see Cara being pushed by the university researcher (BT) to think more broadly about what counts as language. Cara is encouraged to reposition AAL as a viable mediational tool for learning. While Cara is uncertain about which "English learner" to focus on, BT (the university researcher) mediates an alternative path (lines 1–13):

```
01 BT:     He's [Sheldon] so interesting too. I mean he's not an ELL but he's
02         definitely with the African American vernacular
03 Cara:   Uhm uhm uhm.
04 BT:     I think you can definitely write about him.
05 Cara:   Uhm [...]
06 BT:     I think it's really good stuff in this unit 2. Don't be afraid of
07         looking more at the AAVE issues then ELL
08 Cara:   There's definitely a lot of that in there [...]
09 BT:     Even a couple of those lines you could go back and look at and say
10         like okay I need to emphasize a couple words here put like the
11         colons [reference to transcription conventions]
12 Cara:   colons
13 BT:     colons just to draw out the talk (comes moment later after a
14         slight tangent)
15         And even though you don't have students using Spanish you have
16         students using like the African American vernacular English is
17         huge in that unit 2 with Sheldon um so
18 Cara:   [LAUGHS]
```

Throughout this exchange, Cara is listening attentively as BT encourages her to shed her fear (line 6) and approach AAVE issues with the same intensity and legitimacy as more recognized bilingual issues such as Spanish–English. Her cryptic laugh at the end (line 18) signals a pleasant surprise that a new possibility has opened up—the possibility that AAVE/AAL is a legitimate tool on par with Spanish to mediate learning in the classroom. This becomes the springboard for a diametrically different perspective on Sheldon's learner identity. In her Unit 2 report, Cara concludes, "I saw a role shift from novice to expert from my student Sheldon. He speaks African American Vernacular English, and sometimes it is difficult to understand him because of this and because he stutters." Cara began to see his expertise in gardening practices, which we will show later in this chapter.

From Weslandia to Urban Gardening

The gardening unit was part of a thematic unit on "community," a theme that emerged from surveys of student interests, experiences, and problems. Susan had experience planning and teaching interdisciplinary units and recommended a book about gardening for Cara to use in unit 2. To begin the unit, Cara read to the class Paul Fleischman's *Weslandia* (1999), a children's book about an outcast boy who is dissatisfied with the status quo and decides to build an alternative society by conducting experiments, designing a garden, and ultimately building his own civilization. In groups, the students planted parsley and cilantro seeds in sand and soil and made predictions about which would grow.

Tension and participation shifts were common teacher findings in the unit. Through her action research and work with the other cohort teachers, Cara would come to recognize her deficit view of the students and reposition them as experts. This is where Cara would first notice the tension between her script and some students' counterscript (Gutiérrez, Rymes, & Larson, 1995). From this story, she discovered the students had funds of knowledge regarding gardening, Egyptian writing, and gender perceptions, which created an opportunity for third spaces to emerge. Reading the *Weslandia* text opened opportunities for Cara to become familiar with their funds of knowledge. She noted a range of student observations after observing videos and reviewing field notes. For example, one student makes an explicit connection to the *Weslandia* script created by the main character, Wesley, stating that it was similar to "Egyptian writing." While Cara was "pleasantly surprised" by this discovery, she was also regretful that she didn't notice it earlier and expand on this learning opportunity. In a study group, she describes this as a "missed opportunity to expand and create a third space." We will go into greater detail on this later in this chapter.

After becoming cognizant of missed opportunities in Unit 2, she became more intentional about mediating these opportunities in Unit 3. Cara was very conscientious about countering stereotypical and deficit views of gender roles. The *Weslandia* text provided opportunities for reimagining stagnant identities into more dynamic ones. For example, during the first lesson, she observed a third space episode where the main character Wesley's wearing a skirt, dress, and the color pink was the subject of ridicule because he was not conforming to gender-role expectations. Cara, posed questions that led to students sharing personal narratives about how their fathers and uncles also wore pink. More important, it opened up counterhegemonic conversations about what it means to be an outcast or a divergent thinker within dominant society. Students in the class began to open up about their "outcast" and "nonconventional" practices. This opened the door for students like Sheldon to share their nonschool epistemologies, in this case gardening. The *Weslandia* activity inspired Cara's students to express their full linguistic and cultural identities toward building a new community. More important, it allowed Cara to see how their funds of knowledge could be leveraged for academic purposes by creating *Weslandia*-inspired civilizations.

Language Learning Domain: Recognizing Multiple Languages and Discourses

The lessons incorporated the four language domains with a focus on speaking and writing in small groups. It is quite possible and probable that Sheldon's knowledge of urban gardening comes from a richer tradition; however, Cara does not think to access this. Toward the end of the unit Cara recognizes Sheldon's expertise is grounded in communities of practice. Teachers need to recognize that Black leaders have been activists. In order to develop linguistically and culturally responsive pedagogy, it is essential to recognize multiple languages, discourses, and nondominant linguistic funds.

Social Organization of Learning

Cara's activity triangle illustrates her unit plan for socially organizing learning around the object of creating sustainable gardens in urban communities (Figure 6.2). The triangle outlines the activity design; the fundamental question that guides the learning process; the *object*, or immediate learning goal of the activity; the *mediational tools* (both material and ideational artifacts) that facilitate movement toward the learning goal; *the subjects* or immediate classroom participants; the *community* or distal participants; *the rules* that establish parameters for participation within the activity system; *the division of effort*, which establishes roles and responsibilities for each learner toward accomplishing the learning goal; and finally *outcomes*, which are longitudinal effects suggesting a deeper shift in learner identity and consciousness. Outcomes help teachers think about practices and skills that transfer beyond the immediate learning goals or object of the activity.

In this design, Cara begins with a broad question: *How do we create sustainable gardens in urban communities?* This question is broad enough to generate robust opportunities for student participation and leveraging their full linguistic and cultural repertoires. The mediational tools include: reading *Weslandia*, using Black language, epistemologies, science funds, gardening materials (i.e., soil, sand,

Tools and Artifacts
- *Weslandia*
- paper, markers, tape
- marshmallows, spaghetti
- soil, sand, cups, seeds
- students' funds of knowledge (gardening)
- Black language

Subjects
- 2nd graders
- Boys 10 Girls 13
- EL students
- Age range 7-to-8-years
- Cara
- Other teachers in the cohort (Susan and Eva)

Community
- Adams Elementary
- Latinx community
- Bilingual students (Spanish)
- African American students
- Children's Museum
- Female Carpenter

How do we create sustainable gardens in urban communities?

Object
- Make predictions about growing seeds in soil and sand.
- Plan and conduct an investigation to determine if plants need sunlight and water to grow.
- Describe how characters respond to major events and challenges.
- Make text to self-connections in the book.

Rules
- take turns talking and listening
- negotiated expert roles
- peer interaction
- students decide who takes roles in groups

Division of Effort
- Teacher selected heterogenous groups of 4 students by ability and language
- Teacher whole group instruction
- Student-centered activities
- Small group discussions

Outcomes
- Practice food justice.
- Develop an awareness of the quality of food we eat.
- Expand their cultural competencies by learning from others.
- Transform vacant or underutilized properties into productive landscapes that provide places to gather and share knowledge about

FIGURE 6.1   Cara's Activity Triangle

cups, seeds), and materials for building a civilization model (i.e., papers, markers, tape, marshmallows, spaghetti). Reading the *Weslandia* text opened opportunities for Cara to introduce the mandated, official science curriculum. However, she unexpectedly discovered her students' science funds of knowledge related to gardening.

Cara heterogeneously organized the *subjects*, who were second graders between the ages of 7 and 8, English learners, evenly split in terms of gender (10 boys, 13 girls), and mostly Latinx with several African-American learners who were bussed in from surrounding communities where neighborhood schools were closed. The *community* was predominantly working class, Latinx, and some children's museums. Cara purposefully designed ways to access community expertise in terms of visiting the museums as well as inviting experts in building and design. For example, Cara intentionally invited a local female carpenter to leverage her expertise in construction while dispelling gender stereotypes. Cara strategically positioned her to share her carpentry tools and conduct demonstrations of designing buildings. She organized the students into groups of four by ability and language and explicitly established *rules* for participation, including turn-taking, rotating leadership roles, and encouraging peer interaction.

Cara then outlined the *division of effort* to provide students with a framework of how to participate in whole-class discussions as well as small groups. During whole-group instruction, the discourse was more teacher centered, where Cara nominated students to talk, but the dynamic shifted in small groups, where peers experimented with planting herbal seeds in sand and soil. The *object* of this activity was for students to use appropriate scientific discourse practices such as making predictions about growing seeds in soil and sand, making connections to the text as well as themselves, planning and conducting an investigation to test their hypothesis regarding plant growth, and describing how characters in the story responded to major events and challenges. Finally, Cara delineated longitudinal and transformative *outcomes* for learners such as developing an awareness of food quality, expanding cultural and linguistic competence, practicing food justice, and converting additional vacant or underutilized properties into productive landscapes and productive sources of food for the community. Thus, learners become agents of positive change in their communities and beyond.

Sheldon's Gardening Funds of Knowledge

During a study group meeting, Cara shared a video of her reading aloud *Weslandia* and students discussing gardening (Study Group #15). She explained how students had shared their funds of knowledge and expertise connected to themes in the book. From her video she selected a clip of two students describing their experiences building brick and paper houses with family members. On the coding sheet she marked *funds of knowledge* throughout the video and wrote in AAVE, for African American Vernacular English, in two places (Figure 6.2).

Time	a. Peer Assistance	b. Funds of Knowledge	Multiple Languages & Discourse	Questions	e. Tension	f. Third Space	g. Participation Shifts	h. Role Shift	i. Rule Negotiation
0:00:00									
0:02:00									
0:04:00									
0:06:00									
0:08:00									
0:10:00									
0:12:00									
0:14:00									
0:16:00									
0:18:00									
0:20:00									
0:22:00									
0:24:00									
0:26:00									
0:28:00									

FIGURE 6.2 Cara's Coding Sheet Part 1

During the meeting, we noticed other codes marked on the sheet and asked Cara to take a closer look at the ones she had tallied concurrently with *funds of knowledge*. BT pointed to an example where she had tallied multiple codes, including *third space, tension, rule negotiation, questions*, and *multiple languages*. She recalled how Sheldon, an African-American student in the focal group, had shared his funds of knowledge about gardening. When BT asked her what was happening with the other codes during this sharing, she was not sure. Together we watched the recording and discussed it with her.

In this episode, Cara read aloud *Weslandia* to the whole class on the carpet. Cara paused to ask the class to raise their hand if they had planted flowers and vegetables, and most of them had. Many of the students could relate to the main character, Wesley, who plants seeds in a garden. Students could be heard talking over one another and speaking loudly in order to be heard. Each had an expertise they wanted to share. Here Cara led the conversation about planting.

```
01 Cara:     What's the first thing you have to do with the ground?
02 Sheldon:  Oh (.) I know!(1 sec) [You
03 Jerry:                          [You water it. Then you put the plant.
04           Then you put then you put the seed.
05 S:        Then you put the soil.
06 Jerry:    You put the dirt.
07 Cara:     Soil? (1 sec) What if there's soil already out there?
08 Sheldon:                          [No::: /that's wrong Ms. C.
09           I know what you do with it.
10 Ss:       (students raising hands)
11 S:        Dirt.
12 Cara:     Dirt.
13 Sheldon:  I know what you do with it.
```

Cara asks prior knowledge questions to see what the students know about planting in lines 1 and 6. Sheldon is excited to share in line 2. Jerry provides some planting steps in lines 3 and 6. However, Sheldon disagrees with the correct order of the steps Jerry provides and wants to share his experience (line 8, 13). Students continue to provide responses previously stated (line 11).

```
14 Cara:      What if there's already dirt out there outside like in your yard?
15 Sheldon:   (moves in front of teacher) You you you plant it in the dirt
16            right. You put the seeds in
17 Cara:      That's what Jerry said.
18 Sheldon:   On you put water on it and it grow like carrots
19 Cara:      Absolutely then you can grow carrots or whatever you plant
```

Cara does not call on Sheldon to share, but continues to ask the class about planting using the dirt in your yard (line 14). Sheldon gets up off the carpet and moves in front of the teacher to get her attention. He stutters as he explains planting the seeds in the dirt from his own yard (15). Cara does not ask him to elaborate, but refers to what another student had already said (17). Sheldon continues to explain the next step, watering the plant so that it can grow (18). He specifically names carrots. Cara acknowledges the steps but does not ask him about his experience growing carrots (19).

```
20 Cara:      Uhm. Okay when you take out the dirt. But are you just digging a
21            hole and then you throw in the seeds in?
22 Ss:        No:::
23 Cara:      What do you have to do with that whole area?
24 Sheldon:   You have you have you have to dig first and put the seeds in,
25            cover it back up, pour water on it
26 Cara:      Pick the spot.
27 Jerry:     You gotta make the line
28 Cara:      Right
```

Cara continues to talk to the whole class, asking an IRE question in lines 20–21, which elicits a loud "no" from the students. Sheldon shares four sequential steps in the planting process (24–25). Cara does not respond to Sheldon but answers her question from line 23 to pick a spot to plant (26), and she affirms Jerry's response to make a line in the soil (28).

```
29 Sheldon:   No:: Ms. C. You're supposed to dig in the mud. Put the seeds in
30            first.
31 Cara:      Ye::s
32 Sheldon:   Cover it back up.
33 Cara:      Yes
34 Sheldon:   Pour water. Then you
35 Cara:      Yes you do have to water them but there's one little thing that
36            you do kind of be::fore.
37 S:         Sun
38 Cara:      Yes you do need sun also. Depending on the type of plant you
39            might need a lot of sun
40 Ss:        Air
41 Cara:      Air.
```

```
42 Sheldon:    (standing) And I got one more thing Ms. C. [If you put too too
43             much water on it, it won't grow.]
44 Cara:       [trying to think about the spot you have to pick and why] So
45             if you put too much water on it it won't grow. Right. Some
46             plants don't need a lot of water, right.
```

Sheldon makes another attempt to share his planting knowledge (29). When Cara affirms his position (31), he repeats some of the planting steps and adds cover up the seed (32) and water it. He begins to say the next step (33) when Cara interrupts him. She affirms watering the plant but looks for another step (35–36). Students shout out sunlight and air. She agrees that plants need sun and air. Sheldon stands up in line 42, determined to share his knowledge about watering the plants (42–43), but Cara talks over him about picking a spot again.

After we watched the video in the study group during unit 2, we discussed what was happening. The interaction with the study group allowed Cara to reflect how she had coded the clip.

Coding for Third Space During Study Groups

During subsequent study group sessions we probed further about Sheldon's role regarding peer assistance, shifts in participation, tension, and the possibility of third space in the previous episode. Identifying potential third spaces require substantial mediation because it is the intersection of several codes, intertextual spanning several episodes, and not readily visible. For the most part, third space theory in teacher education has been presented from the university-based researchers' perspective (e.g., Klein, Taylor, Onore, Strom, & Abrams, 2013). It has also been used to better understand the dynamics of university–school partnerships and self-study (e.g., Martin, Snow, & Franklin Torrez, 2011). Rarely have teachers actually coded for third space (Razfar, Troiano, Allebach, & Koustas, in press). Reading about third space and actually coding for third space was an integral part of becoming teacher researchers.

Troiano (BT), probes further by drawing attention to the section Cara marked as *tension* on the coding sheet from minutes 44:00 through 48:00 (lines 1–3). BT also probes for the possibility of participation shifts and third space. Cara states that she "would have to go back and watch it because I didn't know what happened. I don't remember" (lines 4–5).

```
01 BT:      Just from looking at this, okay I was interested to know what was
02          happening around 46:48 with a lot of tension and possibly potential
03          third space and shifts in participation and expertise…
04 Cara:    Okay. Well I would have to go back and watch it because I don't
05          know what happened. I don't remember
```

BT continues to probe Cara's coding process and how she selected an episode for a more detailed transcription and discourse analysis (lines 6–15). However, Cara's

attention shifts toward Kamila and Daniel, who are explicitly referring to content
from the *Weslandia* text (lines 13–15). Kamila and Daniel were on task and had
a reputation for being high-performing, expert students (line 14). The source of
the tension and counterscript was Sheldon. It seemed as if Cara didn't see much
value in delving deeper into what the tension was all about. Sheldon's contributions were regularly dismissed as off-task behavior or tangents not related to the
activity's learning goal.

```
06 BT:     Let's look at it. So you're not using this to pick the clips, or
07         you didn't this time. You just…
08 Cara:   Yeah.
09 BT:     Okay, so what number was that? 30?
10 Cara:   Yeah, like 31.
11 BT:     Okay, so what made you take this as opposed to this where a lot of
12         action is happening?
13 Cara:   Just because I thought that it was important that Kamila and Daniel
14         we're talking about, were kind of becoming the experts on doing,
15         building their paper houses and brick.
```

Coding for third space requires more focus on implicit social learning processes
rather than the more observable explicit content such as "building their paper
houses and brick" (line 15). Third space theory draws our attention to what is
not said or seen that is often in the margins of our social structures (Bhaba, 2003;
Soja & Chouinard, 1999). Seeing the nuances of implicit social processes that are
typically unseen and more complex requires greater mediation. For teachers it
generally means going beyond their initial framing of counterscript practices as
off task and transforming them into hybrid spaces of possibility (Gutiérrez, 2008).
BT redirects Cara away from the students and content expertise she wants to
focus and toward Sheldon's counterscript discourse (lines 16–20):

```
16 BT:     So, okay, what I'm asking you to do is not to think about the
17         content right now but just what's happening here on paper. This to
18         me looks really interesting on paper, but the content you might say
19         like this is actually what's the most interesting content wise.
20 Cara:   Okay.
```

At this point Cara watches the clip with her colleagues (lines 21–25), and BT
builds on Cara's perspective while pointing to something that is potentially more
significant but not clearly visible (line 25):

```
21 BT:     Let's just look really quick at 46 and see because this coding
22         sheet, this is how we use it and sometimes it's helpful and
23         sometimes we don't, we do something else because like you said,
24         maybe the content of what they were talking about was more
25         significant. [Plays video clip at minute 46 for everyone]
```

As they watch the clip together BT points out Sheldon's talk about planting (lines
26–27). While Cara doesn't initially remember the full context of Sheldon's talk

and doesn't understand why she didn't notice it (lines 29–30), she recognizes that she has to review (lines 33–34, 38). In addition, she begins to verbalize Sheldon's role as an expert engaged in providing peer assistance as BT notes (line 35).

```
26 BT:      he's (Sheldon) talking about planting here so that was the. Who said
27          pick the spot?
28 Cara:    I don't know. That's Sheldon (.) Oh yeah. I don't remember why I
29          am… trying to get into think about like the spot they have to
30          pick and why. I can't remember.
31 BT:      Okay so, what was the peer assistance you saw there? That was
32          around 46 right?
33 Cara:    I don't know I think somebody was talking and then Sheldon was
34          trying to explain it or something, I'm not sure.
35 BT:      So Sheldon was the one giving the peer assistance?
36 Cara:    I think so.
37 BT:      And then what was the tension that you saw there?
38 Cara:    I don't know, I would have to go back and watch it again.
```

When BT asks what they think they saw (line 39), Eva responds, "third space" (line 40).

```
39 BT:      What did you guys see?
40 Eva:     The third space the tension is
```

BT asked the other teachers why they thought Cara used the code *tension*. Eva asked where in the clip a third space was, and Susan points out how tension was impeding the creation of a third space (lines 41–47):

```
41 Susan:   I think the tension is the students overlapping, the talking. I
42          mean that's the way I would see it. They want to be engaged. They
43          want, they all want to participate in there and the tension is, in
44          my opinion, the tension is that they don't have those
45          opportunities. I mean think like if say we were in small groups
46          talking about it or pair shares or something, then that tension
47          wouldn't be there because they would have that opportunity to talk
```

In her analysis, Susan moved beyond the transcript and drew attention to missed opportunities (lines 45, 47) and ways to reposition Sheldon's role so that his contribution is included in the process by creating a third space. Susan noted that Cara did not give students opportunities to share their experiences with planting, but maintained her authority. Susan pointed to students' overlap talk as the source of tension impeding authentic interaction and evidence that a shared space for learning was not created. She suggested that students need an opportunity to share their experiences and that having students share in pairs or small groups before opening discussion up to the whole class could mediate the tension. Most important, Susan defined third space as the shift in teacher talk into a negotiated space where expertise is shared, something Cara did not do.

However, Eva and Cara continue to struggle with the concept (lines 48–54). Eva is worried about not getting it correct (line 50), and BT proposes rewatching the clip (lines 52, 54):

```
48 Eva:    But where is the third space? Which was on the use of the third
49         space because I might do something wrong in my class. You put in
50         your third space right?
51 Cara:   I don't remember why I put in a third space. I'm trying to think
52 BT:     Want to watch it again?
53 Cara:   Sure.
54 BT:     Where is the third space? 46, okay. Let's look at 46 again.
```

Cara's Action: Sheldon Repositioned as the Expert in the Third Space

As Cara, Susan, and Eva continued to make sense of the complexities of this episode through third space theory, three themes emerged. First, like many of the teachers in our action research program (e.g., Allison, Chapter 5), Cara became aware of how teacher control and her teacher-centered discourse is impeding a space of possibility for engaging Sheldon. Second, Cara moved beyond passive teacher inquiry and exhibited the practices of a teacher researcher by displaying more agency in the analytic process. The role of the university-based research team was essential for this step. Third, by becoming a more engaged teacher researcher, she became aware of the critical levels of discourse analysis. By going beyond the transcript and the coding sheet, there is a greater understanding of going beyond the code of language and embracing meaning (semiotics) and values (ideologies) (Razfar, 2013). The aggregate of all these factors constitute both a physical and psychological third space where a more refined analysis, deeper relationships, and sociocritical consciousness emerge (Cuenca et al., 2011; Gutiérrez, 2008; Zeichner, 2010).

During the study group (SG #15), as Cara reflects on her control over the activity and how she didn't address Sheldon's knowledge of planting (lines 55–56), Eva makes the possibility of a third space explicit (line 57) by noting how Cara's actions may have prevented Sheldon from sharing (line 58).

```
55 Cara:   Maybe because I didn't address Sheldon's whole routine of how to
56         plant.
57 Eva:    I was thinking about that. It can be that a third space, Sheldon
58         has something, she (.) she kind of stops him
```

At this point Cara realizes how she failed to "acknowledge him" (line 59) because she was trying to stay on the official script but doesn't recall why it was important (lines 61–62).

```
59 Cara:   I don't acknowledge him [Sheldon] at all. I'm trying to go with my
60         whole thing about picking a spot for some reason and I don't
```

```
61          remember where we are in the story or why that was important to me
62          [at that time]
```

Susan affirms Cara's observation (lines 63–64), and Eva also realizes that she also does the same thing (line 67). The collective laughter (line 64) and Eva's alignment with Cara is reflective of collegial solidarity that has developed through the action research. They can provide each other with critical feedback openly and authentically.

```
63 Susan:  [That's right and you just don't acknowledge him at all.
64         Look. (laughs)
65 Cara:   Usually I do, but I'm trying to give. He gets so much attention
66         all the time and he]
67 Eva:                              [I'm doing the same thing in the class.]
```

Finally, we see how Cara's stance toward Sheldon shifts from a deficit view toward content expertise (lines 68–69). This is also further indication of her own transformation from passive inquiry toward a teacher researcher identity when she says "I have to pay more attention (line 70). The selection and deep analysis of this clip is confirmed by BT (line 71) and highlights the critical role of the university based researchers in mediating a deeper and more importantly applied understanding of third space theory (Figure 6.3).

```
68 Cara:   even though this, usually it's just other attention. This time
69         it's academic. I mean he is like trying to explain… I don't know
70         I would have to re-watch it and kind of pay more attention.
71 BT:     I think it's a good clip
72 Cara:   (writes on her coding sheet '46:46 Expert Sheldon')
```

Cara writes, for the first time, on the margins of her coding sheet that Sheldon has demonstrated a shift toward being an expert in the interaction (line 72, Figure 6.3). During one of the study group sessions she shared her coding sheet with the group (see Figure 6.2) and began to notice several patterns. In this segment "Funds of Knowledge," "Participation Shifts," and "Role Shifts" were heavily marked within one minute intervals. Thus, we can see how the

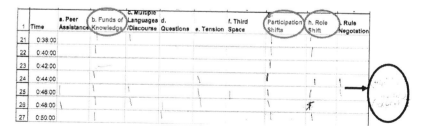

FIGURE 6.3 Cara's Coding Sheet Part 2

coding process, especially the aggregate of codes, led to identifying a third space episode. More precisely, Cara didn't directly observe the third space taking place (only one tick mark), instead the conversation about this vignette during study group sessions with her colleagues and university based research team (BT) generated the possibility of third space. In addition, Sheldon's participation shifts were so noticeable that she went outside the coding sheet template to mark this shift (Figure 6.3, circled). After a detailed transcription of this vignette, Cara's initial observation became more vividly and empirically demonstrable.

With Susan's and Eva's assistance, Cara recognized how her teacher authority had impeded Sheldon's talk about his gardening expertise and, thus, the possible creation of a third space. I had stepped back, saying very little as Susan and Eva helped Cara arrive at her new understanding. While the interaction was collegial, the intellectual conflict that could be seen in the teachers' different understandings of Cara's excerpt pushed Susan and Eva to challenge Cara's interpretation of her excerpt. Ultimately, Cara agreed that she had impeded the development of a third space and later would talk about her failure to appreciate students' funds of knowledge. The teachers' work, however, had cohered into a community that was able to withstand and even draw on any disagreements that they had to create constructive controversy that could drive their own learning.

Blossoming in the Third Space

Later, during one of the final study groups (#14), the teachers talked about a lack of third spaces in the second unit. Cara talked about what had gone well in her class and what she still needed to work on. She read aloud from her transcript how Sheldon explained, "PUT A CARROT AND TOMATO SIGN. YOU HAVE TO LABEL IT. YOU, YOU, YOU AND THEN PEOPLE CAN GO IN THE GARDEN … LIKE WE DO AT HOME." Cara had expanded the previous transcript to include how Sheldon had labeled the plants in his garden at home. She said she provided opportunities for students to share their funds of knowledge but did not move into negotiated spaces where the student expertise informed the curricular goals. In addition, she had not planned for students to bring in their funds of knowledge during the read aloud, but she later redesigned the unit so that students could experiment with planting their own seeds and talk about how their families plant gardens.

After the *Weslandia* read aloud, the class planted herb seeds in sand and soil. Students wrote their predictions about which medium would be better for growing. Most students made predictions that the soil would produce growth by drawing on their gardening expertise. In the transcript 2.2, Sheldon, Isabela, Ian, and Crystal worked together, but there was a lot of tension. The focus group had difficulty negotiating leadership roles and providing peer assistance. The excerpt begins with Crystal taking the packet of seeds from Sheldon.

```
01 Crystal:   (Takes the packet of seeds from Sheldon.)
02 Sheldon:   Ms. C:::
03 Crystal:   No. Isabela. Isabela give him that one (pointing to cup with
04            soil)and you open this and plant it.
05 Isabela:   (Takes the packet of seeds)
06 Sheldon:   No:::o (reaching for packet of seeds)
07 Isabela:   (pulls seeds away from Sheldon)
08 Sheldon:   Let me do i::::t!
09 Crystal:   [Ms. C.]
10 Sheldon:   [Ms. C.]
11 Crystal:   Ms. C, Sheldon wants to do that (pointing to the cup of soil)
12            and this (pointing to the seeds).
13 Sheldon:   No::o
14 Crystal:   (reaches for the cup of sand from Ian)
15 Teacher:   What do you have to do? (turns toward Sheldon)
16 Sheldon:   Put like dirt. The seed is covered back up. Then put water in
17            it.
18 Teacher:   So you have to bury them, right? You have to put them under
19            the soil. Good.
20 Sheldon:   (in a soft voice looking at teacher) Can I take some dirt out?
21 Teacher:   You can take some dirt out. (.) Here, let me get you some
22            newspaper.
```

The students call for Ms. C. to mediate the group work. When Cara arrives she engages Sheldon asking him to explain the experiment (15). He explains the procedures to add dirt to the cup, place the seed and cover it up, and then add water. Sheldon knows he needs to take some dirt out of the cup to be able to cover the parsley seed (16). He asks for permission (20) to remove some dirt. At the end of the transcript, Sheldon gets to be the expert and shares his knowledge in gardening without tension from the group members. Figure 6.4 shows the students planting the parsley seeds in soil and sand.

In the final study group (#19), Cara reflected on the gardening unit and how she changed.

> There was a lot of opportunity with the funds of knowledge. I was very surprised in the unit 2 video they are planting seeds in soil and sand. They are making predictions about which medium is going to help produce a plant more easily.

Third space theory provided a framework for Cara along with her colleagues and the university research team to go beyond the official script of the classroom. When dominant and nondominant scripts intersect, there is an opportunity for a generative third space to emerge (Gutiérrez, 2008). However, as this chapter illustrates, it probably will not happen spontaneously and requires purposeful design and adaptability to contestation (Razfar, 2012; Schuck, Kearney, & Burden, 2017). Coding videos of classroom activities, study group discussions, and discourse analysis were tools that mediated such awareness within the teachers at Adams Elementary. Cara, in particular, showed how these tools can help teachers move

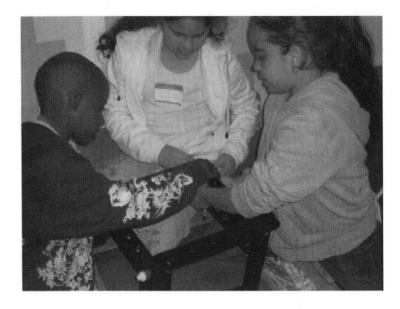

FIGURE 6.4 Sheldon, Crystal, and Isabela Plant Seeds in Soil and Sand

from passive inquiry to engaged teacher researchers (Taylor, 2017). By repositioning Sheldon as an expert, Cara learned to both see and leverage his linguistic, cultural, and scientific funds of knowledge that were otherwise invisible.

Conclusion

Chris Emdin (2020) argues that the absence of a relationship that is rooted in shared culture impedes many students from reaching higher levels of academic rigor. He coined the term *reality pedagogy*, which interrupts the notion that teaching is about managing students and their behavior. It's about reaching students where they really are, making sure that their lives and backgrounds are reflected in the curriculum and in classroom conversations. To do this, teachers need opportunities to video record and discuss their teaching with others. Susan's mediation in the study group allowed Cara to see that she was not listening to Sheldon during the read aloud. Cara realized that she wasn't valuing or effectively leveraging Sheldon's full linguistic repertoire (i.e., Black English). She also realized that she missed opportunities to learn about students' gardening funds of knowledge and incorporate them into the science and literacy lessons. Having the opportunity to discuss and reflect, led her to reposition Sheldon as the expert planting the seeds during the science experiment.

Although at the time Cara and the research team were not aware of the possibilities of urban gardening and science learning in the classroom, there is a growing body of empirical research supporting critical urban gardening and science education. Incorporating this research at the beginning of the action research cycle would be helpful toward countering deficit views of community funds of knowledge and in particular Black epistemologies (Emdin, 2020). Critical urban gardening opposes mainstream environmental politics; it implies the use of biological material as a form of political expression (Certomà, 2011). The origins of critical urban gardening can be traced back to the 1970s in New York, when communities reappropriated green space for building projects and the enjoyment of nature. Activism practices encourage people to garden flowers, trees, and vegetables in any available city space as an alternative to conventional use of space and the system of food production, distribution, and consumption (Certomà, 2015). Tornaghi (2014) proposes a critical geography research agenda around the cultural and political meaning of gardening. Certomà and Tornaghi (2015) examine the link between political gardening and the politics of space with a range of reflections that constitute the basis for furthering urban politics from the ground up. Urban gardening can be an "agent of change" for communities by providing opportunities for strengthening social bonds, expressing and maintaining cultural heritage, and engaging in activities promoting social and political change (Holland, 2004).

Guerilla gardening projects have evolved out of the neighborhoods and communities in which they are located and are led by residents who enjoy the greatest level of participation and commitment and, by extension, confer the most benefit (Certomà, 2011). By transforming vacant or underutilized properties into productive landscapes that provide places to gather and share knowledge about food, residents not only enhance the beauty of their neighborhood through greening, but they also expand their cultural competencies by learning from others. Guerilla gardening is seen by many as integral to practicing food justice.

With a growing awareness of the quality of food we eat, urban gardening provides families with the freshest food right from their homes. In the final focus group #4, we asked: What are some of the key issues or challenges that you see conducting action research? Cara responded:

> My kids, I just realized how creative they are. And that really came out in unit 3 and how I think I talked about this before, really how smart they were. I had misjudged them at the beginning and I had made comments; which I am sorry and I do apologize. I just didn't think that they were going to be capable of it. I was really impressed with them. I think they really enjoyed it.

It is not unusual for white educators in urban communities to struggle with leveraging the linguistic and cultural funds of Black students. Like Cara, many educators begin with deficit views of African American Language and are often uncomfortable and conflicted in terms of how to name the phenomena (Razfar et al., 2020). However, as opportunities to navigate these issues are mediated by university researchers and expert colleagues, the possibility of linguistic and cultural solidarity emerges. A deeper understanding of African American Language, especially as it is related to STEM education, will help us move toward nurturing a more just learning environment and foster a transformative consciousness (Baker-Bell, 2020; Baldwin, 1997; King, 2020). Cara's journey through community gardening and her recognition of the value of Black language, culture, and epistemologies is a first step toward such transformative possibilities.

Additional Resources

1. Madison Metropolitan School District "Outdoor Learning and Gardening" https://science.madison.k12.wi.us/garden-based_ed
2. An Introduction to Urban Farming http://vitalysthealth.org/wp-content/uploads/2017/07/WrkBk-UrbnAgrcltr-FNL-Edited.pdf

Discussion Questions

1. How can students' funds of knowledge be leveraged to plan culturally and linguistically responsive gardening lessons?
2. In what ways can literature be integrated into science teaching and learning?
3. How might critical urban gardening be incorporated into science learning in the classroom?

References

Alim, H. S., Rickford, J. R., & Ball, A. F. (2016). Introducing raciolinguistics. In H. S. Alim, J. R. Rickford, & A. F. Ball (Eds.), *Raciolinguistics: How language shapes our ideas about race* (pp. 1–30). New York, NY: Oxford University Press.

Baker-Bell, A. (2020). *Linguistic justice: Black language, literacy, identity, and pedagogy.* New York, NY: Routledge.

Baldwin, J. (1997). If Black English isn't a language, then tell me, what is? *The Black Scholar, 27*(1), 5–6. [Originally appeared as Baldwin, J. (1979, July 29). If Black English isn't a language, then tell me, what is? *New York Times.* New York.

Bhaba, H. (2003). *The location of culture.* London & New York, NY: Routledge.

Certomà, C. (2011). Critical urban gardening as a post-environmental practice. *Local Environment, 16*(10), 977–987.

Certomà, C. (2015). Critical urban gardening. In M. Pimbert, R. Shindelar, & H. Schösler (Eds.), *Think global, eat local: Exploring foodways* (pp. 13–17). LMU Munich and the Deutsches Museum: RCC Perspectives 1.

Certomà, C., & Tornaghi, C. (2015). Political gardening transforming cities and political agency. *Local Environment, 20*(10), 1123–1131.

Cuenca, A., Schmeichelb, M., Butlerd, B. M., Dinkelman, T., & Nichols, J. R. (2011). Creating a "third space" in student teaching: Implications for the university supervisor's status as outsider. *Teaching and Teacher Education, 27*(7), 1068–1077.

Emdin, C. (2020, July 24). Teaching isn't about managing behavior. *The Atlantic.* Retrieved from https://www.theatlantic.com/education/archive/2020/07/reality-pedagogy-teaching-form-protest/614554/

Finely, R. (2013, March 6). *A guerrilla gardener in central LA* [Video]. TED Conferences. Retrieved from https://www.ted.com/talks/ron_finley_a_guerrilla_gardener_in_south_central_la?language=en

Fleischman, P. (1999). *Weslandia.* Cambridge, MA: Candlewick Press.

Flores, N., & Rosa, J. (2015). Undoing appropriateness: Raciolinguistic ideologies and language diversity in education. *Harvard Educational Review, 85*(2), 149–171.

Gutiérrez, K. D. (2008). Developing a sociocritical literacy in the third space. *Reading Research Quarterly, 43*(2), 148–164.

Gutiérrez, K. D., Rymes, B., & Larson, J. (1995). Script, counterscript, and underlife in the classroom: James Brown versus Brown v. Board of Education. *Harvard Educational Review, 65*(3), 445–471.

Holland, L. (2004). Diversity and connections in community gardens. *Local Environment, 9*(3), 291.

Irvine, J. T., & Gal, S. (2000). Language ideology and linguistic differentiation. In P. V. Kroskrity (Ed.), *Regimes of language: Ideologies, polities, and identities* (pp. 35–84). Santa Fe, NM: School of American Research Press.

King, S. (2020). From African American vernacular English to African American language: Rethinking the study of race and language in African Americans' speech. *Annual Review of Linguistics, 6*, 285–300.

Klein, E. J., Taylor, M., Onore, C., Strom, K., & Abrams, L. (2013). Finding a third space in teacher education: Creating an urban teacher residency. *Teaching Education, 24*(1), 27–57.

Lipman, P., & Haines, N. (2007). From accountability to privatization and African American exclusion: Chicago's "Renaissance 2010." *Educational Policy, 21*(3), 471–502.

Martin, S. D., Snow, J. L., & Franklin Torrez, C. A. (2011). Navigating the terrain of third space: Tensions with/in relationships in school-university partnerships. *Journal of Teacher Education, 62*(3), 299–311.

Razfar, A. (2012). ¡Vamos a jugar counters! Learning mathematics through funds of knowledge, play, and the third space. *Bilingual Research Journal, 35*(1), 53–75.

Razfar, A. (2013). Multilingual mathematics: Learning through contested spaces of meaning making. *International Multilingual Research Journal, 7*(3), 175–196.

Razfar, A., Rumenapp, J. C., & Torres, Z. (2020). Administrating language: The language ideological voices of urban school administrators in urban education. *Urban Education, 00*(0), 1–29. DOI: 10.1177/0042085920959136.

Razfar, A., Troiano, B., Allebach, B., & Koustas, D. (in press). From languishing to languaging in the third space: Teachers applying linguistics to mediate language and STEM learning. In T. B. Peele-Eady (Ed.), *Integrating home and heritage languages in schools: Pedagogy and promise.* New York, NY: NCTE/ Routledge Research Series.

Razfar, A., Troiano, B., Nasir, A., Yang, E., Rumenapp, J. C., & Torres, Z. (2015). Teachers' language ideologies in classroom practices: Using English learners' linguistic capital to socially re-organize learning. In P. Smith (Ed.), *Handbook of research on cross-cultural approaches to language and literacy development* (pp. 261–298). Hershey, PA: IGI Global Publications.

Rickford, J. R. (2016). *Raciolinguistics: How language shapes our ideas about race.* New York, NY: Oxford University Press.

Schieffelin, B. B., Woolard, K. A., & Kroskrity, P.V. (Eds.). (1998). *Language ideologies: Practice and theory.* New York, NY: Oxford University Press.

Schuck, S., Kearney, M., & Burden, K. (2017). Exploring mobile learning in the third space. *Technology, Pedagogy and Education, 26*(2), 121–137.

Soja, E. W., & Chouinard, V. (1999). Thirdspace: Journeys to Los Angeles & other real & imagined places. *Canadian Geographer, 43*(2), 209.

Taylor, L. A. (2017). How teachers become teacher researchers: Narrative as a tool for teacher identity construction. *Teaching and Teacher Education, 61*, 16–25.

Tornaghi, C. (2014). Critical geography of urban agriculture. *Human Geography, 38*(4), 551–567.

Woestehoff, J. (2016, September 13). *The violent legacy of Chicago's mass school closings | Parents Across America.* Retrieved from http://Parentsacrossamerica.Org/ Violent-Legacy-Chicagos-Mass-School-Closings-2/. http://parentsacrossamerica. org/violent-legacy-chicagos-mass-school-closings-2/

Zeichner, K. (2010). Rethinking the connections between campus courses and field experiences in college and university-based teacher education. *Journal of Teacher Education, 61*(12), 89–99.

7

SUSTAINING TEACHING EXCELLENCE AND PROFESSIONAL IDENTITY ACROSS TIME AND SPACE

From Reporting to Sharing

I saw Leah (teacher from Warner School) in Target this weekend. We had a great chat and caught up. I must say, I am super excited because she was talking about some of the changes that have happened at Warner since I was last there. She said that because she and the others have been talking so much about student expertise and problem-based education, that all of the teachers now implement some type of problem-based unit in their instruction. I don't know exactly what this entails, but she said she pulls out the activity triangle to help them … so win for us! Anyway, it was super encouraging that LSciMAct has made a lasting difference. I plan to follow up with her and the others at Warner to get a better idea of what has made a lasting impact some 4–5 years later.

(Joseph Rumenapp email to Aria Razfar, September 8, 2015)

This spontaneous encounter with Leah at a local department store more than 3 years after the formal completion of the program, captures the essence of this book. Action research is about building relationships that cross traditional professional boundaries. While Leah was not one of the teachers highlighted in this book, her narrative is another illustration of how action research can have longitudinal impact. While we haven't been able to follow up with all the participating teachers, mainly due to logistical and financial constraints, those that we have been able to follow up with formally or informally have provided additional insights into how action research can help us reimagine a more enhanced teacher professional development. In this chapter, we examine how reporting

DOI: 10.4324/9781351001168-7

and sharing their action research findings helped mediate longitudinal impact, outcomes, and a new professional identity grounded in teaching excellence, authentic curriculum design, and a culture of academic rigor mediated by their university partnership.

Change in Site: Findings from Action Research Reports

In their final action research reports, each cohort of teachers reflected on several levels of change: change in self, change in students, and change in site (see Appendix H for sample Action Research Report outline). In terms of our current focus on objects and outcomes of the action research activity system, we examined what teachers focused on when it came to changes they were able to document at their school sites and beyond. In this section we examine seven themes that emerged from the action research reports with regard to longitudinal outcomes of conducting action research:

1. Improved test scores and advocacy
2. Administrative support
3. Home and school connections and collaboration
4. Teacher collaboration and expertise
5. Building relationships with the school
6. Challenges, constraints, and limitations
7. Recommendations for future action research

Improving Outcomes Through Test Scores and Advocacy

One of the indicators of longitudinal impact are test scores and organized advocacy. Our action research project was designed to be responsive not only to student and community epistemologies but also to administrative and societal expectations regarding standardized test scores. Obviously, this does not stem from our belief in the legitimacy of standardized tests as a valid measure of learning and development. Nor does this indicate a desire to have fidelity to them or build a curriculum that "teaches to the tests." Instead, one of our professional development goals was to empower teachers theoretically and methodologically to engage the language of standards and standardized tests through a sociocultural lens. The rationale was that if we focus on creating optimum learning opportunities, high test scores would be an indirect by-product of our action research process rather than the target of instruction it tends to be. As a result, the naysayers and skeptics will have nothing to stand on. The Adams cohort of teachers modeled this approach. In fact, given there was ideological alignment on the validity of standardized tests with their own administration, they were targeting the broader community-, district-, and state-level officials with this type of data. They discussed this in great detail in their final action research report:

When students are provided opportunities to use technological tools and artifacts to problem-solve in new ways, they are given the skills to succeed in school and society. This was demonstrated in our improved scores in our state tests in the areas of literacy, mathematics and science.

(Final Action Research Report)

The following figures taken from Susan's final action research report shows the significant improvement for her focal EL students. Figure 7.1 is the overall reading and mathematics scores for the class.

Overall, there was a 12.3% increase for reading and a 13.5% increase for mathematics (Figure 7.1). For the focal EL students, Grace, Sonia, and Iris, there was a slightly higher increase for Grace and Iris (18% and 15%, respectively). More significantly for Iris, she went from "meeting grade level" to "exceeding grade level" in reading. All three students "exceeded grade level" in reading and mathematics, with Sonia's mathematics score not being available (Figure 7.2).

At Warner Elementary School, Allison's class improved an astounding 9 percentile points in mathematics and 11 percentile points in reading. She would mention that this was "the best test scores" she had ever had in all her years of teaching. Other teachers in the cohort also exhibited significant increases in reading (e.g., 13 percentile points for Jan). With these concrete improvements in test scores, teachers were able to advocate for their students and the curriculum they built with their respective administrators.

Another way teachers advocated for their students is through letter writing to the legislative representatives. This was most clear at Genesis Elementary, where

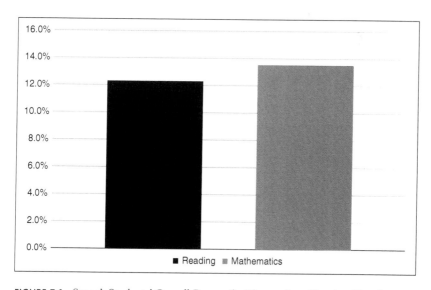

FIGURE 7.1   Susan's Students' Overall Percentile Change from Year 1 to Year 2

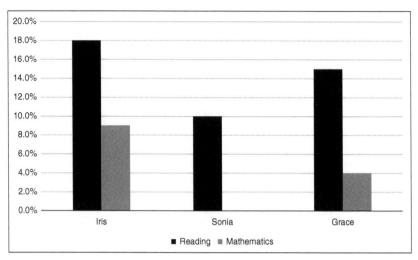

Note Sonia's Mathematics Score Not Available

FIGURE 7.2 Susan's Focal Students' Overall Percentile Change from Year 1 to Year 2

Karen and Abby discuss how the students composed letters advocating for a playground. Karen, for example, cites a student from her observational field notes exclaiming, "I have the power to change history." They further provide a summative finding regarding how advocacy to create a playground unfolded through collaboration with other teachers and representation on the school council:

> In the beginning of the year, students understood that there was a problem at their school because there was no place for them to play. During our units, we encouraged them through stages of community activism. This child's statement, his realization that he has the power to change something, embodies the spirit of a community activist. We joined forces with other teachers who were advocating for a playground at Genesis. We discovered that three other teachers (two of whom are our Local School Council representatives) were working together toward getting a grant for a playground.

Administrative Support

While administrative support at the school and district levels varied initially, each cohort of teachers talked about how essential this was toward making changes within their own classrooms and schools. The range of support or lack thereof also illustrates how action research is about adaptation, flexibility, and possibility. All of our schools were "neighborhood schools" in the same district, so we can safely say that the variation was primarily due to the principals' views of teacher professional identity and their approach to learning and development in light of district and state curricular mandates. Adams Elementary was an example of a school where the administration was extremely aligned and supportive of teacher autonomy and less restrictive in terms of curriculum mandates. Jarman Elementary was somewhere in the middle, with the administration requiring "fidelity to the mandated science curriculum" yet also providing an opening for funds of knowledge–based activities through "extension projects time." Genesis Elementary exemplified the other side of the spectrum.

At Adams the teachers reported feeling "trusted" by their administration. Not surprisingly, they were the school with the highest test scores as a by-product of their school culture:

> We were truly grateful for the support and interest of the administration in our action research. They gave us the autonomy to implement our curriculum and trusted us as professionals to succeed in our teaching.
>
> (Final Action Research Report, Adams)

However, at Genesis, they talked about having to be "sneaky" teachers in the face of a curricular schedule that had little flexibility.

At Jarman Elementary, the administration, while maintaining fidelity to the mandated curriculum, also had some structured flexibility in the form of "extension activities." These teachers were also able to change their administration's stance toward action research:

> We found that doing action research within mandated curricula is possible. Our school, like most [District] schools, requires us to maintain fidelity to the science curriculum, set rigorous expectations and scaffold instruction for all learners. We concluded that incorporating the students' funds of knowledge through extension projects was possible, even with mandated curricula. These activities can be interwoven within the curricula to address learning standards and create authentic learning experiences for the students. This change in thinking came about when we took control of the curricula and implemented it in a way that was best for our students.
>
> (Final Action Report, Jarman)

At Genesis, there was constant fear that someone would be paying a surprise visit to make sure that the teachers were "on-task" and "identical pacing."

> As the year progressed, our Chief Area Officer demanded that all grade levels maintain identical pacing with curriculum. In other words, if someone were to visit our rooms, we were expected to be teaching the same lesson as the other teachers in our grade level.
>
> (Final Action Research Report, Genesis)

This type of curricular surveillance undoubtedly placed tremendous pressure on the teachers to engage in authentic curricular design. Nevertheless, "the sneaky teacher" metaphor points to teacher agency and autonomous professional identity. In this case, the role of the university research team was pivotal. The research team and the teachers met several times with the principal early on in order to lay the foundation for the teachers' funds of knowledge–based curriculum. We assured the principal that our activities were based on tried and tested learning principles and shared successful outcomes through the research literature and our own case study models. The following excerpt shows how the "fear" of being on task for the teachers was palpable. Both Karen and Abby felt they were the "sneaky teacher" because they would plan with:

> their grade levels, but not necessarily teach what was planned. To compound the issue, the administration required a clear time schedule that outlined the specific minutes for each subject. Failing to adhere to these minutes would result in punitive measures (i.e., being written-up). While we felt that the students' learning was worthwhile, we were in a state of constant fear that the administration would walk in and disagree. The administration had put money into programs (i.e., FOSS) and thus expected us to follow this curriculum in the mandated and planned way.
> (Final Action Research Report, Genesis)

They developed a type of parallel curriculum and avoided any punitive administrative measures. Throughout the year they cultivated their approach with documented evidence. In fact, one of the great changes was how they were able to shift the mindset of the administration toward "project-based learning" to the point where they encouraged it across the school;

> Throughout the course of the year, we managed to teach our developed curriculum about the playground without being reprimanded. In fact, at the year's conclusion during a professional development with our staff, our assistant principal acknowledged the work we had done. He noted that our curriculum was rooted in project-based learning. Not only did he commend this, but suggested to the entire staff that this is what should be done in the future (MEMO: Unit 3). They are very strict on teachers that they believed were wasting instructional time, and I would not want them to think I am wasting instructional time sharing their funds of knowledge.
> (Final Action Research Report, Genesis)

Home and School Connections and Collaboration

All of our participating teachers resonated with the concepts of funds of knowledge and leveraging them for the purpose of curriculum design. There was variation in how each cohort went about accessing and integrating such knowledge.

There was also significant variation in how comfortable teachers were crossing the "fourth wall" as indicated in their final action research reports. From teacher–parent conferences at the school to home-visits, teachers developed their own strategies in order to make greater home–school connections and collaborations.

At Adams Elementary, teacher–parent conferences were the principle method of connecting with students' homes. It was through these conferences that the teachers discovered how video games could be a viable mediational tool for curricular activity in their classrooms. In addition, the parents were very supportive and provided positive feedback:

> The enthusiasm of the students in regards to video games and the parents' support of our project was another change in our site. During parent-teacher conferences and all-school events, our parents often mentioned how excited their child was about using video games in the classroom.
>
> (Final Action Report, Adams)

There were definitely challenges in attempting to build viable home–school connections beyond the participating teachers. The Jarman teachers found how teachers at their school "have been reluctant to embrace the funds of knowledge process." However, they were confident that "as teachers became more familiar and confident with the curricula" that more teachers would utilize it (Final Action Report, Jarman).

The teachers at Genesis thought the playground initiative started by the students would generate great interest from the parents. However, they were "disappointed that we received little participation." Specifically, given the large number of parents who had expertise in construction, they anticipated greater involvement. Despite their disappointment, they remained "hopeful that the playground initiative was a stepping stone toward a genuine partnership with parents" (Final Action Research Report, Genesis).

At Warner Elementary School, Allison demonstrated one of the strongest commitments to home visits. She and her family were well rooted in the Chinatown community, with her cousin's restaurant serving as a hub for project meetings and building collegial and personal bonds. Allison shared several stories of how as a kid she "resented" having to share her room and other things with her cousin's family when they first immigrated to the United States. It led to a type of anti-immigrant sentiment and a type of "self-hate." She grew up not speaking Mandarin or Cantonese and over time became distant with her heritage language and culture as she became more and more assimilated into "white and English only" American culture. Her story echoed similar themes of "language and culture loss" in many first-generation immigrant children. However, as she became a more experienced teacher, she moved from feelings of self-loathing and resentment for her immigrant experiences and more toward empathy and solidarity. As she learned about how her dad made sacrifices and helped their immigrant relatives to settle in the United States, she became filled with pride and appreciation with her own immigration narrative As a result, she learned to leverage her own "immigrant" funds of knowledge. Each home visit was an opportunity to reconnect to something within herself that she had suppressed. She loved going to the parents' homes and opening herself up to help them in any way she could:

> At first, I was hesitant since; I have not done this in 15 years! However, it is like "riding a bike" … you starts peddling and GO!!!!!!!!!!!!!!!!!!!!!!!!!!!!!!!!!!!! !!!!!!!!!!!!!! If you would like me to go w/any of you at night … just ask! It has been great to meet the parents and the ultimate goal of all the parents; "We want our child to succeed in school" … It is now my job to make this possible w/their support!
>
> (Final Action Research Report, Warner Elementary)

The home visits fundamentally altered her view of the parents and her stance on the immigrant experience:

> The visits took place over 2 months (Figure 7.3) which was a lot of work for a teacher working full time and taking classes; however, I was able to make it to all of my students' homes and was greeted with food, drinks,

HOME VISIT DATE	STUDENT
10-7	Brant
10-8	Jessi, Min Hin, Oscar
10-11	Wan Nang
10-14	Nin, Yu Nin
10-15	Jimmy, Brandi
10-19	Diane, Ying Ping
10-21	Amy
10-22	Martha, Emily Po
10-25	Melanie
10-27	John, Kelvin, Vincent
11-5	Sue
11-10	Xioling
11-16	Xi Yiu
11-22	Chenja

FIGURE 7.3 Allison's Home Visit Log

and even gifts. I noted on October (Unit 1) about how I began to view my relationship with them and their parents.

(Final Action Research Report, Warner Elementary)

She had a detailed log of each home visit as well as a calendar where the dates were circled (Figure 7.3).

Overall, Allison met with 22 families in their homes over a 2-month period. She talked about how home visits made her "humbled," "grateful," how it was "special" and led to "several changes" within herself and the broader community.

> While on a whole I learned that parents wanted students to succeed, I noted in another post (Blackboard Post Fall) "It was very 'humbling' to go inside someone's home." These home visits were a very special time for me to learn about my students, and I noticed several changes in the way that I viewed them and was very grateful that their families supported me.
>
> (Final Action Report, Warner)

Upon completing the action research reports, we celebrated with dinner at her cousin's restaurant in Chinatown. Allison's deep commitment to home visits and general openness with her experiences helped mediate our collective growth. It alleviated much of the hesitation and fear other teachers shared about home visits and ultimately led to strengthening student and community relationships.

Teacher Collaboration, Interdisciplinary Expertise, and Learning Disabilities

Our cohort model purposefully grouped teachers from diverse disciplines, learner expertise, and even grade levels. We made sure that in each cohort there was a mix of language arts and STEM expertise. In the case of Adams, Susan, the secondary school language arts teacher, worked with Eva, the secondary school STEM teacher, and Cara, the early childhood and elementary teacher. They all benefited from this collaboration at the theoretical and design levels. Susan and Eva even shared the same students, and they noted the impact of this:

> The greatest change came from the collaboration of the interdisciplinary cohort and the implementation of the activity theory and how it changed our strategies in teaching.
>
> (Final Action Report, Adams)

The Genesis cohort had a similar observation and additionally had a bilingual language expert as part of their cohort, which was "integral to our collaboration and learning experience":

> Teacher collaboration is a practice that assists on multiple levels, including planning phases, analysis of student work, modifications to instruction, assessment opportunities, and reflection on ourselves as professionals and individuals. Especially if you are teaching English learners, we advise you to collaborate with a colleague who is a language and/or content expert. Within our cohort, we had the fortune of having a mix of experts within our group. This greatly assisted us as we planned to teach our ELs both language and content. We cannot express how integral this was to our collaboration and learning experience.
>
> (Final Action Report, Genesis)

In addition to content and language learning expertise, the Jarman cohort benefited from expertise in learning disabilities and special education. Dana's expertise in special education mediated a more expansive understanding of how to organize learning that was responsive to nontraditional learners. They could be more mindful and strategic about "nontraditional learning styles and modalities." The teachers at Jarman noted how this collaboration helped them "improve the quality of instruction":

> Having a general education and a special education teacher collaborate to teach the units allowed us to improve the quality of instruction for the students. Dana's knowledge of special education teaching practices complimented Elisa's knowledge of the curriculum. Together we were able to teach to nontraditional learning styles and modalities, which supported a classroom of diverse learners, including ELs and students with learning disabilities.
>
> (Final Action Research Report, Jarman)

The impact of this collaboration was one of those longitudinal outcomes that extended beyond the immediate goals of the project. It helped lead to more "inclusive" and "improved instructional practices" across the school with benefits for all types of learners:

> This type of collaboration continued to grow into the next school year as the middle school grades switched to full inclusion to better serve their special education students. Dana went into the classroom with her students, this necessitated an ongoing collaboration between special education and general education teachers. This resulted in improved instructional practices that benefited both special education and EL students. Collaboration empowered teachers to advocate for their students.
>
> (Final Action Research Report, Jarman)

The Jarman teachers would become leaders of their middle school professional development team. They mentored their colleagues in how to "integrate science, reading, and writing." They empowered the other teachers at Jarman to "embrace the challenge of using the mandated curricula in a way that was responsive to student needs." This led to schoolwide curricular development geared toward ELs, students with learning disabilities, and traditional learners:

> This led to units of study that were taught across the science, reading and writing classes. Even in a setting where subjects are departmentalized, integration of topics is possible. This overlapping instruction was highly effective and especially beneficial for EL students and students with disabilities, providing more exposure and more time to grasp the big concepts and show mastery.
>
> (Final Action Report, Jarman)

The Jarman teachers had appropriated many of the action research practices discussed in this book. They not only sustained them but enhanced them. Their identities as teacher researchers allowed them to see beyond the restrictions of mandated and scripted curriculum.

Building Relationships Within the School

Our research team shared narratives of empathy and solidarity for us as researchers working with the teachers. There was a similar theme with our teachers and their students. One of the enduring lessons we learned doing action research was how critical it was to build relationships outside the classroom and school site. The Adams teachers noted how "the project strengthened the professional relationships and friendships." They also mentioned the presence of the research team nurturing this growth, "Ms. Troiano became a natural presence in our classrooms helping and supporting us in various ways" (Final Action Report, Adams).

Teachers could be more open and critical with each other without fear of professional consequences. The Jarman teachers stated how the "project created an environment that was open to self-evaluation and reflection." They further added how collaborative relationships with their colleagues led to "exchanging ideas freely and receiving constructive feedback that allowed for teachers to grow and develop in order to meet the needs of their students" (Final Action Report, Jarman).

At Genesis this intimate relationship extended to the administration, which for us was a welcome surprise given their initial resistance and their feeling the need to be "sneaky teachers." They stated in their final report, "What began as a relationship of uncertainty and indifference has continued as one of support with a common goal." They reminded future adopters of action research that building relationships with fellow colleagues and administrators leads to positive academic outcomes:

> In our experience, building relationships with administrators is essential to provide the best education experience for students. While ours started as an uncertain one, our journey is proof that it is possible. Being open and confident about the opportunities that you will afford your ELs by teaching in a way that capitalizes on both language and content will keep lines of communication open so that a positive relationship remains possible.
>
> (Final Action Research Report, Genesis)

The Genesis cohort's journey toward building a playground was made possible in part by inviting a skeptical administration into the process. Being open and authentic with administrators who wield power over a teacher's career requires them to feel confident in their own professional identity. They left future teachers with this recommendation:

> As you embark on your journey of teaching in this way, be sure to share it with your administration (and perhaps offer to update your staff through a professional development!). Remember that you are knowledgeable about your craft as a teacher and what you learn is worth communicating to others!
>
> (Final Action Research Report, Genesis)

Challenges, Constraints, and Limitations

Teachers conducting action research will encounter a number of challenges. We have throughout this book discussed the challenges of mandated curriculum, lack of administrative and/or parental support, as well as limited technology. We have also demonstrated how these challenges were transformed into opportunities through the resilience of teachers and the strength of our university partnership. That said, action research requires constant critical self-reflection in order to adapt to emerging challenges. Genesis teachers reported the challenges of a mandated curriculum that required "a uniform pacing chart for all teachers at the same grade level," teaching "twice the load" (mandated curriculum and action research project), as well as other content areas like "social studies being sacrificed" (Final Action Research Report, Genesis). Adams teachers were constrained by the lack of appropriate technology to implement their selected video games (Final Action Research Report, Adams). They also lamented about their struggles as "novice teacher–researchers" during the early stages of the program:

Our role as action researchers was a learning process and throughout the year there were numerous challenges. As we tallied our videos we found over time that we changed how we recognized the categories. The role of an inexperienced teacher–researcher was challenging. Journaling and taking field notes was difficult to do during class time. There was a time gap between learning the concepts in our action research class and the time when we implemented our plan.

(Final Action Report, Adams)

Action research is a learning process so it's natural for teachers to grapple with the research practices early on. In fact, both Adams and Jarman teachers discussed the prospects of longitudinal sustainability. Jarman teachers struggled with logistics and planning, while large class size made organizing learning at Adams difficult. These are institutional factors that must be addressed for action research to be adopted more broadly. For the larger goals of action research to take foot, like content integration, building culturally sustainable curriculum, and fostering teacher–researcher and professional identities, this approach needs to be central to the district's and state's plans for education. It cannot simply be an add-on or "extension project" like it initially was at Jarman. While the administration became supportive, time, space, and resources were always mitigating factors in the process at all the sites. This doesn't have to be the case. Given these institutional and personal constraints, the challenges of doing action research for "the first time" are to be expected:

Time continued to be a factor throughout our work. To keep on track at times we could not give the students more time to take their extension projects further. Also, our co-teaching and collaboration were often done during our preparation periods and therefore we gave up this time in the school day to conduct this research. This would not be sustainable in the long term because preparation periods time is a needed part of the school day for teachers. We also retrospectively felt limited by this being the first time we conducted work like this. This project started out very differently than it ended.

(Final Action Report, Jarman)

Recommendations for Future Action Research

The teachers collectively offered valuable recommendations in their final reports for future educators adopting action research:

- Seek ways to empower students as experts so that they can move beyond what Freire (1970) calls the "banking model of education," where learners are assumed to be empty slates to be filled. Students and their communities must be viewed with a greater sense of agency, autonomy, and active constructors of knowledge.

- There must be a longitudinal commitment to data collection, assessment, and mediation.
- Teachers do not need to speak their students' languages or be members of their communities in order to "value their linguistic, cultural, and STEM funds of knowledge."
- A vital characteristic for conducting action research and designing authentic curriculum is "flexibility" and "adaptability to the inevitable challenges that arise. Be "comfortable being uncomfortable" because "we can guarantee that authentic learning/curriculum "won't follow the script."
- Create a welcoming space and safe space for parents by any means necessary through making the "the embodied identities of engineer, community activist, and Spanish proficiency" accessible.

Conclusion

Participatory action research (PAR) is collaborative in nature, and it encourages sharing, developing consensus, and designing curriculum that often pushes the boundaries of static models of schooling. From standardized assessments to mandated state curriculum, there is often a fundamental tension and even a contradiction between individualistic norms and the collectivist ethos of PAR. Sustaining teaching excellence through fostering a collective teacher–researcher identity can seem like trying to fit a square peg into a round hole. How does one reconcile the inherent contractions of norm-referenced standardized assessments that are not sensitive to English learners and the linguistic and cultural epistemologies available to them? Further, teachers face punitive consequences for underperformance as measured by fidelity to curricular mandates and standardized test scores. Reporting and sharing are practices that are essential to mediating effective professional development that can lead to long-term change. Reporting and sharing helps teachers develop stronger relationships with their colleagues, the community, and their administration (Wenner & Campbell, 2017). Through various evaluation and assessment tools such as surveys, questionnaires, and standardized test scores, teachers can better advocate for their students, especially those who have been systematically marginalized (Mertler, 2019).

The action research reports demonstrated how the teachers at Genesis, Jarman, Adams, and Warner negotiated some of these inherent systematic tensions. They used quantitative and qualitative data as well as their university partners to empower their schools' administration. These processes helped them answer questions from district, state, and other outside observers. Improving schools through action research requires transparency and trust. Formative sharing and reporting changes the purpose of evaluation from a culture of fear and exclusion toward a culture of solidarity and inclusion. For this reason, teachers saw the value of a longitudinal commitment to more robust forms of data collection and assessment.

Building partnerships with families, communities, and university-based researchers requires a fundamental shift in how we organize and evaluate schools. Conducting home visits, doing discourse analysis, and participating in study groups outside of school space and time are practices that need to become an explicit metric in how we determine resource allocation, budgets, and successful learning (Pape & Lerner, 2016). As the teachers reported, they are time intensive and emotionally taxing. Breaking the fourth wall in schools does not need to be spontaneous. Given what we have learned about the effectiveness of teacher development outside the school building, these spaces can be more explicitly supported. When administrators value these connections and collaborations in the professional development of their teachers and student learning outcomes, they will naturally dedicate time, space, and resources to such activities (Grant & Ray, 2019; Grant, Bell, Yoo, Jimenez, & Frye, 2017).

As stated in the action research reports, leveraging teacher, student, and community expertise enhances teacher professional identity, develops leadership, and enhances student learning. This is particularly true for second language and special needs learners (Dove & Honigsfeld, 2010; Nguyen, 2012). Teachers' expertise is optimized when they are working collaboratively across disciplines, especially language arts and STEM (Civil, 2016; Razfar & Nasir, 2019). The teachers in their reports demonstrated how centering teacher expertise and trusting them to design, implement, and assess culturally sustaining curricular activities can yield demonstrably positive results for all stakeholders. Action research reports provide an empirical method for centering teacher expertise and evaluating longitudinal professional growth (Berliner, 1988; Farrell, 2013).

Discussion Questions

1. What is the role of standardized test scores in advocating for designing and implementing a culturally responsive curriculum?
2. How can administrators support teacher professional development and make action research sustainable in their schools?
3. How can teachers create home school and collaborations through action research?
4. What are some strategies for "breaking the fourth wall" with your students?

Additional Resources

1. Writing Action Research Report Tutorial
   https://www.Actionresearchtutorials.Org/11-Writing-Your-Report
2. Data Presentation and Visualization Resources
   http://www.shodor.org/interactivate/lessons/HistogramsBarGraph/

3. National Center for Education Statistics: Forum Guide to Data Visualization
https://nces.ed.gov/pubs2017/NFES2017016.pdf
4. National Center for Education Statistics: Forum Guide to Taking Action with
Education Data
https://nces.ed.gov/pubs2013/2013801.pdf

References

Berliner, D. C. (1988). Implications of studies on expertise in pedagogy for teacher education and evaluation. *New directions for teacher assessment: Proceeding of the 1988 ETS Invitational Conference* (pp. 39–68). Princeton, NJ: Educational Testing Service.

Civil, M. (2016). STEM learning research through a funds of knowledge lens. *Cultural Studies of Science Education, 11*, 41–59. DOI: 10.1007/s11422-014-9648-2

Dove, M., & Honigsfeld, A. (2010). ESL coteaching and collaboration: Opportunities to develop teacher leadership and enhance student learning. *TESOL Journal, 1*(1), 3–22.

Farrell, T. S. (2013). Reflecting on ESL teacher expertise: A case study. *System, 41*(4), 1070–1082.

Freire, P. (1970). *Pedagogy of the oppressed.* New York, NY: Continuum Press.

Grant, K. B., & Ray, J. A. (Eds.). (2019). *Home, school, and community collaboration: Culturally responsive family engagement* (4th ed.). Thousand Oaks, CA: Sage Publications.

Grant, L., Bell, A. B., Yoo, M., Jimenez, C., & Frye, B. (2017). Professional development for educators to promote literacy development of English learners: Valuing home connections. *Reading Horizons: A Journal of Literacy and Language Arts, 56*(4), 1–25.

Mertler, C. A. (2019). *Action research: Improving schools and empowering educators* (6th ed.). Thousand Oaks, CA: SAGE Publications.

Nguyen, H. T. (2012). General education and special education teachers collaborate to support English language learners with learning disabilities. *Issues in Teacher Education, 21*(1), 127–152.

Pape, M., & Lerner, J. (2016). Budgeting for equity: How can participatory budgeting advance equity in the United States? *Journal of Public Deliberation, 12*(2). DOI: 10.16997/jdd.261

Razfar, A., & Nasir, A. (2019). Repositioning English learners' funds of knowledge for scientific practices. *Theory Into Practice, 58*(3), 226–235.

Wenner, J. A., & Campbell, T. (2017). The theoretical and empirical basis of teacher leadership: A review of the literature. *Review of Educational Research, 87*(1), 134–171.

8

BREAKING THE FOURTH WALL

Rebuilding University and School Partnerships Through Action Research

I do get emotional doing this work because you do change as a person. There is something about learning through other people that makes you learn and change yourself. So I welcome you to learn about yourself and things you may have never known and embrace a field that is really rooted in making a difference in your students and yourself. So yes, this program is hard, but it is also inviting to have the power to change. Action research is not just writing to get a degree, but to share what you are doing with the rest of the world. For me research is for change and its passionate work, I hope I can ignite that passion in you and it is going to be a bumpy road, but it will also be fun. I want us to be close to each other and we all need to be here for one another.

(Nasir, 2013, p. 254)

A major theme presented throughout this book is how participatory action research radically changes relationships between teachers, students, administrators, families, communities, and university-based researchers. It fundamentally challenges the notion of an objective, outside observer peering onto people without any personal stake or interest in what's happening. In cinema, theater, television, and literature, the concept of a "fourth wall" refers to the invisible barrier that exists between performers and the audience (Mangan, 2013). A similar barrier exists in formal schooling (McLaren, 1999; Quantz, 1999). Teachers, students, administrators, and even university-based researchers perform their roles as if the other participants don't have lives outside the school building. This stance leads to a decontextualized form of teaching and learning. Linguistic, cultural, and nondominant epistemologies are rendered invisible, which has a profound negative effect on learning and development. While this negative effect impacts

DOI: 10.4324/9781351001168-8

all learners, the consequences are greater for learners who come from nondominant communities. We have used this theater convention as a metaphor for discussing how participatory action research foregrounds strategies for "breaking the fourth wall."

In this chapter we discuss longitudinal outcomes, personal growth, and development as university-based researchers, and how we constantly stepped away and into each other's lives in order to learn. It is an opportunity for us to self-reflect, examine what we learned from working with teachers, what we learned from teachers, and model reflexive practice in how action research developed us personally and professionally (Bloome & Green, 2015; Schön, 1991). We purposefully "step back" in order to provide a metanarrative of how university-based researchers engaged in reflexivity and what's known in organizational theory as *double-loop learning* (Argyris, 1977, 1991). To do this, we examined longitudinal impact and outcomes from our external evaluation, revisited outcomes from a cultural historical theoretical perspective, and examined our narratives of change as a university research team. We conclude with a summary of lessons learned and new directions for participatory action research, teacher professional development, and teacher education programs.

Stepping Back: Longitudinal Impact and Outcomes From External Evaluation

Two years after the first two cohorts of our action research project was completed, an external review team conducted surveys and focus groups with all the participating teachers (Razfar & Li, 2014). This included all the teachers highlighted in this book as well as their cohorts with whom they collaborated. The external reviewers asked questions about the impact of the action research project on the teachers, their students, and schools. All teachers strongly agreed that they put less emphasis on decontextualized mathematical activities such as basic numeracy, rote memorization of rules, and formulaic algorithms in instruction. They reformed their science and mathematics teaching and curriculum design to emphasize conceptual development. They continued to develop collaborative action plans for transforming mathematics and science learning for English learners. In fact, they continued to use many of the activity design tools presented in this book. Some form of action research became a permanent part of their orientation toward curriculum design and instruction. Almost all the teachers reported purposefully engaging their students in high levels of literacy, developing proficiencies in English and Spanish as they engaged in making sense of mathematical problems and explaining their problem-solving strategies through writing. All teachers continued to use discourse analysis to develop more appropriate pedagogy for English learners, especially in the content areas of mathematics and science. While all the teachers reported appropriating many of the core values and practices of an action research approach, about a quarter of the

TABLE 8.1 Final Evaluation of the Action Research Project Impact

As a Result of Training Received From the LSciMAct Action Research Project, I Have:	Strongly Disagree	Disagree	Agree	Strongly Agree
put *less* emphasis on worksheets, decontextualized numerical problems, and memorization of rules and algorithms in my instruction	0	0	8	20
reformed science and mathematics teaching by emphasizing conceptual development and reasoning	0	0	8	20
developed my students with high levels of literacy and proficiencies in English and Spanish as they engage in making sense of mathematical problems and writing explanations of their work	0	1	14	13
used discourse analysis to develop more appropriate pedagogy for English language learners in content areas such as math and science	0	1	11	15
developed a collaborative action plan for transforming math and science instructional practices for English language learners	0	0	11	17
used a form of action research to aid in curriculum design and instruction	0	0	6	21
shared my new knowledge and skills with other teachers	0	1	15	12
modeled and disseminated my improved instruction to other teachers	0	7	12	9

teachers (7/30, 23%) reported challenges with sharing, modeling, and disseminating their newly acquired knowledge and skills with other teachers at their school (Table 8.1).

The focus group conversations confirmed several longitudinal themes among the participating teachers. These themes spoke to the object and outcomes of the professional development activity we designed from the outset (see Figure 8.1). First, the *teacher researcher* identity was appropriated in terms of continuing the practices used throughout the project, namely activity design, discourse analysis, and leveraging students' mathematics and science funds. The following comment illustrates the rigor of action research as well as the benefits of reviewing videos, analyzing field notes and transcripts, and coding:

> I really have enjoyed the action research courses. Even though they were a lot more work, I've been learning more about my students and myself as I review videos from my classroom and analyze field notes, transcripts, and coding sheets. I feel like I have become more aware of my teaching strengths and weaknesses as well as the questions that I address my students.

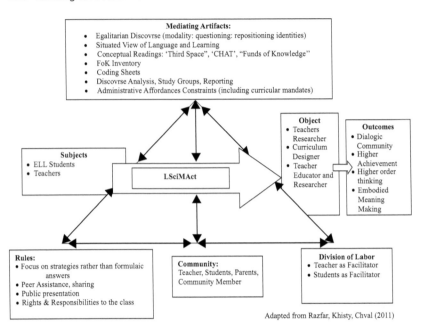

FIGURE 8.1   Original Activity Triangle Objects and Outcomes

Teachers talked about continuing to refine their research practices and becoming "more efficient and meaningful." This shows how teachers displayed agency by making the tools "their own," a shift that they become more acutely aware of with time, "My awareness is more efficient when it comes to collecting data and observing students evolving in their learning." Becoming a teacher–researcher meant regularly using research to inform teaching as one teacher said, "I learned many new teaching practices and ways to reflect on my teaching through research." Furthermore, research helped them become "more aware of what to look for when analyzing student learning."

A second theme was how action research helped teachers integrate content between mathematics, science, and language arts. Reading research articles related to ELs and STEM helped teachers develop new strategies and deepen their understanding:

> I felt the articles, journals, and research I read on teaching ELs math and science were extremely beneficial and refreshing. I learned many new strategies to use when teaching ELs. It also helped to deepen my understanding of how ELs learn math and science and how to teach it in an innovative and effective way.

There was also a significant shift in how they moved toward more expansive views of literacy and ways to mediate English learning. One teacher commented on the benefits of collaborating with their STEM colleagues: "I am not a math teacher, so these courses [action research and bilingual/ESL courses] opened up a new world for me of how to integrate math/science into my curriculum."

The third theme was leveraging student funds of knowledge in designing curriculum. One teacher commented, "I have learned how to effectively bring students' funds of knowledge to make instruction relevant and meaningful." By moving toward a culturally relevant, responsive, and sustaining pedagogy, teachers "learned about the historical, political, and theoretical" aspects related to English learners. Most important, they talked about "becoming better teachers" and moving toward empathy and linguistic solidarity with English learners, "I have never been an EL and I didn't really know how to help them. Now I feel that I have many strategies to help me reach and support them."

Overall, the teachers commented on how action research made them "life-long learners through self-reflection and continuous education." The changes made them more effective teachers not only for ELs but "mainstream students" as well. This was an important outcome that we hoped to achieve even though the project was primarily designed to address the needs of ELs and bilingual/ESL learners. Through continuous reflection, collaboration across disciplines, leveraging community resources, and working with university-based researchers, teachers talked about how LSciMAct "changed our teaching" and helped them "become better teachers." In the following section, we revisit these themes in light of our own analysis drawing on the original Cultural Historical Activity Triangle (CHAT) we used to design the action research process.

From Learning Goals and Objects to Enduring Outcomes: Revisiting the CHAT Triangle

Upon the completion of the project, in addition to the external review, our research team spent several years reflecting on the 30 action research reports, the 3 case-study dissertations, the professional development sessions, and the 24 conference presentations. Based on our initial design, using the CHAT triangle, we focused on the *object* and *outcomes* of our professional development activity system. Our initial object was to mediate the process of becoming teacher researchers and curriculum designers and turn ourselves into a more responsive teacher educator program. Longitudinally, we aimed for outcomes that were meaningful for all stakeholders: teachers, students, families, administrators, and university partners. Initially, we translated these desired outcomes as fostering a dialogic community, higher achievement in terms of test scores, higher order/academic thinking, and situated/embodied meaning-making. To a large degree, we demonstrably achieved these outcomes to some degree, especially with the cases presented in this book. We settled on the fact that this type of professional development, grounded in authentic meaning-making and relationship building, continues well beyond the "final" action report.

Like the teachers who reflected on changes in their students, themselves as teachers, and their schools, we examined the data for evidence of long-term impact. We found that the most critical aspect of our professional developments was in *how* we fostered deep relationships with teachers and their respective communities. Understanding the process was essential to making changes to our professional development design going forward. After all, we are also participants in the action research process. One of the most critical shifts we made from our original design was to open up ourselves to the lives of the teachers outside of the classroom. There was variation in how this was done across the cohorts due to logistical limitations. Each of the cases presented in this book benefited from a doctoral student researcher who ultimately completed a dissertation based on those cases. In the true spirit of ethnographic research, we were able to develop an emic view of the participating teachers.

For example, in Troiano's dissertation, she noted a significant qualitative shift in the analytic process once the cohort started meeting outside of school (Troiano, 2012). Shifting from on-site meetings in the school building to outside of the school noticeably changed the tenor of the meetings. There were no more hurried anxious looks and constant administrative and student "interruptions." Here is a vignette of the first study group held outside of the school building:

> They [the teachers] arrived and for the first 15 minutes or so we exchanged greetings and settled into my dining room after taking a tour of my small apartment. I had prepared some food and drinks, and Eva had brought me a chocolate bunny and wooden brightly colored eggs. "It's a tradition in my country to bring something," she said. We admired the fine craftsmanship in the eggs painted designs, and then talked about the photos that were displayed in the room and enjoyed the food and drinks. And for the first time since we began our study groups, we began our work and didn't stop for over an hour. For the rest of the school year, we met frequently outside of school, moving the meeting from one person's home to another's. We each appeared to take pride in inviting the rest of us into our homes, and always began by sharing food and drinks and relating something personal about ourselves that had nothing to do with who we were as teachers. Typically photos or belongings would elicit comments and a story would follow.

This vignette illustrates how our view of the teachers fundamentally shifted from instructional technicians to people who were travelers, cooks, mothers, wives, caretakers, and women with different interests, abilities, and worldviews. While we often talk about teachers "teaching empathetically" with students (Mirra, 2018), this is just as critical for teacher educators working with teachers (e.g., Jackson, 2020). A similar pattern emerged in the other examples as well, where researchers would meet with teachers at family-owned restaurants and their homes (Nasir, 2013; Rumenapp, 2013). This shift, however, was not limited to the dissertation focal schools, as similar adjustments were made with other cohorts.

The Sociocultural Framework and the CHAT triangle (Figure 8.1), oriented the participants to community relations, the leveraging of nonschool-based mediational tools, and diachronic outcomes grounded in relations based on mutual understanding, empathy, and solidarity (Engeström, 1999; Mirra, 2018). The activity triangle template helps teachers design a systematic curricular process while also being mindful of deeper impact based on best practices and going beyond the latest professional development fad (Wells, 2009).

The original activity design established roles and responsibilities for each learner toward accomplishing the learning goal and also established longitudinal *outcomes* that reflected deeper shifts in student and teacher identity and consciousness. In the years following the implementation of action research, we asked ourselves, "What practices had become a regular part of the teachers' lives? Did teachers continue to create a dialogic classroom community (and the mediating tools to analyze it), mediate higher-order learning, and design culturally responsive curriculum?" Some of these questions were answered earlier through the external evaluation. We also independently collected evidence of such outcomes when some participating teachers from the first two cohorts came back to serve as mentors for the new cohorts, did guest lectures in our action research and bilingual/ESL courses, presented at conferences, connected on social media, and even held spontaneous meetings in the community.

Breaking the "Fourth Wall": Narratives of Empathy, Solidarity, and Relationship Building

As stated earlier, building relationships with teachers and communities was a key component of accomplishing the goals of our professional development. In order to enhance teacher professional identity and student learning outcomes, we as university-based teacher educators and researchers had to significantly embed ourselves in the day-to-day practices of our teachers' lives. Building solidarity with teachers is a considerable investment of time, resources, and most significantly mental and emotional energy.

From attending funerals of murdered sons to sharing immigrant struggles at teachers' family restaurants, our research team as a collective built enduring bonds of solidarity that went far beyond typical professional development tasks and roles. It was late spring of 2012 when we received the tragic news from one of our participating teachers (Kim) at Warner Elementary School that her son (Michael) was senselessly murdered in the parking lot of a local McDonald's leaving behind five children. From that fateful moment, all of us, researchers and participating teachers from all the schools, embraced Kim during this dark period and as a collective moved through the various stages of grief. From shock and anger to acceptance and empowerment, this cathartic experience critically changed how we viewed our role as teacher educators and our relationships with our teachers that continues to the present. It broke what in theater is often referred to as the "fourth wall," the imagined, metaphorical wall that exists between the audience and the actors.

The fourth wall is a performance convention where the actors perform as if the audience is not listening and doesn't exist. Breaking the fourth wall, meant we could no longer pretend to be invisible, passive spectators but vested participants with authentic interest in the lives of our teachers. We can no longer pretend, under the guise of professional distance, that we don't see or hear each other. It was not just about embracing Kim in her moment of grief, but also embracing each other and our communities in our full humanity. Participating in Michael's funeral in a predominantly African-American church, on a Saturday morning, in one of the most historically segregated cities in the United States broke more than the fourth wall. It broke the walls that separate "objective" university researchers from their passive subjects, teachers and students, schools and communities, religious and secular, Black and White, and on and on. It was truly like lightning in a dark valley providing a glimpse into how deep-seated barriers can be transformed into bridges.

Our teachers in their final reports shared narratives of how they felt understood and supported by the research team. Katie's story demonstrates one of the significant longitudinal outcomes of our action research. Upon completing her action research project, Katie would continue to participate as a guest lecturer and a mentor for future cohorts. In the years after she completed the program, she called upon us for business advice, continued to use discourse analysis, and eventually returned to her hometown and began teaching in public schools. Katie was an example of a teacher who, while going through the pressures of divorce, was inspired to start a tutoring business with a friend in part due to the "empowerment" she felt from participating in the action research project. In her final action research report, she shared with us several vignettes that showed how her participation in action research prepared her theoretically, methodologically, and personally for such an endeavor: She would years later text us on Facebook Messenger (2017):

> My friend wants to work with me [to design and develop] approaches and philosophy to use, deciding on outcomes for classes, teacher training, hiring/evaluating … making college branded courses for kids like anthropology, philosophy, sociology … I **LOVE** where she's going with this!
>
> (Katie, Facebook Messenger Text, 2017)

The pressures of a divorce and starting a business meant we as a research team had to become more flexible with project deadlines as well as how Katie could continue to participate with her colleagues. Katie shared with us, "I'm single momming it (filed in June, high conflict, it sucks, but don't be sorry, it's much better for us), but I'm wondering what I should be thinking about." This level of openness demonstrated the rapport we had built in order to be responsive to our teachers' needs and continued development through various personal and professional challenges.

In the aftermath of our original action research project, social media has allowed us to maintain and sustain the relationships that made the initial transformative shifts possible. Centering community spaces and relations outside of the school (both virtual and physical spaces) was essential toward mediating deeper relations of empathy and solidarity. These were relationships we aimed for teachers to nurture with their students in order to leverage funds of knowledge for building curricular units. Whether it was helping Susan with moving to a new apartment, participating in Cara's new baby shower and emerging literacy development, providing moral and sometimes logistical support for Julie while battling breast cancer, Karen's life as a yoga and mindfulness instructor, or Kim's regular posts about Michael, social media platforms such as Facebook and Instagram have allowed us to be continuously engaged participants and witnesses to longitudinal outcomes of narratives of mutual understanding, empathy, and solidarity. The movement from on-site to off-site meetings in the homes and community was a significant crossing of cultural, spatial, and emotional boundaries that made documenting longitudinal outcomes possible. In the following section, we examine how teachers documented the scaling of change from self to site.

Changes in University Researchers: Findings From Dissertations

Over the last 10 years, eight doctoral dissertations have been written about the teachers, their schools, and their communities that we had the privilege of working with. Naturally, the impact on us (project director, research assistants, and graduate students) was and continues to be profound. Our roles as researchers, educators, learners, colleagues, and ultimately friends was driven by a mutual commitment to a transcendent vision, goal, and outcome. This work was supported by the U.S. Department of Education, Office of English Language Acquisition (OELA) NPD (National Professional Development) program (Razfar, 2007, 2011). While this work would have been impossible without this support and we are grateful, there are several implications for national professional development efforts of this type. Just like the teachers at Genesis, who initially felt like they had to be "sneaky teachers" in order to fulfill both the expectations of our project and their district's mandated curriculum, or the teachers at Jarman, who stated that action researcher was an "add-on" to what they really had to do, our commitment to the research component felt the same way.

It is worth noting that the "research component" that we undertook was not an expectation for this type of grant. In fact, when the project director would be at national meetings of other grantees, many, including the project officers, were surprised to learn about such an in-depth focus on research. The evaluation expectation for these grants generally focuses on outcomes such as "completers," meaning how many teachers earned a Bilingual/ESL endorsement. As university-based researchers, we came to the conclusion that this hard divide between research and professional development at the federal level needs to change in order to foster a deeper culture of research and developing teacher researchers in K–12 spaces. This can be addressed by how grant agencies value research, assessment, and evaluation when it comes to teacher development in conjunction with university partnerships. As a research university, we had relatively more autonomy to creatively integrate the research foundation for the project. However, we would definitely have benefited from having more research expertise and intellectual support on the grant agency's side. This can be easily accomplished by having more researchers or former researchers involved in the conceptualization and implementation of teacher professional development grants.

As a project director and dissertation chair, I had to balance the tensions between the expectations of the granting agency, the demands of a research university, and the objectives of our K–12 partners. The changes within ourselves as university-based partners occurred in four ways: (1) changing our stance as researchers, (2) humanizing the researcher role within the academy as well as the community, (3) moving from research subjects to participants, and (4) reflecting on our own racial identity. Each of the dissertations exemplified these shifts in us and hence constituted one of the main longitudinal outcomes of the action research project.

Changing Our Stance as Researchers

Many of us university-based researchers began our training with the assumption that the researcher should be a distant, neutral, and objective observer of the social phenomena we are investigating. The positivistic scientific method dominates our stance as to who and how we position ourselves in relation to our subjects. Practically, this means that we should not connect with research "subjects" at all in order to maintain objectivity and not "bias" our results. The action research paradigm we adopted categorically rejects this framing. As a result, we expect to not only be involved in the lives of so-called research subjects, but also become full-fledged participants in their contexts. Furthermore, because we anticipate shifts in our own stances and practices, analyzing these changes is an essential component of our reporting, whether it be dissertations, conference presentations, or publications. One of the profound changes reported in the dissertations was how our view of research changed. The purpose of research went from drawing predetermined "black and white categories and citing all the right people to generating new knowledge and redrawing black and white lines with gray ones" (Rumenapp, 2013, pp. 235–236). This opened us up to designing our research for the purpose of experiencing change consciously and directly within ourselves.

It became an integral part of our positionality as researchers at every stage of the process. Our distinct role and relationship with the teachers also became clarified. Because we were deeply embedded as participants within the context of our teachers' lives both in and out of the classroom, it was important for us to have a clear sense of our role. This is consistent with our cultural historical perspective in terms of the division of labor and rules of participation. For example, Troiano (2012) reflects on how despite many years of K–12 urban teaching experience, her identity as a university researcher with a unique role and expertise needed to be defined in order to make curricular decisions that were outside the range of the mandated curriculum such as "choosing lessons to video record, selecting what to transcribe, and working with focal students" (p. 55). This awareness of how we position ourselves as university researchers with an essential expertise for teacher professional development helped enrich our collaboration.

Humanizing the Researcher Role Within the Academy as Well as the Community

Humanizing the researcher role within the academy as well as the community was another illustration of how we as university-based researchers shifted our stance toward the purpose of research. Rather than being neutral, objective describers of a social phenomena, participatory action research pushed us to consciously reflect on our own subjective position. At the same time, we also had to become cognizant of our distance and how we navigated the spectrum of objective and subjective positioning. As university-based researchers, we generally enter schools with simple models of who teachers, students, and researchers are. We have expectations and biases about what they do and what they ought to do. However, these models are often essentialist and based on generalized samples that are far removed from the community schools we work with. Rumenapp (2013) testified, "I am an example of this entire dissertation. It was through seeking to understand that I finally repositioned the people in this study into their dynamic changing roles." He further explains how his role shifted from coming in as a distant "research assistant" toward becoming "a friend, a colleague, and a researcher. I have endured some of the most difficult times with the people in this study" (p. 236). It was during this period that one of the teachers at Warner (Kim) had her son murdered, and Joseph at the same time lost his mother. Discourse analysis was not just a methodology but a "dramatic dance of social positioning in action." Throughout the project, we mourned, grieved, and celebrated together (several newborns and marriages). We learned to appreciate and how to build solidarity through the mundane and extraordinary.

In many of our university research projects, especially when we are in stricter experimental design-based environments, we experienced a tendency to emphasize maintaining objective distance from research subjects and implementing uniform procedures. We attempted to control the environments and subjects we were studying in order to better understand how independent variables affected dependent ones. While this is done in order to limit bias and error, it often leads to further alienation of the researcher and is an obstacle to becoming an authentic participant. As researchers, we become more distant from the perspective of the teachers we are working with. Our research goals and objectives may lead us toward a static and linear view of time. Prior to coming to this action research project Troiano was part of another research project that apprenticed her into this way of interacting with teachers. This led to initial hesitation and discomfort with crossing the researcher/teacher boundary.

The following vignette (lines 1–13) taken from Troiano's dissertation (2012) shows how Eva, the STEM teacher at Adams Elementary, who identifies as an EL, raised the issue of how our researcher presence changed her teaching from "something natural," organic, and spontaneous (lines 2–3) to "pressure" (line 8) and the feeling of being "analyzed" (line 11):

```
01 Eva:   You know what I really like it when you come in my class late to
02        tell the truth. When you are late I start the lesson and it's
03        not so much pressure on me. I go with the flow, I forget about
04        you coming and then it's okay I can be me because (.) to tell
05        you the truth for me, teaching is something natural. I have a
06        plan in my mind but I never learn something in the beginning.
07        It's what I have in that moment and what I'm going and then if I
08        am very, I am pressure, I kind of block myself and it's not me
09 BT:    What's the pressure?
10 Eva:   and I don't like it when I'm not … kind of somebody you know
11        (.) analyze me wherever I'm doing what I did the moving, what
12        it's any kind of you know every steps.
```
(Troiano, 2012, p. 59)

Troiano further observed how Eva expressed her preference for the researcher to come in "late" (lines 1–2), and as a result modified her arrival to after the lesson had already started. This was particularly difficult given her "pride in being on time" and assuming that the teachers "appreciated" her promptness. While she lamented the two times that she was late, Eva was most appreciative of her late arrival, and it made her teaching more effective. In contrast, the other teacher in the cohort, Cara, who was a novice teacher, appreciated Troiano's "early arrival to help with classroom management." The most important takeaway here was that we as researchers learned to adjust our own notions of time in order to adapt to the needs of the teachers we worked with. This is less about research methods and more about our stance toward the phenomenon and participants of a study. Experimental and quasi-experimental design methodologies have made significant contributions toward understanding youth voice and youth participatory action research (Berg, Coman, & Schensul, 2009; Branquinho, Tomé, Grothausen, Gaspar de Matos, 2020; Herr & Anderson, 2014). Quasi-experimental design methodologies can play a critical role in gaining a deeper understanding of youth voice and teacher engagement (Cater, Machtmes, & Fox, 2008).

Moving from Research Subjects to Participants

As we move toward a more humanizing research model, the roles of researcher and research "subjects" also shift. In a more humanizing framework, research subjects, in our case the teachers, become participants in the overall design. Each of our dissertations highlighted this finding. In addition, while the university-based research team leveraged their experience as former teachers within the same district, it was also important to realize that we were no longer teachers (Nasir, 2013; Troiano, 2012). Troiano and Nasir talk about how their experiences as teachers mediated a genuine sense of solidarity with the project's teachers. At the same time, in adopting a university-based research stance, they needed some level of distance and objectivity in order to mediate reflection, analysis, and the teacher–researcher identity. This more neutral stance was critical to navigating the inherent tensions between the mandated curriculum objectives and the more culturally responsive participatory action research model. We were always cognizant of how to transform these tensions into spaces of possibility. While difficult to accept at first, the stakes of noncompliance with administration and district expectations were much higher for the teachers. This made us more conscious of our researcher identity and our unique role in teacher professional development.

Historically, positivist philosophies and medical models have had a major role in shaping how social science and education researchers viewed their role in designing, conducting, and talking about research (Caldwell, 2015). These approaches have increasingly been questioned (Evans & Benefield, 2001); however, the legacy of separating research from practice still has its effects. While there is a tendency at university-based research programs to socialize young scholars to shed their teacher identity as they move toward becoming scholars, action research approaches have been shifting the paradigm across disciplines in higher education (Levin & Greenwood, 2008; Prober & Khan, 2013; Zuber-Skerritt, 1992).

Our participatory action research design was more in line with ethnographic and phenomenological approaches that emphasize the researcher as a coparticipant rather than a distant observer. Furthermore, it was explicitly designed to foster egalitarian discourse practices and linguistic, racial, and social justice (Johnson & Parry, 2016). Each of our doctoral dissertations talked about this fundamental shift as they all began with a positivist orientation. Rumenapp (2013) noted his shift: "research isn't about being 'right' or proving a theory, it is about understanding others and creating knowledge, and building relationships [with teachers and students]" (p. 236). He discussed how initially his participation was positioned as "interfering." His observations were consistent with what is described as *grounded theory* where conceptual frameworks are developed through participation with people in authentic activities (Glaser & Strauss, 2017). While grounded theory is historically distinct from participatory action research (PAR) and has some positivistic tendencies in that the researcher is a detached objective observer, integrating grounded theory with participatory action research has led to a more inclusive research process that is generative and consistent with its aim of achieving greater authenticity and understanding (Teram, Schachter, & Stalker, 2005).

Participatory research can often feel like interference or disruption of the research site. As a new doctoral student, Troiano (2012) recorded how during the pilot stage she always "avoided interfering," tried to "remain apart," and often "tried to create a barrier" between her role as a researcher and the teachers' role to do analysis (p. 67). This barrier would eventually fall through the "rules of engagement" that guided our project. In other words, the teachers helped us develop our identities as university researchers. As she opened up about her own vulnerability as a novice university researcher, the cohort teachers helped her navigate these frustrations, hence demonstrating their emerging researcher identity (lines 1–6):

```
01 Susan:   But I remember one time Bev that you didn't know where you
02          where going to go with this and I said that's just part of
03          the process (laughs)
04 BT:      Was I frustrated?
05 Susan:   Yes you were very frustrated!
06 All:     (laugh hard)
```

As Susan points out, the outcome of research is not predetermined (line 1), and being frustrated was all right (lines 5–6). This is an example of how cohort teachers and doctoral students co-constructed knowledge. It was evident that the teachers had moved beyond research subjects. They not only shared their own frustrations with their action research curriculum, but also provided support for the frustrations of their university partner working on her dissertation project. We should underscore a critical lesson we learned here: It is important to be open about epistemological vulnerabilities. Doing so leads to solidarity and mediating the researcher identities of all participants.

Establishing solidarity with teachers by sharing one's epistemic vulnerabilities requires movement from objective researcher toward subjective participant. This shift was exhibited in Nasir's dissertation focusing on her work with Karen and Abby and Genesis Elementary (Nasir, 2013). Nasir's identity as a bilingual learner, daughter of immigrants, and years as a teacher within the district led her to see her role as someone who could seamlessly "help teachers navigate both the teacher and students' communities." As someone who grew up in a predominantly English monolingual, white suburban community, she assumed that she could connect with Abby and Karen. These insider assumptions that Nasir noted were tested as Abby struggled with the funds of knowledge (FoK) component of the project. She assumed that the teachers should have no difficulty doing home visits and eliciting FoK; however, this assumption proved to be limited when the expectation to fulfill the requirements of the project led her to the realization that, "I have pushed too far" (lines 1–4; Nasir, 2013, p. 255):

```
01 The critical moment for me was when Abby returned ten minutes later
02 with her eyes red full of tears and her body shaken up. I could
03 clearly tell there was more to the story than I knew about her.
04 Seeing her reaction, made me realize that I have pushed too far.
```

This was a critical moment of deeper reflection about the objective and distant researcher role. Abby's discomfort and "fear" with home visits for the purposes of funds of knowledge inquiry was rooted in a personal experience that she didn't feel comfortable sharing. Nasir reported that eventually Abby would later share with Nasir via email stories about how in the past "fathers have tried to hit on me and I do not want to put myself in an uncomfortable situation." This revelation put Nasir in a bind in terms of her identity as a researcher. She had a real dilemma between continuing her research in an objective and detached manner, or becoming intimately involved and an "advocate" for Abby.

```
05 I changed to advocate for the teachers by respecting their comfort
06 which allowed me to recognize that my study is more than detached
07 research, but it's about fostering relationships with the teachers,
08 on a personal level and beyond our identities as teacher but as
09 people with complex lives.
```
(Nasir, 2013, p. 255)

Reflecting on Our Own Racial Identity

Participatory action research can have a significant impact on our racial consciousness and relationships with racial "others" (Cahill, 2007; Torre, 2009). This was most evident in Nasir's work at Genesis. She self-identified as a racial-linguistic and working-class minority, "a Pakistani-American, Muslim, female, who was also raised in a low income neighborhood" (Nasir, 2013, p. 255). She also thought that this would position her to assume an expert stance while advocating for "language minority" students. In addition, Nasir grew up in a predominantly English, monolingual, white, small town in the midwestern part of the United States. Both Abby and Karen grew up in white, middle-class communities and continued to live in similar neighborhoods while teaching at Genesis Elementary. This led to a feeling of "cultural disconnect of working with students whose FoK did not resemble their own" (Nasir, 2013, p. 255). Nasir initially believed that her own intimate knowledge of dominant and nondominant spaces as well as her status as a university-based expert would help her "bridge the gap" for Karen and Abby. She conducted study groups and leveraged articles such as Genzuk (1999) in order to alleviate their fears and concerns and "the elephant in the room."

The elephant in the room for Karen and Abby, as well as for many middle-class, white, female teachers, is the fear and discomfort they have of communities of color (Lensmire, 2012; Picower, 2009). In order to counter hegemonic understandings of urban racial subjects and the maintenance of what some have termed *white innocence* (Wekker, 2016), it is necessary to address this elephant in the room in order to leverage linguistic, cultural, and STEM funds of knowledge. Culturally sustaining forms of curriculum design in urban schools requires moving through these fears that are historical and a collective burden that is too heavy for individual teachers to navigate (Paris & Winn, 2013; Picower, 2009).

Nasir recognized her role as a university researcher and a minority subject could mediate through these fears and discomforts. She described a critical episode where she moved from her own naivete and romanticizing home visits toward critical understating of racial identity and building solidarity with Karen and Abby (lines 1–4):

```
01 However, in my moment of cheerleading for home visits, I was naïve
02 to the personal situations of my teachers. After saying these
03 words, Abby began to cry and immediately left the room to a private
04 area. Karen followed after her, while Lorena and I stayed back.
```
(Nasir, 2013, pp. 255–256)

Lorena's role and understanding of both the community and her colleagues help Nasir gain a deeper appreciation for her own racial blind spots. While Abby and Karen moved away, Lorena helped Nasir see the need to acknowledge their experiences as "minority women" and how she "was blinded to the cultural demands [she] was requesting Abby and Karen to do" (lines 5–13):

```
05 I remember asking Lorena if she thought I said anything offensive
06 because I was confused at what could spark Abby with such emotion
07 to leave. Lorena reminded me of the cultural differences between
08 our experiences as minority women. She told me that I was blinded
09 to the cultural demands I was requesting Abby and Karen to do. She
10 said that she has lived in this neighborhood for several years so
11 she knew how friendly the parents can be, but that, in her opinion,
12 Abby and Karen had not been exposed to the neighborhood the way she
13 had.
```
(Nasir, 2013, pp. 255–256)

Discussing whiteness and making sense of its impact on members of both dominant and nondominant groups must unpack the inherent fears and frustrations that come with it. Many white teachers in schools with a majority nonwhite populations often fear that engaging in such dialogue makes them look racist or bad people (McIntyre, 1997). Embracing the uncomfortable is an essential part of participatory action research for everyone involved, and the Genesis cohort learned to engage the tensions, "the uncomfortable zones," and the "bumpy road" inherent in racial topics:

I do get emotional doing this work because you do change as a person. There is something about learning through other people that makes you learn and change yourself. So I welcome you to learning about yourself and things you may have never known and embracing a field that is really rooted in making a difference in your students and yourself.

(Nasir, 2013, p. 256)

As discussed in earlier chapters (e.g., Cara's case in Chapter 6), racial tensions can be leveraged to mediate third spaces of learning.

Conclusion

Our objective at the outset of this book was to provide a detailed demonstration of how a range of teachers working with their university research partners engaged in action research that was theoretically informed, methodologically rigorous, and personally meaningful. Drawing on cultural historical activity theory for professional development, we sought to advance teacher inquiry, autonomy, and agency. We aimed to socially reorganize learning, reimagine curriculum design as interdisciplinary (STEM and literature), and build sustainable practices that endured beyond our program. Our cohorts were organized to optimize the interdisciplinary expertise of the teachers that included STEM, language arts, and social studies. In two of the cases (Jarman, Chapter 3; Genesis, Chapter 2), we demonstrated the benefits of not only interdisciplinary teacher collaboration but also teachers with content expertise collaborating with teachers who specialize in diverse learning styles, English as second language (ESL), and special education. In addition, we learned to collectively "break the fourth wall" that inhibits professional growth.

The teachers at Genesis, Jarman, Adams, and Warner became reflective teacher researchers who appropriated practices that would help them design curriculum that leveraged students' funds of knowledge and at the same time incorporated the goals of state standards and mandated curricula. As teacher–researchers they learned how to navigate and negotiate the tensions between designing authentic learning and implementing scripted curriculum. They learned to advocate for student- and community-centered activities grounded in empirical evidence and scholarship. In addition, several of the cases, like Warner and Genesis, more explicitly moved from teacher-centered to community-centered discourse practices linking mathematics, science, and language within the larger community.

The cases of action research presented in this book coincide with many of the new directions in action research, professional development, and teacher education. Over the years action research has sought to enhance the professional identity of teachers by foregrounding their content and pedagogical expertise, valuing community knowledge, and centering student learning. Each of the chapters illustrated the power of action research to remediate teacher professional identity in more substantial and longitudinal ways (Wells, 2009). Youth participatory action research (YPAR), in particular, has more explicitly aimed to empower youth and communities stakeholders to engage in transformative activities that address issues of equity and environmental, racial, and linguistic justice (e.g., Baker-Bell, 2020; Morales-Doyle 2017). This was more clearly visible at Genesis Elementary (Chapter 2) as students, teachers, community advocates, and university-based researchers worked collectively to build a safe and sustainable playground from scratch. At Genesis the youth embodied the spirit of YPAR by taking on greater leadership responsibility at every stage of the action research process: conceptualization, data collection, design, advocacy, financial planning, and implementation.

Participatory action research (PAR) and more recently youth participatory action research (YPAR) have led to more egalitarian models of learning, teaching, and curriculum design across the globe. This conceptual and ideological shift has ushered in a new era of education that is more socioculturally, historically, economically, and politically conscious. From the so-called third world or *global south* to the first world *global north* (Di Nicola, 2020), these novel theoretical and methodological approaches have and are closing the learning and opportunity gaps that have historically persisted between dominant and nondominant communities and nations (Lomeli & Rappaport, 2018; Milner, 2012; Rowell, 2017). Egalitarian epistemologies and the democratization of knowledge serves to push the boundaries of traditional research that sustain the status quo and rearrange hegemonic relationships (Anderson, 2017).

Since the landmark case of *Brown v. Board of Education* (1954) that purportedly ended legal segregation, there have been numerous efforts in the United States to desegregate education and society (Kluger, 2011). It was the basis for another landmark case 20 years later, *Lau v. Nichols* (1974) that connected civil rights to the linguistic rights of multilingual children (Gándara, Moran, & Garcia, 2004). However, more than 50 years later, these types of legal reform efforts have largely fallen short of their stated and/or perceived goals because they lacked the moral, ethical, and relational foundations necessary to categorically end racism and linguicism in the hearts, minds, and day-to-day relations of society. Instead, these legislations were driven by the politics of the moment, the politics of neutrality, and a temporary moment of interest convergence between dominant white society and minority groups (Bell, 1980). They were mere procedural acts and a temporary tourniquet to quell the growing American and global disbelief that the United States was not truly a land of equity and equal opportunity.

As we conclude this book, we find ourselves in uncertain and turbulent times. The recent killings of George Floyd, Ahmaud Arbery, and Brianna Taylor have sparked a national and global movement for social, economic, and racial justice. For arguably the first time, there is a growing cross section of people demanding sustained and systematic efforts to bring about change (Schell et al., 2020). This movement has engendered widespread youth participation and leadership at the grassroots and national levels. At the 2021 U.S. Presidential inauguration ceremony, 22-year-old African American Amanda Gorman was chosen as the poet laureate, and her poem, *The Hill we Climb*, embodied this ethos with immediate implications for classrooms (Jago, 2021). YPAR is well positioned as a conceptual and methodological framework to help address these issues as well as push the boundaries of what is curricularly appropriate for children and youth (Ritterbusch et al., 2020).

A global pandemic has dramatically shifted education. As remote learning becomes normative, students' funds of knowledge, parents, and teacher expertise to elicit and use them to create dynamic learning becomes more pivotal. The new First Lady, a former teacher and educational researcher, was blindsided by having her academic legitimacy questioned publicly by the *Wall Street Journal* (Alexander, 2020). The disrespect and deprofessionalization of teachers and the education community undermines our commitment to truth, fairness, and dignity. We have shown throughout this book that participatory action research is fundamentally about breaking barriers and building strong relationships among teachers, students, communities, and their university-based partners. Breaking the psychological, cultural, and linguistic walls of segregation requires a model that transcends legal policies based on interest-convergence. Instead, breaking the fourth wall in education and society demands a collective commitment to humanistic ideals and a bottom-up approach to fostering solidarity with those we deem as "other" (Malaurent & Avison, 2016; Jackson 2020). Action research is not just technical skills; it is relationship building, becoming comfortable with that which makes us uncomfortable, transformative justice–centered curriculum, and an emancipatory paradigm shift (Brydon-Miller, Kral, & Ortiz Aragón, 2020; Wood, McAteer, & Whitehead, 2019).

Discussion Questions

1. What are some ways you can mediate conversations about systematic racism, racial and linguistic disparities, and racial identity in your classroom?
2. How does action research affect the researcher and help us move "beyond positivism"?
3. In what ways can relationships be fostered to break the fourth wall in conducting action research?

Additional Resources

1. Why racial equity and justice? • Talking race • Tools for assessment, strategic planning and action
   https://neaedjustice.org/wp-content/uploads/2018/11/Racial-Justice-in-Education.pdf
2. Activities for Research Paradigms: Philosophy Terms
   https://philosophyterms.com/positivism/

Beyond Positivism
https://study.sagepub.com/mukherjiandalbon3e/student-resources/chapter-5/activities
3. Breaking the Fourth Wall: Activities
https://www.eltnews.gr/education/2017-breaking-the-fourth-wall-in-teaching
Breaking the Fourth Wall Lesson Plan—BYU Theater Department
https://spanport.byu.edu/GoldenAgeTheater/documents1/4th_Wall_Liz_Sands.pdf

References

Alexander, B. U. T. (2020, December 20). Jill Biden was blindsided by Wall Street Journal call to drop "Dr." title: "It was really the tone of it". *USA TODAY*. Retrieved from https://eu.usatoday.com/story/entertainment/tv/2020/12/17/jill-biden-speaks-out-wall-street-journal-column-drop-dr-title/3952529001/

Anderson, G. L. (2017). Can participatory action research (PAR) democratize research, knowledge, and schooling? Experiences from the global South and North. *International Journal of Qualitative Studies in Education, 30*(5), 427–431.

Argyris, C. (1977). Double loop learning in organizations. *Harvard Business Review, 55*(5), 115–125.

Argyris, C. (1991). Teaching smart people how to learn. *Harvard Business Review, 69*(3), 99–109.

Baker-Bell, A. (2020). *Linguistic justice: Black language, literacy, identity, and pedagogy*. New York, NY: Routledge.

Bell, D. (1980). Brown v. Board of Education and the interest-convergence dilemma. *Harvard Law Review, 93*(3), 518–533. DOI. 10.2307/1340546

Berg, M., Coman, E., & Schensul, J. J. (2009). Youth action research for prevention: A multi-level intervention designed to increase efficacy and empowerment among urban youth. *American Journal of Community Psychology, 43*(3), 345–359.

Bloome, D., & Green, J. (2015). The social and linguistic turns in studying language and literacy. In J. Rowell & K. Pahl (Eds.), *The Routledge handbook of literacy studies* (pp. 19–34). New York, NY: Routledge.

Branquinho, C., Tomé, G., Grothausen, T., & Gaspar de Matos, M. (2020). Community-based Youth Participatory Action Research studies with a focus on youth health and well-being: A systematic review. *Journal of Community Psychology, 48*(5), 1301–1315.

Brown v. Board of Education, 347 U.S. 483 (1954).

Brydon-Miller, M., Kral, M., & Ortiz Aragón, A. (2020). Participatory action research: International perspectives and practices. *International Review of Qualitative Research, 13*(2), 103–111.

Cahill, C. (2007). Repositioning ethical commitments: Participatory action research as a relational praxis of social change. *ACME: An International Journal for Critical Geographies, 6*(3), 360–373.

Caldwell, B. (2015). *Beyond positivism*. New York, NY: Routledge.

Cater, M., Machtmes, K., & Fox, J. (2008). An examination of youth voice via quasi-experimental methodology. *Journal of Youth Development, 3*(2), 38–49. DOI: 10.5195/JYD.2008.305.

Engeström, Y. (1999). Innovative learning in work teams: Analyzing cycles of knowledge creation in practice. In Y. Engeström, R. Miettinen, & R.-L. Punamäki (Eds.), *Perspectives on activity theory* (pp. 377–404). New York, NY: Cambridge University Press.

Gándara, P., Moran, R., & Garcia, E. (2004). Chapter 2: Legacy of Brown: Lau and language policy in the United States. *Review of Research in Education, 28*(1), 27–46.

Genzuk, M. (1999). Tapping into community funds of knowledge. In *Effective strategies for English language acquisition: Curriculum guide for the professional development of teachers grades kindergarten through eight* (pp. 9–21). Los Angeles, CA: Los Angeles Annenberg Metropolitan Project/ARCO Foundation.

Glaser, B. G., & Strauss, A. L. (2017). *Discovery of grounded theory: Strategies for qualitative research*. New York, NY: Routledge.

Herr, K., & Anderson, G. L. (2014). *The action research dissertation: A guide for students and faculty*. Thousand Oaks, CA: Sage Publications.

Jackson, D. (2020). Relationship building in a black space: Partnering in solidarity. *Journal of Literacy Research, 52*(4), 432–455.

Jago, C. (2021, January 20). Lesson of the day: Amanda Gorman and "The Hill We Climb". *The New York Times*. Retrieved from https://www.nytimes.com/2021/01/20/learning/lesson-of-the-day-amanda-gorman-and-the-hill-we-climb.html

Johnson, C.W., & Parry, D. C. (Eds.). (2016). *Fostering social justice through qualitative inquiry: A methodological guide*. New York, NY: Routledge.

Katie (personal communication, Facebook messenger, January 2017).

Kluger, R. (2011). *Simple justice: The history of Brown v. Board of Education and Black America's struggle for equality*. New York, NY: Vintage.

Lau v. Nichols, 414 U.S. 563. (1974).

Lensmire, A. (2012). *White urban teachers: Stories of fear, violence, and desire*. Lanham, MD: Rowman & Littlefield Publication Group.

Levin, M., & Greenwood, D. J. (2008). The future of universities: Action research and the transformation of higher education. In P Reason & H. Bradbury-Huang (Eds.), *The SAGE handbook of action research: Participative inquiry and practice* (pp. 211–226). Thousand Oaks, CA: SAGE Publications.

Lomeli, J. D. R., & Rappaport, J. (2018). Imagining Latin American social science from the global south: Orlando Fals Borda and participatory action research. *Latin American Research Review, 53*(3), 597–612.

Malaurent, J., & Avison, D. (2016). Reconciling global and local needs: A canonical action research project to deal with workarounds. *Information Systems Journal, 26*(3), 227–257.

Mangan, M. (2013). *The drama, theatre and performance companion*. New York, NY: Palgrave Macmillan.

McIntyre, A. (1997). *Making meaning of whiteness: Exploring racial identity with white teachers*. Albany: SUNY Press.

McLaren, P. (1999). *Schooling as a ritual performance: Toward a political economy of educational symbols and gestures*. Lanham, MD: Rowman & Littlefield Publishing Group.

Milner IV, H. R. (2012). Beyond a test score: Explaining opportunity gaps in educational practice. *Journal of Black Studies, 43*(6), 693–718.

Mirra, N. (2018). *Educating for empathy*. New York, NY: Teachers College Press.

Morales-Doyle, D. (2017). Justice centered science pedagogy: A catalyst for academic achievement and social transformation. *Science Education, 101*(6), 1034–1060.

Nasir, A. (2013). *Teachers theorizing English learners' math-science funds of knowledge through community activism* [Unpublished doctoral dissertation]. University of Illinois at Chicago.

Paris, D., & Winn, M. T. (Eds.). (2013). *Humanizing research: Decolonizing qualitative inquiry with youth and communities.* Thousand Oaks, CA: Sage Publications.

Picower, B. (2009). The unexamined whiteness of teaching: How white teachers maintain and enact dominant racial ideologies. *Race Ethnicity and Education, 12*(2), 197–215.

Prober, C. G., & Khan, S. (2013). Medical education reimagined: A call to action. *Academic Medicine, 88*(10), 1407–1410.

Quantz, R. A. (1999). School ritual as performance: A reconstruction of Durkheim's and Turner's uses of ritual. *Educational Theory, 49*(4), 493–513.

Razfar, A. (2007). *Transforming literacy, science, and math through action research (LSciMAct).* Washington, DC: Grant funded by the U.S. Department of Education.

Razfar, A. (2011). Action research in urban schools: Empowerment, transformation, and challenges. *Teacher Education Quarterly, 38*(4), 25–44.

Razfar, A., & Li, R. (2014, September). *Transforming, literacy, science, and mathematics through action research (LSciMACT): Final evaluation report of national professional development program.* Washington, DC: U.S. Department of Education.

Ritterbusch, A. E., Boothby, N., Mugumya, F., Wanican, J., Bangirana, C., Nyende, N., … Meyer, S. R. (2020). Pushing the limits of child participation in research: Reflections from a youth-driven participatory action research (YPAR) initiative in Uganda. *International Journal of Qualitative Methods, 19*, 1–12.

Rowell, L. (2017). Knowledge mobilization and action research in global contexts: Towards a comparative orientation. *Educational Action Research, 25*(3), 333–336.

Rumenapp, J. C. (2013). *RE-positioning English learners in teacher development: A language ideologies approach to urban education* [Unpublished doctoral dissertation]. University of Illinois at Chicago.

Schell, C. J., Guy, C., Shelton, D. S., Campbell-Staton, S. C., Sealey, B. A., Lee, D. N., & Harris, N. C. (2020). Recreating Wakanda by promoting black excellence in ecology and evolution. *Nature Ecology & Evolution, 4*(10), 1285–1287.

Schön, D. A. (1991). *The reflective turn: Case studies in and on educational practice.* New York, NY: Teachers College Press.

Teram, E., Schachter, C. L., & Stalker, C. A. (2005). The case for integrating grounded theory and participatory action research: Empowering clients to inform professional practice. *Qualitative Health Research, 15*(8), 1129–1140.

Torre, M. E. (2009). Participatory action research and critical race theory: Fueling spaces for nos-otras to research. *The Urban Review, 41*(1), 106–120.

Troiano, B. L. (2012). *Developing professional teacher researchers: Transforming language learning through discourse analysis* [Unpublished doctoral dissertation]. University of Illinois at Chicago.

Wekker, G. (2016). *White innocence: Paradoxes of colonialism and race.* Durham, NC: Duke University Press.

Wells, G. (2009). Dialogic inquiry as collaborative action research. In S. Noffke & B. Somekh (Eds.), *The SAGE handbook of educational action research* (pp. 62–73). Thousand Oaks, CA: SAGE Publications.

Wood, L., McAteer, M., & Whitehead, J. (2019). How are action researchers contributing to knowledge democracy? A global perspective. *Educational Action Research, 27*(1), 7–21.

Zuber-Skerritt, O. (1992). *Action research in higher education: Examples and reflections.* London: Kogan Page Limited.

EPILOGUE

Over the last decade, action research has become a global phenomenon in teacher education. From action research networks throughout Africa, Asia, and the Middle East to Freirian-inspired networks in South America, Europe, and North America, the global south and north are converging around a common call to not just talk about, hope for, or reimagine another world, but to make it happen. Amidst a global pandemic and public protests against systemic environmental and racial injustices, the urgency to rise up, organize, and make a difference is only growing in scope and scale.

On the night of November 5, 2008, as the United States was electing its first Black president, distinguished professor of curriculum studies William "Bill" Ayers, was present as an observer in our class and noted our conversation about Stuart Hall's notion of third space, especially as it related to agency and responsibility. He noted how "the conversation [about third space] continued for an hour and a half at a high pitch of participation even though everyone was excited to leave—this was, after all, election night 2008." We decided to, as a class, walk together to Grant Park to be witnesses to the "Audacity of Hope," America's "postracial" turn, and experience a third space in the making. At the time, our action research projects were just beginning.

By 2012, in response to massive school closures in urban neighborhoods and corporate-led privatization efforts, the Chicago Teacher Union (CTU) inspired nationwide protests calling for smaller class sizes, needed student services, and the dignity of a profession that was constantly under attack from corporations that placed profits over people. Our classrooms during this period became "a sea of red shirts" signifying solidarity and active participation in this movement. They drew attention to poverty as one of the biggest roadblocks to academic achievement; disparities within the city, especially the lack of resources in schools serving

DOI: 10.4324/9781351001168-9

low-income Black and Latinx students; and how more than 160 schools had no library and many lacked playgrounds.

This model for professional development focuses on integrating instructional knowledge from the fields of bilingual and English as a second language (ESL) education, mathematics education, and science education, with teachers doing action research and developing collegial communities. Furthermore, these cases have broader applicability and implications beyond the schools and communities in which they were situated. They are part of a teacher professional development movement that goes beyond methods fetish and seeks to fundamentally humanize education by centering teacher expertise, student learning, and community epistemologies.

In 2020, delays in housing inequalities, educational and health disparities, and environmental injustices can no longer be tolerated by teachers everywhere. Teachers in urban and rural communities from the Southern to Northern Hemispheres are collectively saying, *"¡Basta ya! Enough is Enough!"* As the calls for justice and equity intensify, educators and the communities they serve are at a crossroads of realizing the long-awaited changes. Action research, STEM education, language learning, and university–school partnerships are viable vehicles for bringing about transformative change. The action research stories presented in this book are about leveraging funds of knowledge, integrating STEM education and language learning, and building sustainable university–community partnerships. They are collectively part of a broader movement to humanize teacher education and professional development by intentionally and strategically moving away from deficit views of teachers and K–12 education. They are intended to inspire teachers, administrators, and university professors to reconsider and reclaim their central role in building an equitable, just, and loving society.

APPENDIX A: ACTIVITY TRIANGLE TEMPLATE

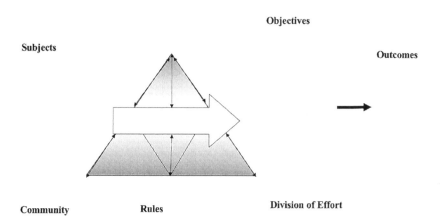

Tools and Artifacts

Objectives

Subjects

Outcomes

Community   Rules   Division of Effort

APPENDIX B: FUND OF KNOWLEDGE INVENTORY TABLE

Standards-based Practices	Content Objectives	Funds of Knowledge	STEM Cultural Practices and Values

APPENDIX C: SOCIAL ORGANIZATION OF LEARNING PROTOCOL (ADAPTED FROM RAZFAR)

Date: _____ Observer: _____

Site: _____

Began observation at: _____

Concluded observation at: _____

Part I: The Social Organization of Learning

1) Describe the activity:
2) Number of participants: _____ #male: _____ #female: _____

Describe any other salient identity markers that describe these students:

3) Spatial Arrangement (Diagram)
4) Instructional Arrangement
   a) Small group
   b) Whole class
   c) Individualized work
   d) Other: _____

Notes:

5) Nature of activity
   a) Teacher defined
   b) Student defined
   c) Negotiated

Notes:

6) Nature of participation:

1	2	3	4	5
Teacher centered		Student centered		Community centered

7) Management/Rule Negotiation
   a) Explicit teacher established/enforced rewards/sanctions
   b) Implicit teacher established/enforced rewards/sanctions
   c) Community established/enforced rewards/sanctions
   d) Other:

Description:

Part II: Language Practices

1) Language(s) used for this activity: (a) English (b) Spanish (c) Other:
   _____

2) If more than one language was used, describe the language mixing:
   a) code switching
   b) native language used to clarify/extend
   c) preview/review
   d) speakers divided by language
   e) topics divided by language
   f) other: _____

3) Speaker Designation:
   a) Teacher designates
   b) Student leader designates
   c) Self-nomination
   d) mixed

Notes:

4) Extent of participation:
   a) A few students dominate talk
   b) Small core participates in talk
   c) Most students participate in talk
   d) No students participate in talk

Salient identity markers of most vocal participants:

5) Discourse Pattern:
   a) IRE
   b) Instructional Conversation
   c) Other: _____

Notes:

6) Assistance/Expansion:
   a) Teacher expands on student thinking
   b) Students expand
   c) Missed opportunities for expansion.

Examples:

7) Discourse(s) used
   a) Math
   b) Science
   c) Students' funds of knowledge
   d) Other: _____

Examples:

8) Potential third spaces
   a) Tension
   b) Shifts in participation
   c) Expert/novice role shifts
   d) Other: _____

Examples:

APPENDIX D: FIELD-NOTE OBSERVATION TEMPLATE

Date:

Site:

Activity:

Participants:

Length of Observation:

Summary

Write a one-paragraph summary or abstract of the day's events. Include analytic description, such as today was a good example of code-switching.

Narrative

Write a detailed narrative of what you observed. Use (OC: _____.) for observer comments.

Questions/Things to Follow Up With
Types of Field Notes

Field Note Type	Definition	Approach	Example
Descriptive	The most objective (as objective as it can be) and the fieldworker is as detached as they can be from the participants they are describing.	Empiricist	I have a newcomer, 11 students in the bilingual program, 8 students that are transiting out of the program, and 7 other students in my class. Three students that are in the bilingual program also have IEPs for a learning disability.

Field Note Type	Definition	Approach	Example
Interpretative	This is the observer's stance of what they are observing.	More value-laden, subjective, and evaluative	My students are always working with each other and helping each other learn. Some students are hardworking, others are lazy, and others go beyond their means to ensure a good grade.
Reflexive	More introspective. Thinking about the change that is occurring to the fieldworker.	The observer's commentary **(OC)** Analysis, interpretation, and reflection happening in this part	OC: As a community, we've experienced a few issues this year that dealt with culture—there has been some conflict between a girl of Indian descent and a few of the girls who are Mexican American, and it required some intervention and discussion. My partner and I are concerned about bullying and intimidation in general and have seen fifth-graders show social aggression before.

(Adapted from Merriam, 2007)

APPENDIX E: CODING SHEET TEMPLATE

Time	PA	FoK	MLD	Q	T	3rdSp	PartSh	RSh	RN
0:00:00									
0:02:00									
0:04:00									
0:06:00									
0:08:00									
0:10:00									
0:12:00									
0:14:00									
0:16:00									
0:18:00									
0:20:00									

PA—Peer Assistance; FoK—Funds of Knowledge; MLD—Multiple Languages Discourses; Q—Questions; T—Tension; 3rdSp—Third Space; PartSh—Participation Shift; RSh—Role Shift; RN—Role Negotiation

APPENDIX F: DISCOURSE ANALYSIS TRANSCRIPTION CONVENTIONS

Numbered Lines	Each line is numbered beginning with 01.
Speakers	Name of speaker:
[ ]	Overlap talk
All CAPS	Reading text aloud.
Bold	Louder voice
:	Vowel elongation (stress comes after vowel)
-	Raising/Falling Intonation
?	Questioning intonation
Italics	Recitation of any kind (reading out loud)
(.)	Micropause less than 0.2 seconds
(2 sec)	Longer pause–Write the number of seconds in parenthesis
Uhm/uhuh	Backchanneling—Use colon to show length
Describe in ( )	Nonverbal cues (gestures)
/	Self-repair
//	Other repair
" "	Mock voice—speaker assumes voice of another speaker.

APPENDIX G: UNIT PLANNING

Phase	Description	Tools
Planning	During this phase bring your planning ideas and get feedback from colleagues. You will turn in the following materials before beginning the unit:	• Inventory Table • Activity Triangle
Implementing	During implementation you will be teaching the unit and recording your lessons.	• Lesson plans • Field notes • Coding sheet
Analyzing	During the analysis phase use the codes to analyze the data set. Use the coding sheet to select and transcribe episodes.	• Select and transcribe episodes • Individual report • Group report • Student work

APPENDIX H: FINAL REPORTING TOOLS

Questions for Final Cohort Report

1. Do you see differences from the first to the second video with respect to the protocol (i.e., shifts in participation)?
2. Look at modality (shift from uncertainty to certainty) in terms of knowledges students bring to the activity. Look for the move from definite to indefinite linguistic features, such as a move from using *may* or *might* to *is*.
3. Have the learning outcomes been achieved? If so, what is the evidence?
4. What would you change/modify based on what you observed and learned?
5. What missed opportunities for expansion did you identify?
6. Are there examples of repair that you noticed?
7. Did the activity system work with respect to math, science, and literacy?
8. What new things emerged?
9. Are there other aspects of the protocol you would like to discuss?
10. How have your views of action research, sociocultural theory, discourse analysis, identity (i.e., learner, English learners) developed over the course of the semester?

Completion of this book should provide teachers a foundation for how to conduct action.

Sample Action Research Report Outline

Abstract

Chapter 1: Introduction
    Purpose Statement
    Significance of Study
    Definition of Terms
    Research Questions

Chapter 2: Conceptual Framework
  Identity
  Agency
  Gradual Release Model
  Funds of Knowledge
  Sociocultural Theory
  Zone of Proximal Development
  Racial and Social Justice
  Discourse
  Action Research

Chapter 3: Methods
  Context
  Participants
  Curriculum
  Data Collection Procedures
  Data Analysis

Chapter 4: Findings
  Theme One:
      Change in Students
      Change in Self
      Change in Site
  Theme Two:
      Change in Students
      Change in Self
      Change in Site
  Theme Three:
      Change in Students
      Change in Self
      Change in Site

Chapter 5: Discussion
  Summary of Findings
  Limitations
  Conclusion
  Recommendations

References

Appendix

INDEX

Page numbers in *italics* denote figures, page numbers in **bold** denote tables.